OECD Sovereign Borrowing Outlook 2022

This work is published under the responsibility of the Secretary-General of the OECD. The opinions expressed and arguments employed herein do not necessarily reflect the official views of the Member countries of the OECD.

This document, as well as any data and map included herein, are without prejudice to the status of or sovereignty over any territory, to the delimitation of international frontiers and boundaries and to the name of any territory, city or area.

The statistical data for Israel are supplied by and under the responsibility of the relevant Israeli authorities. The use of such data by the OECD is without prejudice to the status of the Golan Heights, East Jerusalem and Israeli settlements in the West Bank under the terms of international law.

Note by Turkey
The information in this document with reference to "Cyprus" relates to the southern part of the Island. There is no single authority representing both Turkish and Greek Cypriot people on the Island. Turkey recognises the Turkish Republic of Northern Cyprus (TRNC). Until a lasting and equitable solution is found within the context of the United Nations, Turkey shall preserve its position concerning the "Cyprus issue".

Note by all the European Union Member States of the OECD and the European Union
The Republic of Cyprus is recognised by all members of the United Nations with the exception of Turkey. The information in this document relates to the area under the effective control of the Government of the Republic of Cyprus.

Please cite this publication as:
OECD (2022), *OECD Sovereign Borrowing Outlook 2022*, OECD Publishing, Paris, https://doi.org/10.1787/b2d85ea7-en.

ISBN 978-92-64-88968-2 (print)
ISBN 978-92-64-36500-1 (pdf)

OECD Sovereign Borrowing Outlook
ISSN 2306-0468 (print)
ISSN 2306-0476 (online)

Foreword

This edition of the *OECD Sovereign Borrowing Outlook* presents analysis of the impact of the pandemic on sovereign borrowing needs and outstanding debt for 2020 and 2021, and provides projections for 2022 for the OECD area. It also reviews sovereign debt issuance trends in Emerging Market and Developing Economies (EMEs) in 2021, and provides an update on the impact of the COVID-19 crisis on issuance conditions of EME sovereigns. It then takes the perspective of a public debt manager and discusses approaches to incorporating ESG factors into public debt management, identifying key challenges and risks as well as the common features of emerging leading practices in both OECD and non-OECD countries.

The publication draws mainly on responses received to an annual survey on the borrowing needs of OECD governments circulated by the OECD's Bond Market and Public Debt Management Unit. This includes an update on trends and developments associated with sovereign borrowing requirements, funding strategies, market infrastructure and debt levels from the perspective of public debt managers. The Outlook makes a policy distinction between funding strategies and borrowing requirements. Central government marketable gross borrowing needs, or requirements, are calculated on the basis of budget deficits and redemptions. Funding strategies entail decisions on how borrowing needs are going to be financed using different instruments (e.g. long-term, short-term, nominal, indexed, etc.) and which distribution channels (auctions, tap, syndication, etc.) will be used.

This year, the OECD conducted a special survey study on 'Approaches to incorporating ESG factors into public debt management including labelled bonds' among OECD and selected non-OECD countries. Chapter 2 draws mainly on the responses to this survey.

Comments and questions should be addressed to the Bond Markets and Public Debt Management Unit within the Financial Markets Division of the OECD Directorate for Financial and Enterprise Affairs (e-mail: PublicDebt@oecd.org). Find out more about OECD work on bond markets and public debt management online at www.oecd.org/finance/public-debt/.

Acknowledgements

The OECD Sovereign Borrowing Outlook is one of the activities of the OECD Working Party on Debt Management, incorporated in the programme of work of the Bond Markets and Public Debt Management Unit within the OECD Directorate for Financial and Enterprise Affairs. This Outlook was prepared by the OECD Bond Markets and Public Debt Management Unit; Fatos Koc (Head of the Unit), Gary Mills (Statistician), and Shai Somek (Project assistant). Emanuele Properzi (intern) and Gulgun Arikan (intern and consultant) co authored and provided technical support on the global sovereign bond data in Chapters 2 and 3. Pamela Duffin (Communications Manager) and Liv Gudmundson (Publications and Editorial Lead) supported the team with publishing guidance and editorial support.

A number of OECD colleagues provided feedback: Robert Patalano (Head of the Financial Markets Division) on Chapters 1 and 3; Catriona Marshall (Economist) on Chapter 2; Nigel Pain (Head of the Macroeconomic Policy Division) on Chapter 3; Alvaro Pina (Senior Economist) on Chapter 1; Enes Sunel (Economist) on Chapters 1 and 3, and; Arthur Minsat (Head of Unit) on Chapter 3. The following members of the Working Party on Debt Management provided valuable feedback: Grahame Johnson (Chair, Advisor to the Governor, Central Bank, Canada); Rob Nicholl (Chief Executive Officer, Office of Financial Management, Australia); Sir Robert Stheeman (Chief Executive; UK Debt Management Office), and; Teppo Koivisto (Director of Finance, Treasury, Finland) on Chapters 1 and 2; Cristina Casalinho (Vice-Chair, CEO, Treasury and Government Debt Agency, Portugal); Davide Iacovoni (Director General; Ministry of Economy and Finance, Italy); Frederick Pietrangeli (Director, Office of Debt Management, US Treasury); and, Tomoya Yamashita (Director for Debt Management and JGB Investor Relations; Ministry of Finance, Japan) on Chapter 1; Patricio Sepulveda Carmona (Head of the Debt Office; Ministry of Finance, Chile) and Victor Gonzalez (Senior Advisor of the Public Debt Office, Ministry of Finance, Chile) on Chapters 2 and 3; Maria Del Carmen Bonilla Rodriguez (Head of the Public Credit Unit; Ministry of Finance and Public Credit, Mexico) on Chapter 3; Eldridge Katzenbach (Senior Debt Manager, Office of Debt Management, US Treasury) on Chapter 1; and, Philippe Garrau (Financial Officer, European Commission) on Chapter 1. TCX Fund supported the survey study on 'Approaches to incorporating Environmental, Social and Governance (ESG) factors into public debt management' among non-OECD countries, Harald Hirschhofer (Senior Advisor, TCX Fund) and Axel Racowski (Vice President, Rothschild & Co) provided comments on the draft survey.

Editorial

The necessary and prudent measures taken to soften the economic blow from the COVID-19 pandemic have resulted in large fiscal deficits and a marked consequent increase in public indebtedness. Before the outbreak of the war in Ukraine, economies around the world were recovering strongly with a debt stabilising impact, and fiscal and monetary policy support measures were also gradually phasing out. Coupled with the expectation of a change in global liquidity conditions, the war has further heightened uncertainty and is posing challenges for policy makers by simultaneously threatening economic growth and exacerbating already rising inflation. Against this background, the 2022 *Sovereign Borrowing Outlook* analyses recent trends and possible future developments in sovereign financing requirements. It then sheds light on the implications of evolving monetary and fiscal policies and the broader government agenda including sustainability for public debt management.

The outstanding amount of OECD area central government marketable debt increased by more than USD 10 trillion in the two years following the outbreak of the pandemic and was set to reach an estimated USD 50 trillion by end-2021. This edition of the *Outlook* projects that the outstanding level of central government marketable debt will increase by USD 3 trillion to USD 53 trillion in 2022. This represents a total increase of more than USD 13 trillion (33%) in outstanding government securities since the outbreak of the COVID-19 pandemic. That is more than the total debt growth over the decade before this crisis. Furthermore, given the uncertainties around the impact of the war and potential fiscal support to be provided to consumers and business affected by higher food and energy prices, there is a risk of upward deviation from these estimates, particularly in the Euro area.

An increasing outstanding amount of debt means increases in the amount of debt to be refinanced. In view of the rapid pace of debt accumulation and favourable funding conditions, many countries have sought to rebalance their sovereign debt portfolio maturities to ease near-term redemption pressures and to strengthen the resilience of their debt portfolios against refinancing risk. As a result, the average term-to-maturity of outstanding debt has almost fully returned to a pre-pandemic level, standing at 7.6 years in 2021 and reaching record highs in 16 OECD countries including France, Italy, Portugal, Spain and the United States. Despite the extended maturities of new issuance, debt redemption profiles are expected to be elevated and may pose significant challenges in terms of refinancing risks, as 42% of outstanding marketable debt stock will need to be refinanced or repaid within the next three years.

The cost of borrowing is a key determinant of the sustainability of public finances in any country. The surge in borrowing needs following the outbreak of the pandemic was financed at very favourable conditions, largely due to exceptionally accommodative monetary policies. Going forward, however, sovereign borrowing costs are set to increase for both advanced economies and emerging market economies. As major central banks look to tighten monetary policies in response to rising inflation, both maturing debt and new debt issuance will be financed at higher rates. In addition, the tapering of quantitative easing and unwinding of asset purchase programmes will result in an increase in net issuances that have to be absorbed by other investors who may demand higher yields. Finally, a reduction in activity could increase the search cost of primary dealers, which would increase their risk premia to intermediate trade. All of this points to a need for close monitoring of government securities markets, and more careful planning of government' funding operations, taking into account a possible decrease in market liquidity, investor demand for different maturity segments and the balance sheet capacity of primary dealers.

The change in global liquidity conditions is affecting Emerging Market and Developing Economies in particular. Less favourable liquidity conditions are coinciding with increased refinancing needs and deteriorating credit conditions in some low- and lower-middle income economies. These country groups issued more than USD 3.5 trillion of debt in financial markets on average in both 2020 and 2021, roughly 50% higher than the pre-pandemic three year average. Simultaneously, with the exception of the Asian region, the quality of their debt has been deteriorating with a record of 74 credit rating downgrades, reflecting increased risk premia and borrowing costs. Going forward, it is important that these countries continue to receive financial and technical support from international financial institutions in order to manage their debt in a transparent and prudent way. In this context, OECD's Debt Transparency Initiative can contribute to improving the transparency of bilateral lending to low-income economies, subject to continued support from G20 members, governments in low-income countries and engagement from private sector lenders.

Sustainability, which increasingly drives changes in financial markets more broadly, also has implications for public debt management. Environmental, social and governance (ESG) considerations are affecting government securities markets and public debt management practices by feeding into investment decisions, assessments of sovereign creditworthiness and structural budget changes. In response, debt management offices are increasingly playing a support role in national ESG strategies by acting as an interface between the government and financial markets and through the issuance of ESG-labelled instruments in recent years. Reflecting inputs from both OECD and non-OECD countries, this *Outlook* discusses key challenges and risks related to the incorporation of ESG factors into public debt management, and presents the common features of newly emerging leading ESG-related practices in terms of communication, transparency and liquidity.

Carmine Di Noia,
Director, OECD Directorate for Financial and Enterprise Affairs

Table of contents

Foreword   3

Acknowledgements   4

Editorial   5

Abbreviations and acronyms   11

Executive summary   14

1 Sovereign borrowing outlook for OECD countries   17
   1.1. Introduction   18
   1.2. OECD government market borrowings remain higher than pre-pandemic levels, but are
   showing some signs of stabilisation   19
   1.3. Cost of funding remained low despite the recent rise   23
   1.4. Risk-driven borrowing strategies resulted in an increased the amount of duration supply to
   the market   27
   1.5. Increased refinancing needs has created scope for introducing new securities and maturity
   lines   29
   1.6. Countries are emerging from the crisis with more debt, while strong growth helps stabilise
   debt burdens   32
   1.7. Implications of the pandemic for future debt management   39
   References   46
   Annex 1.A. Methods and sources   49
   Notes   52

2 ESG practices and challenges from a public debt management perspective   55
   2.1. Introduction   56
   2.2. Sustainable finance and public debt   57
   2.3. Incorporation of ESG-considerations in public debt management   63
   References   85
   Annex 2.A. Methodology for data collection and classification   89
   Notes   90

3 Sovereign debt issuance trends in emerging-market economies   93
   3.1. Introduction   94
   3.2. Borrowing from the markets by EMDE sovereigns continued to increase despite tightening
   financial conditions   95

3.3. The share of debt issued in foreign currency continued to decrease in 2021 amid rising borrowing costs 102

3.4. Average maturity of debt issuance in most regions declined as T-Bill issuance prevailed among EMDEs 105

3.5. Redemption profiles remain risky with high amounts of debt due in the next three years 107

3.6. The credit quality of EMDE sovereigns has continued to deteriorate in most regions after the record rating downgrades issued in the wake of the pandemic 108

3.7. Implications of the recent trends in sovereign funding by EMDEs 110

References 111

Annex 3.A. Methods and sources 113

Notes 114

Annex A. OECD 2021 Survey on Primary Markets Developments 117

Annex B. OECD 2021 Survey on Liquidity in Government Bond Secondary Markets 165

FIGURES

Figure 1.1. Fiscal and borrowing outlook in OECD countries, 2007-22 19

Figure 1.2. Gross borrowing through marketable debt as a percentage of GDP 20

Figure 1.3. Annual changes in net borrowings from the markets as a percentage of GDP 23

Figure 1.4. Change in benchmark yields between December 2020 and December 2021 24

Figure 1.5. Volume share of fixed-rate bond issuance by yield category 25

Figure 1.6. Central banks' net purchases and government debt issuance in selected countries 26

Figure 1.7. Maturity composition of central government marketable debt issuance 28

Figure 1.8. Issuance of new securities and maturity lines 30

Figure 1.9. Marketable debt-to-GDP: 2008 financial crisis vs COVID-19 shock 32

Figure 1.10. Changes in selected central government debt-to-GDP ratios across the OECD (percentage point changes between 2019-20 and 2020-21) 33

Figure 1.11. Central government marketable debt and fiscal balances 34

Figure 1.12. Central government marketable debt considering different exchange rate assumptions, 2021 estimates. 35

Figure 1.13. General government interest expenses in relation to GDP 36

Figure 1.14. Maturity structure of central government marketable debt 37

Figure 1.15. Average term-to-maturity of outstanding marketable debt in selected OECD countries 38

Figure 1.16. Redemptions of central government marketable debt in OECD country groupings, as a percentage of debt stock 38

Figure 1.17. Key lessons learned from the COVID-19 crisis 40

Figure 1.18. Potential implications of the pandemic on public debt management 43

Figure 2.1. Main motivation to incorporate ESG related factors into investor relations information-responses from the OECD area DMOs 64

Figure 2.2. Main motivation to incorporate ESG related factors into investor relations information- responses from the non-OECD DMOs 65

Figure 2.3. Information shared to investors by OECD and non-OECD DMOs 65

Figure 2.4. Common tools for disseminating ESG-related information by non-OECD DMOs 66

Figure 2.5. ESG awareness among non-OECD DMOs 67

Figure 2.6. Key areas for capacity building 68

Figure 2.7. ESG bond labels and specificities 71

Figure 2.8. Sovereign ESG bond issuance by advanced and emerging market economies 72

Figure 2.9. ESG sovereign bond issuance before and after the pandemic 73

Figure 2.10. Sovereign ESG issuance by type 75

Figure 2.11. Currency composition 77

Figure 2.12. Volume share of fixed-rate ESG-labelled bond issuance by yield category 78

Figure 2.13. Spread between the German Twin Bonds 84

Figure 3.1. Central government gross debt issuance by EMDEs 96

Figure 3.2. Change in the main policy interest rate of EME central banks and EME local currency bond spreads over ten-year US Government bond yields	97
Figure 3.3. A model of sovereign borrowing, financial intermediaries and asset purchases	99
Figure 3.4. Transmission of a sovereign bond sell-off by non-resident investors	99
Figure 3.5. EMDE sovereign debt gross issuance by regional and income categories	100
Figure 3.6.Net debt issuance by income categories, EMDE countries (USD billion)	101
Figure 3.7. Foreign currency denominated debt issuance within emerging-market economy groups	103
Figure 3.8. Volume share by yield group of fixed-rate USD denominated bond issuance by EMDEs in 2021	104
Figure 3.9. Average term to maturity (ATM) of gross issuance for EMDE regions, weighted by issue amounts	105
Figure 3.10. Maturity composition of debt issuance by investment and non-investment grade categories in 2021	106
Figure 3.11. Outstanding government debt due within the next three years	108
Figure 3.12. Changes in EMDE sovereign credit ratings	108
Figure 3.13. Evolution of credit quality for a selected group of EMDEs	109

TABLES

Table 1.1. NextGenerationEU and its funding strategy	21

Annex Table 1.A.1. Average term-to-maturity country comments	51

Table A.1. Overview of issuing procedures	119
Table A.2. Q1 Overview of issuing procedures – country notes	119
Table A.3. Q1b Overview of recent changes in issuing procedures and techniques	121
Table A.4. Q2 Have you issued or plan to issue any new types of securities like inflation-linked bonds, variable rate notes, green bonds, and longer dated securities?	123
Table A.5. Q2 New type of instrument that was issued in the LAST 12 months	124
Table A.6. Q2 New type of instrument that will be issued in the NEXT 12 months	125
Table A.7. Q2 Other types of securities	126
Table A.8. Q3 Major challenges experienced over the last 12 months	127
Table A.9. Q3 Specified OTHER major challenges experienced over the last 12 months	128
Table A.10. Q3 Major challenges experienced over the last 12 months – Country notes	129
Table A.11. Q4 Major risk factors/events faced in the last 12 months	132
Table A.12. Major risk factors/events which might affect your operations in the next 12 months	134
Table A.13. Q4 Specified OTHER major risk factors/events that might affect the DMO operations in the next 12 months	136
Table A.14. Q4 major risk factors/events that your DMO faced last 12 months or might affect your operations in the next 12 months – Country notes	137
Table A.15. Q5 How do you manage these risks (e.g. contingency funding plans, continuity plan etc.)?	138
Table A.16. Q6 Do you consider potential risk factors when preparing your financing plan (e.g. auction calendar)?	141
Table A.17. Q7 How has the maturity structure of your 2021 issuances changed compared to 2020?	143
Table A.18. Q7 maturity structure of your 2021 issuances – country notes	144
Table A.19. Q8 Have you changed your funding strategies during 2021 compared to any original 2021 funding plan?	146
Table A.20. Q9 How have you adapted your funding strategies and operations in response to the pandemic in last 12 months?	147
Table A.21. Q9 How have you adapted your funding strategies and operations in response to the pandemic – Country notes	149
Table A.22. Q10 Have you observed any changes in investors behaviour in participating in auctions or/ Syndications (e.g. oversized orders)?	150
Table A.23. Q11 Do you have a liquidity buffer?	152
Table A.24. Q12 Please indicate areas of key lessons learned from the COVID-19 crisis.	154
Table A.25. Q13 Do you plan to review the long-term funding strategy as a consequence of increased debt levels following the COVID-19 pandemic?	155
Table A.26. Q14 Potential implications of the pandemic for future debt management	157

Table A.27. Q14 Specified OTHER implications of the pandemic for future debt management 159
Table A.28. Q14 Potential implications of the pandemic for future debt management – Country Notes 159
Table A.29. Q15 To what extent are you concerned about the adequacy of investor demand? 161
Table A.30. Q15 Please indicate situations or factors that give rise to concerns about future investor demand (e.g. changes in global liquidity conditions, regulations)? 162
Table A.31. Q16 Following the pandemic which operations do you now plan to carry out remotely (including at least partially) as standard that you did NOT do remotely prior to the pandemic? 163
Table B.1. Domestic currency bond lines 167
Table B.2. Q2 Do you believe it is necessary/important to maintain certain volumes in specific maturity segments in your country? 169
Table B.3. What has been the overall trend in the liquidity conditions of your domestic sovereign bonds -in terms of bid-ask spread, trading volumes etc.- over the last 12 months? 171
Table B.4. Q4 If you answered there was an improvement or a decline in Q3, please specify the main factors that might affect the changes in liquidity conditions? 174
Table B.5. Q4 If you answered there was an improvement or a decline in Q3, please specify the main factors that might affect the changes in liquidity conditions? 176
Table B.6. Q4 If you answered there was an improvement or a decline in Q3, please specify the main factors that might affect the changes in liquidity conditions – Country Notes 178
Table B.7. Q5 Have you observed changes in liquidity conditions of your foreign bonds over the last 12 months? 179
Table B.8. Q6 Have you observed changes in liquidity conditions of bond related derivate and repo markets over the last 12 months? 180
Table B.9. Q7 Do you have measures in place to motivate dealers to provide liquidity? 182
Table B.10. Q8 Do you undertake any other measures in order to enhance liquidity? 185
Table B.11. Q8b If yes to Q8, please specify the measures that you undertake to enhance liquidity 186
Table B.12. Q8b Other specified measures that you undertake to enhance liquidity measures that you undertake to enhance liquidity 188
Table B.13. Q9 Have you imposed new requirements on market-makers in their provision of liquidity over the last 12 months? 189
Table B.14. Q10 Have you made any changes to your market communication strategies since the pandemic? 190
Table B.15. Q11 How has the transition to alternative reference rates been proceeding in your country? 191
Table B.16. Q12 In your opinion, are market participants in your country generally ready for the transition? 193
Table B.17. Q13 Do you have any plans to issue securities linked to an alternative reference rate? 195

Follow OECD Publications on:

http://twitter.com/OECD_Pubs

http://www.facebook.com/OECDPublications

http://www.linkedin.com/groups/OECD-Publications-4645871

http://www.youtube.com/oecdilibrary

http://www.oecd.org/oecddirect/

Abbreviations and acronyms

AEs	Advanced Economies
AFT	Agence France Trésor
ATM	Average Term-to-Maturity
BCP	Business Continuity Plan
BFS	Benchmark Financing Strategy
BoE	Bank of England
BOJ	Bank of Japan
BTP	Buono del Tesoro Poliennale
CB	Central Bank
CDS	Credit Default Swap
CFA	Communauté financière d'Afrique
COVID	Coronavirus disease (COVID-19)
CPI	Consumer Price Index
CUSIP	Committee on Uniform Security Identification Procedures
DMO	Debt Management Office
DSSI	Debt Service Suspension Initiative
ECB	European Central Bank
EMDEs	Emerging Markets and Developing Economies
EME	Emerging Market Economy
ESG	Environmental, Social and Governance
EU	European Union
EUR	Euro
FRN	Floating Rate Note
FX	Foreign Exchange
GBP	Great Britain Pound
GBP	Green Bond Principles
GBR	Gross Borrowing Requirement

GDP	Gross Domestic Product
GFC	Global Financial Crisis
GNI	Gross National Income
HICs	High Income Countries
ICE	Intercontinental Exchange
ICMA	International Capital Market Association
IIF	Institute of International Finance
ILBs	Inflation-Linked Bonds
IMF	International Monetary Fund
ISIN	International Securities Identification Number
ISK	Icelandic Krona
KPIs	Key Performance Indicators
LAC	Latin America and Caribbean
LICs	Low Income Countries
MENA	Middle East and North Africa
MOF	Ministry of Finance
NBR	Net Borrowing Requirement
NDP	National Development Plan
OAT	Obligation Assimilable au Trésor
OECD	Organisation for Economic Co-operation and Development
PDM	Public Debt Management
PEPP	Pandemic Emergency Purchase Programme
PSPP	Public Sector Purchase Programme
QE	Quantitative Easing
RCF	Rapid Credit Facility
RFI	Rapid Financing Instrument
RIC	Reuters Instrument Code
ROR	Rollover Ratio
SBPs	Social Bond Principles
SDG	Sustainable Development Goals
SDRs	Special Drawing Rights
SLBPs	Sustainability-Linked Bond Principles
SNA	System of National Accounts
SPTs	Sustainable Performance Targets
SSA	Sub-Saharan Africa

TTEC	Transition Energétique et Ecologique pour le Climat
UMICs	Upper-Middle Income Countries
UN	United Nations
UNEP	United Nations Environment Programme
USD	United States Dollar
WP	Working Paper
WPDM	Working Party on Debt Management
YTM	Yield-to-Maturity

Executive summary

Borrowing needs of OECD governments are expected to stabilise somewhat in 2022 after rising rapidly in the wake of the pandemic

Fiscal responses to the COVID-19 crisis have necessitated significantly increased issuance of marketable debt over the last two years. In the OECD area as whole, central government gross borrowing requirements, which had remained stable at around USD 9.5 trillion after the 2008 financial crisis, stood at USD 16.4 trillion in 2020, and USD 15.1 trillion in 2021. In 2022, OECD governments are expected to borrow approximately USD 14.4 trillion from the markets, a small decrease compared to the previous two years markedly higher than pre-pandemic levels.

It is important to note that the share of net borrowing – the amount to be raised to cover the current budget deficit – in gross borrowing has significantly reduced, reflecting the gradual improvement in fiscal balances. While net borrowings constituted 50% of total borrowing in 2020, the ratio decreased to 20% in 2021, and it is expected to remain at around the same level in 2022. In absolute terms, central government net borrowing requirement for the OECD area is estimated to be around USD 3 trillion in 2022, double pre pandemic levels.

As countries are emerging from the pandemic with high levels of debt, debt servicing may pose challenges for sovereign issuers

Although the strong economic recovery in 2021 somewhat eased the government debt burden – which surged by more than 16 percentage points in 2020, the debt-to-GDP ratio remains at record high levels in many countries. In this context, the legacy of COVID-19 casts a long shadow on public finances with a significantly high debt to service. Despite the lengthened average-term-to-maturity of outstanding debt, an important indicator of refinancing risk across OECD countries, the amount of debt to be repaid or refinanced is considerable. Governments in the OECD area expected to redeem more than USD 20 trillion worth of maturing debt by the end of 2024.

Recently, financial conditions in the OECD area have tightened amid less supportive monetary policies and aggravated inflationary pressures since the outbreak of the war in Ukraine. For example, average 10-year government bond yields in large advanced economies have increased by more than 1.2 percentage points since January 2022. Going forward, the war in Ukraine is expected to slow the global recovery from the COVID-19 pandemic and further push up inflation worldwide. In addition to already rising policy interest rates, major central banks have revealed plans to unwind their large balance sheets, which would weigh further on yields on long-term bonds and cause an adjustment to the investor base of government debt in several jurisdictions. In this context of elevated uncertainty and a changing funding environment, this *Outlook* highlights the importance of effective communications, both by debt management offices and central banks, to cope with potential challenges in government securities markets. The *Outlook* also recommends that sovereign debt management offices closely monitor the resilience of market intermediaries and co-ordinate with the relevant authorities to promptly address possible stressed market conditions.

With deteriorated credit conditions, emerging market and developing economies are facing greater challenges

Since the outbreak of the pandemic, emerging market sovereign debt has been undergoing a structural decline in credit quality, as a record number of countries in these country groups have been downgraded. This *Outlook* indicates that sovereign debt issued by emerging market and developing economies with an investment grade has been shrinking since the outbreak of the pandemic. At the same time, their borrowing costs have been on the rise since the second half of the 2021.

With deteriorated credit conditions and high refinancing needs, emerging market economies are facing greater challenges. First, the tightening of global liquidity may erode investors' risk appetite towards emerging market economies, which in turn would make accessing international capital markets more difficult for those sovereign issuers. Second, spill-overs from the war in Ukraine are likely to aggravate existing challenges. Rising global energy and food prices, as well as slower global growth as a result of the conflict will negatively affect the economic prospects of emerging market and developing economies. An interaction of the major downside risks would pose considerable challenges for debt management in especially low-income countries with limited room for manoeuvre. In this context, lending and other financial support to these countries, such as grant facilities by international financial institutions, will be critical in terms of the sustainability of their debts and in supporting their economies.

A growing number of sovereign issuers are taking a role in supporting government sustainability agendas amid increased efforts to address the dual crises of COVID-19 and climate change

As Environmental, Social and Governance (ESG) related risks and concerns are growing in importance across all jurisdictions, many governments are including environmental, sustainability, and socio-economic objectives in their policy packages. Public debt management, as an interface between government and financial markets, can play an important role in supporting government sustainability agendas by conveying government commitments to improving environmental and social outcomes to investors and issuing ESG-labelled bonds. This approach has spread rapidly among OECD countries in recent years, in line with increased efforts by countries to address the dual crises of COVID-19 and climate change.

Drawing on a survey of OECD and selected non-OECD countries, this *Outlook* indicates that, when issuing labelled bonds, sovereign debt managers face a number of challenges including a lack of expertise in this area and a lack of availability of eligible projects in budgets, as well as compliance with impact and other reporting requirements. Leading practices to date highlight the importance of stakeholder engagement including cross-department collaboration and communication with market participants, commitment to transparency and reporting disclosures and to sustaining liquidity through issuance volume and instrument design. For sovereign issuers in emerging markets, labelled bonds present the benefit of attracting international investors by meeting their criteria for transparency and ESG issues. However, if not managed properly, this could create further vulnerability for issuers due to the increased currency risk associated with issuing foreign-currency debt.

1 Sovereign borrowing outlook for OECD countries

Following the record rise in 2020, OECD government funding needs stabilised in 2021, although they remained higher than in the pre-COVID-19 period. The cost of government funding increased slightly from historically record lows, as economies gradually recovered from COVID-19 and monetary policy stances became less supportive. Although the strong economic recovery in 2021 has somewhat eased the government debt burden, it remains at record high levels in many countries and the legacy of the crisis casts a long shadow on public finances.

This chapter assesses the impact of the pandemic on sovereign borrowing needs and outstanding debt for 2020 and 2021, and provides projections for 2022. It highlights the benefit of lengthening portfolio duration during periods of low interest rates and maintaining issuance flexibility through the use of a variety of different securities to manage high financing needs. This chapter also points to the risk and policy challenges arising from high refinancing needs, rising inflation and interest rates, changing patterns of investor demand and uncertainties around the projected level of borrowing requirements.

1.1. Introduction

The macroeconomic policy response to the COVID-19 crisis has been the largest and fastest in peacetime. This chapter offers an overview of the impact of these policy measures on the level, composition and cost of sovereign borrowing and debt in the OECD area in 2020 and 2021, as well as the projections for 2022. The analysis presented is based primarily on data collected through surveys.

Key findings

- The gross borrowings of OECD governments, which jumped by 70% in 2020 following the outbreak of COVID-19, are expected to gradually stabilise as economies recover and pandemic-related fiscal support is withdrawn. Aggregate government market borrowing needs are projected to decline slightly from above USD 16 trillion in 2020 to around USD 14 trillion in 2022, with marked differences across countries.

- OECD government net marketable debt issuance is expected to decline from USD 8 trillion in 2020 to around USD 3 trillion in 2021. It is projected to remain at around the same level in 2022, which is double pre-pandemic levels.

- Since 2019, the outstanding level of marketable debt for OECD governments increased by more than USD 10 trillion to USD 50 trillion in 2021, and is projected to reach USD 53 trillion in 2022. As a percentage of GDP, central government marketable debt for the OECD area rose by more than 16 percentage points to 90% in 2020, and is expected to gradually decline to 88% in 2022, driven *inter alia* by stabilised borrowing needs and low interest payments. These estimations for 2022, made before the war in Ukraine, are now subject to the economic effects of the war, as well as the monetary and fiscal policy responses.

- The cost of borrowing has risen, but remains at low levels across OECD countries. In the OECD area, nearly 70% of the fixed-rate government bonds issued in 2021 were for a yield less than 1%. This ratio was 80% in 2020 and 37% in 2019.

- Many countries sought to mitigate refinancing risk by lengthening issuance maturities. The average term-to-maturity of outstanding debt has almost fully returned to a pre-pandemic level standing at 7.6 years in 2021 and reached record highs in 16 OECD countries including France, Italy, Portugal, Spain and the United States.

- Despite the extended maturities of new issuance, debt redemption profiles are expected to be elevated and may pose significant challenges in terms of refinancing risks, with 40% of outstanding marketable debt stock needing to be refinanced or repaid within the next three years.

- Given the refinancing needs, rising yields, inflationary pressures and the prospects of less accommodative monetary policy, it is important for sovereign debt managers to strengthen investor relations and remain transparent and predictable in providing guidance to investors. They may also explore new borrowing instruments to support financing capacity.

- Going forward, downside risks to the outlook include the potential emergence of new COVID-19 variants, persistent inflation and mounting geopolitical tensions. To ensure the continued smooth functioning of government securities markets, debt managers should remain vigilant, closely monitor the resilience of market intermediaries and co-ordinate with the relevant authorities to promptly address possible stressed market conditions. Authorities may benefit from tools such as security lending facilities, flexibility in their approach to issuance and maintaining contingency buffers to be able to absorb possible stress in markets.

1.2. OECD government market borrowings remain higher than pre-pandemic levels, but are showing some signs of stabilisation

Fiscal responses by OECD governments to the COVID-19 crisis necessitated significantly increased issuance of marketable debt. Total gross borrowings from OECD governments, which had remained stable at around USD 10 trillion after the 2008 financial crisis, rose from USD 9.6 trillion in 2019 to above USD 16 trillion in 2020. This was a result of the extensive use of direct fiscal policy tools to mitigate the economic impact of the pandemic (Figure 1.1). This represents the highest increase ever in a single year and almost double the rise related to the 2008 financial crisis. Responses to the 2021 OECD Survey on Sovereign Borrowing indicate signs of stabilisation (see Box 1.3 for the survey definitions and methodology changes). Estimates indicate that OECD governments borrowed approximately USD 15 trillion in 2021 and will borrow USD 14 trillion in 2022 from the markets. This marks a small decrease compared to the amount of borrowing in 2020 but remains markedly higher than pre-pandemic levels. It should be noted that these estimations were made ahead of Russia's war against the people of Ukraine, when the fiscal stance was set to tighten gradually in 2022 mainly due to the gradual withdrawal of pandemic-related support measures. Considering the economic impact of the war and potential fiscal policy responses implemented by some countries, the downside risks to these estimates increase (OECD, 2022[1]).[1]

Gross borrowing needs consist of new borrowing plus refinancing needs. In 2021, a large portion of gross borrowings was used to refinancing maturing debt. The ratio increased from around 50% in 2020 to above 80% in 2021 and is projected to remain around that level in 2022. At the same time, new debt issuance to the markets declined significantly in 2021 and is projected to moderate to USD 3 trillion in 2022, largely due to economic growth and the withdrawal of fiscal support in most OECD countries. Despite the large drop compared to 2020, net borrowing needs remain significantly higher than pre-pandemic levels, which were around USD 1.3 trillion in the five years before the pandemic. It should be noted that projected net borrowing needs are subject to change depending on macroeconomic and fiscal developments during the year. For example, cash buffers in a few countries that were built-up though pre-funding in 2020 were drawn down in 2021, largely due to diminished volatility in cash flows.[2]

Figure 1.1. Fiscal and borrowing outlook in OECD countries, 2007-22

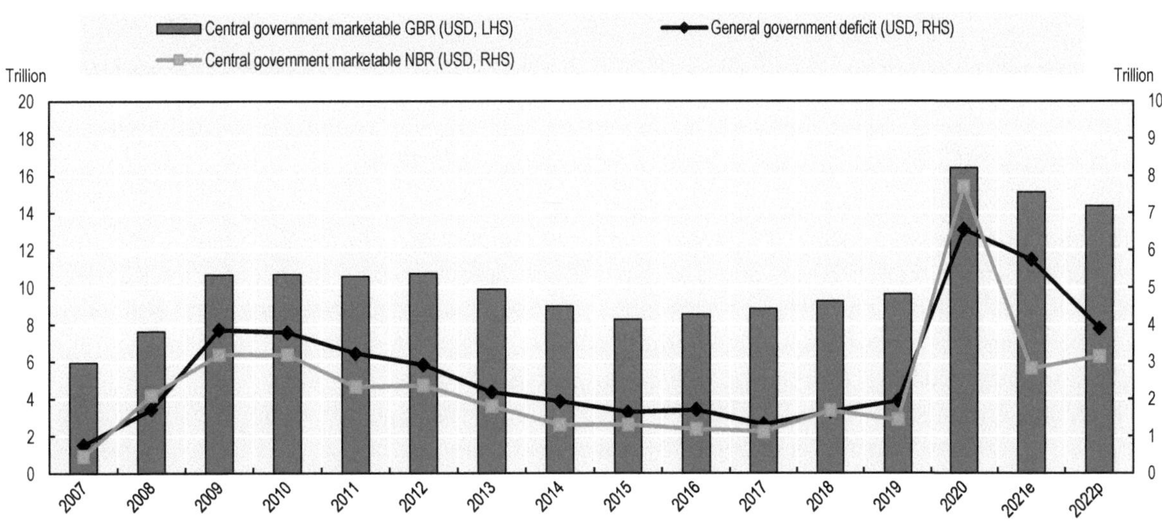

Notes: GBR = standardised gross borrowing requirement, NBR = net borrowing requirement.
Source: 2021 Survey on Central Government Marketable Debt and Borrowing; OECD Economic Outlook (December 2021); IMF World Economic Outlook Database (October 2021); Refinitiv, national authorities' websites and OECD calculations.

Figure 1.2 illustrates the trends in sovereign borrowings from the markets as a percentage of GDP for the OECD area, and for selected OECD groupings. Supported by massive fiscal policy and monetary policy support, economic growth in OECD countries rebounded sharply in 2021. The OECD Economic Outlook of December 2021 expects the GDP growth for the OECD area to reach 5.3% in 2021 and to moderate to 3.9% in 2022 (OECD, 2021[2]). Yet, recent illustrative simulations over the economic impact of the war in Ukraine suggest that GDP growth in the OECD area as a whole could be reduced by around 1 percentage point in 2022, if the shocks to commodity prices and financial markets seen since the outbreak of the war are sustained (OECD, 2022[1]). Against this backdrop, gross borrowing requirements in relation to GDP (which increased by more than 10 percentage points from 2019 to 2020) are estimated to decline by 6.6 percentage points by 2022. Compared to the OECD average, this decline in gross borrowing requirements is expected to be greater for "G7" countries' – where ratios are already relatively high – and largely driven by the United States. Given the uncertainties around the impact of the war and fiscal support, there is a risk of upward deviation from these estimates, particularly those in the Euro area.

Figure 1.2. Gross borrowing through marketable debt as a percentage of GDP

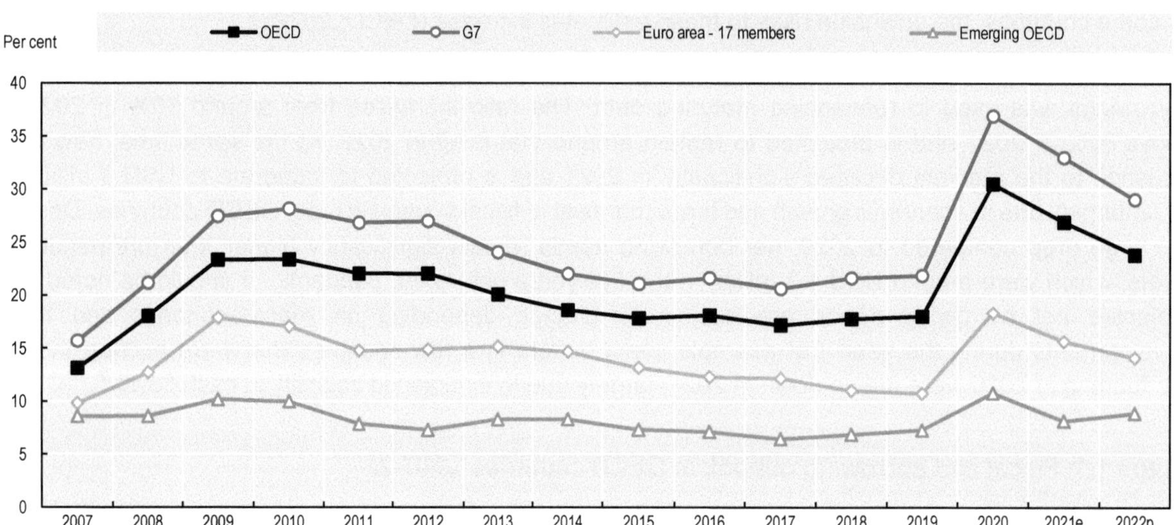

Note: Standardised gross borrowing requirement. Emerging OECD group consists of Chile, Colombia, Costa Rica, Hungary, Mexico, Poland and Turkey.
Source: 2021 Survey on Central Government Marketable Debt and Borrowing; OECD Economic Outlook (December 2021); IMF World Economic Outlook Database (October 2021); Refinitiv, national authorities' websites and OECD calculations.

EU Member countries have received significant financial support through the European Union, mostly in the form of loans from the SURE fund and grants and loans from the NextGenerationEU (NGEU) package. Given that this publication only covers government securities issued to finance central government budget deficits, the figures for Euro-area countries do not account for such funding sources. However, it should be noted that these additional funding sources will contribute to reduced borrowing needs from the markets over the short- and medium-term. In particular, NGEU grants are expected to generate additional fiscal space and reduce the pressure on debt-to-GDP ratio in EU Member countries (Pfeiffer, Janos and Jan, July 2021[3]). NGEU's current financing schemes entail an annual bond issuance of up to an average of around EUR 150 billion per year between 2021 and 2026, meaning that the European Union is becoming one of the major issuers in European capital markets (Box 1.1). With respect to distribution, the support will be mainly directed to the countries that suffered a large negative effect from the crisis. Hence, Italy and Spain are expected to absorb 60% or more of the grant package over 2021-23 (OECD, 2021[2]).[3]

Box 1.1. The European Commission as a capital market participant

The European Commission, on behalf of the European Union, has been running several lending programmes to support EU Member and other countries over a period of 40 years. However, the size and complexity of the NextGenerationEU (NGEU) programme required a fundamental change in the EU's approach to capital markets as an issuer. Hence, the Commission follows the practices used by sovereign issuers which comprise an open and transparent communication to market participants, a diversity of instruments and issuance techniques and the use of a structured network of primary dealers.

NextGenerationEU and its funding strategy:

NGEU is a temporary recovery instrument, which can raise up to EUR 750 billion at 2018 prices or some EUR 800 billion in current prices (5% of EU GDP). It aims to support economic recovery and build a greener, more digital and more resilient European Union.

The issuance of NGEU debt is planned to take place between mid-2021 and 2026. This entails average annual bond issuance of up to EUR 150 billion per year between mid-2021 and 2026. This would make the European Union one of the largest issuers in the Euro area in net terms.

According to the current setting, any NGEU issuance after 2026 will be limited in scale and consist solely of refinancing the maturing debt to smooth the budgetary absorption of liabilities over time. All borrowing will be fully repaid by 2058.

The funding strategy used under NGEU combines:

- An annual borrowing decision which sets the yearly ceilings under which transactions can be undertaken;
- A semi-annual funding plan with the targeted volumes and a tentative calendar for both auctions and syndications, to offer transparency and predictability to investors and other stakeholders;
- Multiple funding instruments (conventional bonds, green bonds and EU-Bills) to maintain flexibility, and to manage liquidity needs and the maturity profile;
- A combination of auctions and syndications, to ensure cost efficiency; and
- Structured and transparent relationships with banks supporting the issuance programme (via a Primary Dealer Network).

Since it became operational in mid-June 2021, the European Commission has issued EUR 96 billion of bonds and bills through syndications and auctions. Weighted average maturity of the issuance reached 9.5 years as of end 2021, higher than the OECD average. In terms of the borrowing cost, the weighted average yield was -0.11% (Table 1.1). The bonds have been trading between yields on corresponding German and French bonds.

Table 1.1. NextGenerationEU and its funding strategy

Funding instruments	Volumes (in EUR billions)	Average maturity at issuance (in years)	Yield at issuance
Bonds	71	12.7	0.13%
Bills	25	0.3	-0.78%
Overall	96	9.5	-0.11%

Note: Issued between mid-June 2021 and end of December 2021

Source: European Commission, https://ec.europa.eu/info/strategy/eu-budget/eu-borrower-investor-relations/.

1.2.1. Net borrowing requirements have eased with significant differences among countries

Projections for gross financing requirements are driven by the refinancing of debt due in the year and new financing requirements for the current year's budget (i.e. net borrowing requirements). Refinancing amounts for maturing debt are known with a high level of certainty in advance. Conversely, projections for net borrowing requirements are inherently uncertain. Even if tax and spending policies remain unchanged, actual gross borrowing needs may diverge from planned amounts due to various reasons, including economic and budgetary outcomes, market conditions and the timing of cash transactions.

In the OECD area, net borrowings from the market decreased by more than 60%, from almost USD 8 trillion in 2020 to USD 3 trillion in 2021. Most fiscal measures in 2020 had been designed to be short-lived. However, repeated COVID-19 outbreaks with new types of variants prompted authorities in some countries to extend fiscal measures further. While many fiscal programs are still providing significant support to the economy, their size and composition have adjusted in several countries as the pandemic evolved. In parallel, government financing forecasts in a number of countries were adjusted throughout the year in accordance with the changes in both budget outcomes and funding. The recent OECD Survey on Primary Market Developments revealed more than two-thirds of debt management offices (DMOs) experienced challenges with the sharp changes in government funding needs, and more than half found cash forecasting in 2021 difficult (Annex A). In 2021, net borrowings for the OECD area as a whole were lower than the planned amount for 2020, which was close to USD 5 trillion (OECD, 2021[2]). This was largely due to better-than-expected tax revenue outturns in several countries and the use of cash buffers in a few countries (e.g. the Netherlands and the United States).

Figure 1.3 illustrates annual changes in borrowing requirements in relation to GDP across countries in the wake of the pandemic. At the total OECD level net borrowing requirements in relation to GDP deteriorated by 11.6 percentage points over 2019-20 and improved by 9.3 percentage points for 2020-21. In 2020, aggregate net borrowing needs surged across the OECD area although the increase in funding needs varied greatly across countries with differences in the pandemic impact on economies. Differences in the capacity to increase direct fiscal spending, financial stability concerns, and the ability to raise additional funds from the markets also contributed to the variation across countries.

Following the acute phase of the pandemic, the size and composition of the fiscal responses have diverged. This reflects differences in automatic stabilisers, pre-pandemic fiscal space, the severity of infections, and policy preferences. Compared to 2020, borrowing needs, as a percentage of GDP, declined in most countries in 2021, and increased further only in a few countries. In some countries, such as Denmark, Japan, Korea, Poland and Portugal, the ratio of net borrowings-to-GDP declined to pre-pandemic levels in 2021.

This comparison also reveals that those countries with the highest annual decline in new borrowing levels in 2021 experienced the highest percentage point increases in 2020. Specifically, new borrowings in relation to GDP in Canada, New Zealand, Japan and the United States fell by more than 10 percentage points in 2021 (having increased by more than 15 percentage points from 2019 to 2020). This is largely due to strong economic growth and the associated improvements in primary fiscal balances. In some cases, the use of high cash balances, built up from pre-financing in 2020, also helped alleviate the need for new debt issuance in 2021, most notably in the second half of the year.

Figure 1.3. Annual changes in net borrowings from the markets as a percentage of GDP

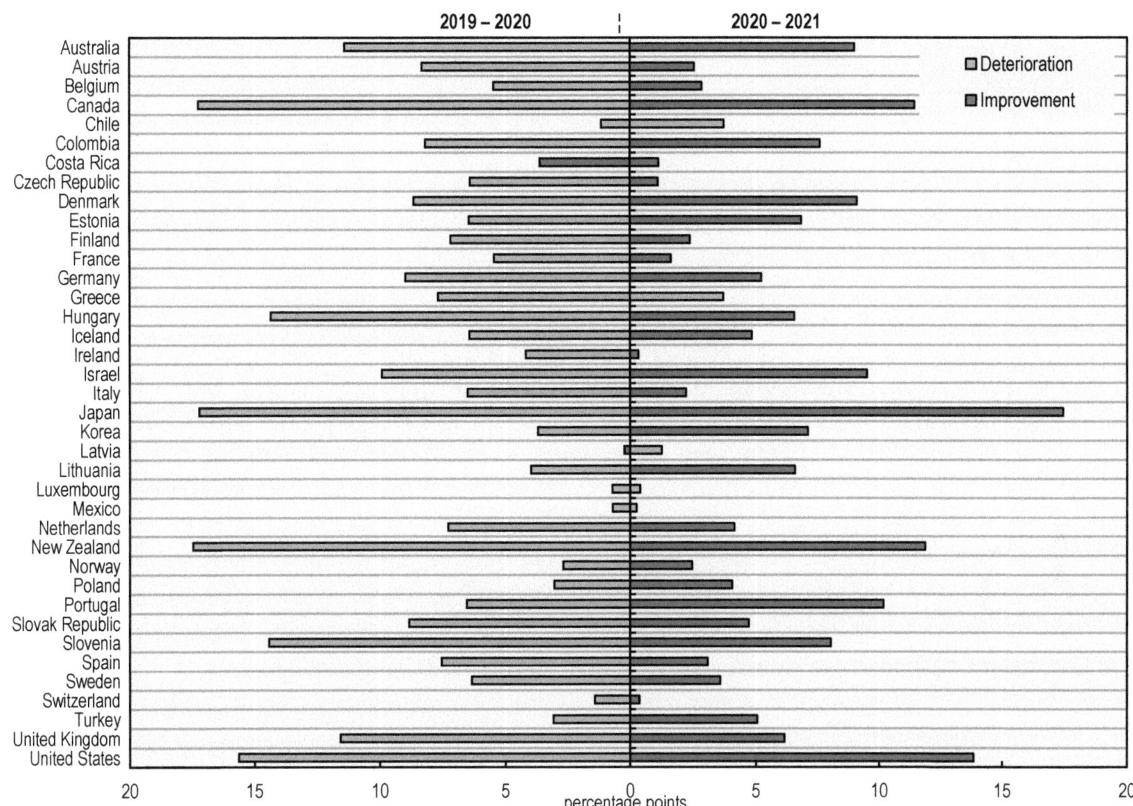

Source: 2021 Survey on Central Government Marketable Debt and Borrowing; OECD Economic Outlook (December 2021); IMF World Economic Outlook Database (October 2021); Refinitiv, national authorities' websites and OECD calculations.

1.3. Cost of funding remained low despite the recent rise

In the OECD area, funding conditions have generally remained favourable despite the surge in pandemic related borrowing. OECD countries were able to issue the substantial amount of new debt required without putting excessive upward pressure on borrowing costs. While this likely reflected, in part, strong market demand for low-risk assets, central banks played a major role in ensuring that sovereign debt markets continued to function smoothly. As well, highly accommodative monetary policies have supported economic activity. Investors' perception of the pandemic as a one-off shock to debt dynamics rather than a structural deterioration in national fiscal positions also contributed to the low and stable borrowing costs.

Recently, financial conditions in the OECD area have tightened somewhat, amid aggravated inflationary pressures since the outbreak of the war in Ukraine. Many central banks have indicated an intention to accelerate the timing of monetary policy normalisation by bringing forward the timing of increases in their policy rates and concluding quantitative easing (QE) programmes (or unwinding balance sheets). It should be noted, however, that the pace of this policy normalisation varies considerably among countries, reflecting different stages of economic recovery from the pandemic, inflationary pressures and the impact of the war.

The Bank of England became the first major central bank to raise interest rates (in December 2021, in folloed by several subsequent increases) and has begun to reduce the stock of UK government bonds purchases by ceasing to reinvest the proceeds of maturing assets in March 2022. The US Federal Reserve ended asset purchases and raised its policy rate by 1/4 percentage point to 0.5 per cent in March 2022 and by half percentage point to 1 per cent in May 2022. At its April meeting, the European Central Bank has kept key its key policy interest rates unchanged and announced that it expected to conclude its asset purchase programme in the third quarter of 2022. Meanwhile, there has been no change in the quantitative easing policy of the Bank of Japan. As central banks try to find the delicate balance between stemming the inflation threat without having a significantly negative impact on economic growth, the changes in monetary policy stance have been clearly communicated so far and appear to have generated relatively little financial market stress.

Stronger growth, higher inflation and the gradual unwinding of highly accommodative monetary policy stances, including tapering of asset purchases by major central banks, have led to higher bond yields. The yields on government bonds finished 2021 markedly higher than the previous two years, although they are still low by historical standards. Over the year to December 2021 for the OECD area, yields on both 2-year and 10-year benchmark bonds rose by around 1% on average (Figure 1.4). Much of the increase for the longer end of yield curves is attributed to a combination of heightened inflation expectations, greater inflation risk premia and rising term premia (BIS, December 2021[4]). Despite that, government bonds were still trading at historically low yields, and sometimes even at negative nominal yields in several OECD countries at the end of 2021 (e.g. up to 5-year maturity in France and Japan, 10-year maturity in Germany).

Figure 1.4. Change in benchmark yields between December 2020 and December 2021

Panel A: Change in 2-year benchmark yields / Panel B: Change in 10-year benchmark yields

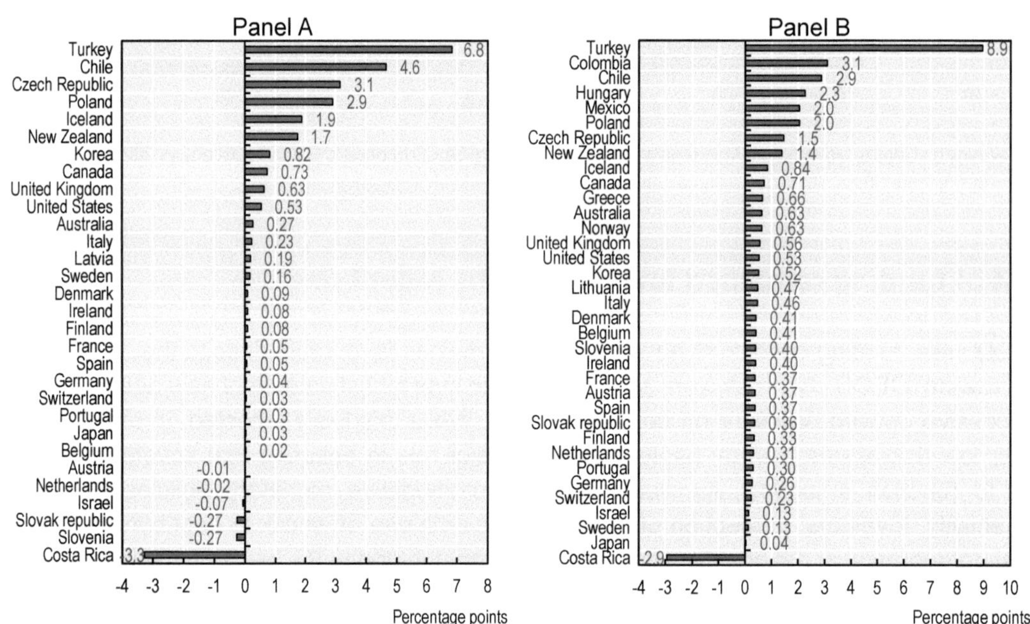

Note: Difference in average yields in December of each year.
Source: Refinitiv.

The figures reflect a significant rise in borrowing costs in some countries including Chile, Mexico, Poland and Turkey. In some cases, country-specific economic and geopolitical factors contributed to stressed market conditions and an erosion of credibility, in addition to the general decreased risk appetite of investors due to heightened global uncertainty.[4] For example, in Turkey the lack of credibility in monetary policy has exacerbated capital outflows and led to currency depreciation and a surge in risk premia. Between 2019 and 2021, the share of non-resident holdings of domestic debt decreased from around 10% in 2019 to 3% in 2021, while the share held by public banks rose from about 26% to 39%. In Chile, concerns over the weakening of public finances, as well as rising political/social pressures led to credit rating downgrades. These downgrades, together with the reduction of public bonds in pension funds have added pressures on market funding conditions. Between 2019 and 2021, non-resident holdings of domestic debt fell from 20% to 13%, while this was compensated by increased domestic bank holdings.

This general increase in interest rates meant that government funding costs rose in 2021, particularly in the fourth quarter. In addition, the longer average maturities for new issuance, as discussed in Section 1.4, contributed to the higher overall cost of borrowing.[5] Figure 1.5 illustrates volume shares of fixed-rate bond issuance by yield category for 2020 and 2021. Despite the increase in interest rates over the last months of the year, nearly 70% of the fixed-rate government bonds in the OECD are were issued with less than 1% yield in 2021. This ratio was 80% in 2020 and 37% in 2019. Compared to 2020, major changes took place in Canada, Italy, the United Kingdom and the United States. The figures also reflect around half of the fixed-rate bonds issued in the Euro area and in Japan, having been allocated in the primary market at negative rates.

It should also be noted that in 2021, the funding activities by some sovereigns were concentrated in the first half of the year. Combined with the gradual improvement in borrowing requirements and increased uncertainty and volatility induced by the repositioning of some investors on the long end of the yield curves, this prompted some issuers to reduce their issuance activity in the second half of the year (Annex A). In some Euro-area countries, the start of disbursements from the European Commission to European countries in the summer also played a role in the reduction of government borrowings compared to planned issuance activities (Box 1.1).

Figure 1.5. Volume share of fixed-rate bond issuance by yield category

Panel A: 2020 / Panel B: 2021

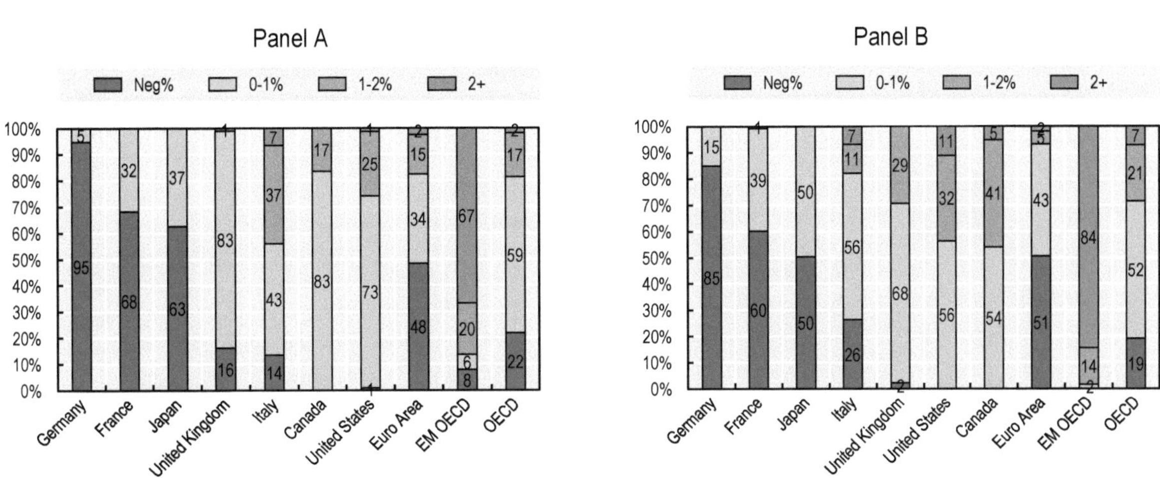

Note: Fixed-rate bond issuances and re-opens denominated in EUR, USD, Japanese Yen, Canadian dollars and British pounds and categorised by yield at issuance. The EM OECD group consists of Chile, Colombia, Costa Rica, Hungary, Mexico, Poland and Turkey.
Source: Refinitiv; OECD Economic Outlook (December 2021); IMF World Economic Outlook Database (October 2021); and OECD calculations.

Looking ahead, financial conditions are likely to tighten further, whether because of central banks continuing to normalise monetary policy or because investors demand higher yields given the economic and inflation outlook. The pace and timing of monetary policy normalisation will be closely watched by investors, who aim to assess risks and opportunities to determine optimal asset allocations. When surveyed, most countries in the OECD expressed little concern over the adequacy of investor demand.[6] That said, if inflation outcomes surprise on the upside and inflation expectations drift up substantially, central banks around the world could be forced to accelerate planned normalisation by increasing policy rates earlier and faster than expected. In turn, this could lead to a substantial repricing in financial markets (OECD, 2021[2]). In this context, even the most liquid government securities markets may come under pressure as investors become more sensitive to changes in macroeconomic uncertainty.

1.3.1. Central bank purchases of and demand for government securities

In the wake of the pandemic, asset purchase programmes have been effectively used by a number of central banks, both to restore market functioning at the initial stage of the crisis and then through to support the economic recoveries. The asset purchases, which have been concentrated in government securities, reached unprecedented levels in several countries. Total net purchases of government securities by major central banks reached USD 4.6 trillion in 2020, moderating to USD 1.3 trillion in 2021 (Figure 1.6). These figures equate to 52% and 17% of long-term debt securities issuance by central governments of these countries in 2020 and 2021 respectively. As a result, in 2021, they remained as the single largest creditor in most OECD countries by holding around 45% of the outstanding stock in Japan and Canada, more than 35% in Australia and New Zealand, and the United Kingdom and more than 20% in most of the EU countries, Sweden and the United States.

Figure 1.6. Central banks' net purchases and government debt issuance in selected countries

Panel A: EU issues and ECB purchases; and US issues and Federal Reserve purchases / Panel B: Japan issues and Bank of Japan (BoJ) purchases; UK issues and Bank of England (BoE) purchases; and Canada issues and Bank of Canada (BoC) purchases

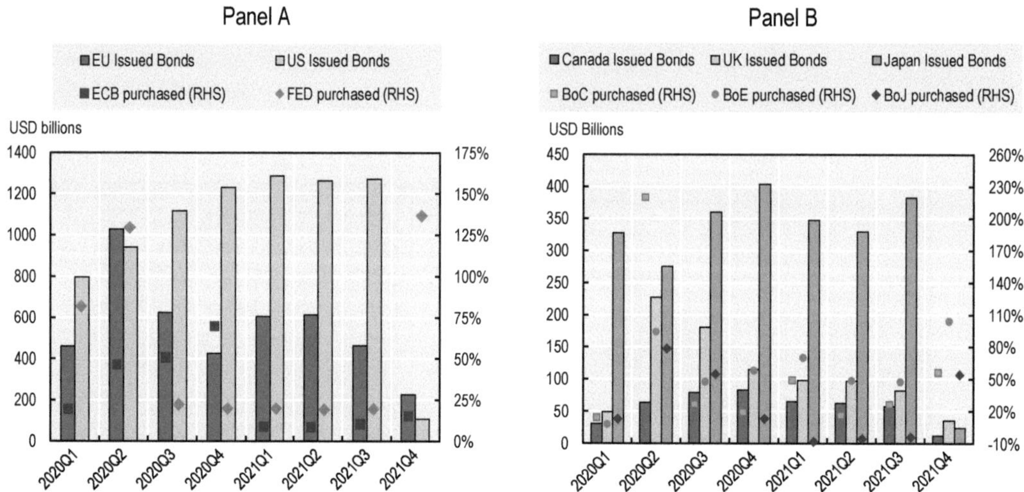

Note: Converted into USD at the end of each month. Calculated from data on security holdings for the Federal Reserve and the BoJ. For the BoE data are calculated from holdings of gilts by the Bank of England's asset purchase facility. Data for ECB are net purchases for the PSPP and the PEPP.
Source: Central banks, Refinitiv and OECD calculations.

The accumulation of bonds through large scale asset purchase programmes has lowered the 'free float' of available government securities to the market and to some extent helped the absorption of additional supply of government securities. Through asset purchase programmes, central banks have lowered the interest rates on bonds and facilitated market functioning by acting as a 'backstop' buyer. While supply of government bonds has surged in the wake of the pandemic, the presence of a large, solvent, predictable and persistent buyer has helped primary dealers (PDs) with their market-making activity in terms of research cost and holding larger inventories.[7]

As the economies have rebounded and inflation concerns built up, a number of central banks began to normalise policy. Several central banks have already stopped net purchases and some either signalled their intention to start, or starting to implement balance sheet reduction since 2021, which, all things equal, increases the net supply of these bonds.[8] This means that their holdings as a proportion of total government bonds outstanding are expected to only decline gradually.

Looking forward, the unwinding of asset purchase programmes would be expected to put some upward pressure on bond yields, although the extent of this pressure would depend on the pace and scale of the unwind. This increase should come primarily through the portfolio balance channel, as the increased net issuance will have to be absorbed by other investors who may demand higher yields. Depending on how the unwinding of the programmes are structured, there may also be a signalling effect if market participants infer that balance sheet reduction carries information about the future path of policy rates. Finally, central banks' reduced level of activity could increase primary dealers' search costs, which would increase their risk premia to intermediate trade.

While central banks have helped to absorb the additional supply of government securities in the market in major advanced economies, the balance sheet capacity of primary dealers may need to be assessed more carefully in planning governments' funding. Overall, government securities market resilience will depend on various factors including Primary Dealers' warehousing capacities, market absorption of additional bond supply and the pace of central banks' tapering and unwinding of their balance sheet.

1.4. Risk-driven borrowing strategies resulted in an increased the amount of duration supply to the market

The primary objective of sovereign debt issuers is to ensure government financing requirements are met at all times and at the lowest possible cost over the medium to long run, consistent with a prudent level of related risk. This well-defined objective requires a number of supply (i.e. Issuer) and demand (i.e. Investor) factors to be considered by sovereign DMOs when setting borrowing strategies. These include i) cost and risk features (*e.g.* interest rate, refinancing, liquidity and currency risks) of the existing debt portfolios; *ii)* projections of the government borrowing needs; *iii)* potential medium- and long-term outcomes of a range of alternative funding strategies in terms of cost and risk parameters; *iv)* expert judgement on market constraints (e.g. investor demand, market development, legal restrictions etc.) and *v)* potential market challenges and opportunities, taking not account the potential for sovereign debt operations to impact home markets (OECD, 2018[5]). Depending on these factors, countries' borrowing strategies, in terms of maturity, interest rate and currency composition of borrowings, evolve over time.

As discussed in the following sections, overall T-Bill issuance has been reduced and most sovereign issuers have shifted towards fixed-rate issuance with long-term maturities, which represented more than half of securities in their funding programmes in 2021. Sovereign debt managers are targeting a similar strategy in 2022, looking to further strengthen the resilience of sovereign debt portfolios to refinancing risks.

1.4.1. Reduction in T-bill issuances: A shift from money market funding to capital market funding

In normal times, short-term debt such as T-Bills act as a cash management instrument, whose issuance volume is determined by the timing and size of government receipts and outlays. During crisis periods, such as the 2008 financial crisis and the recent COVID-19 crisis, T-Bills play an important role as 'shock absorbers' in sovereign financing.[9] When there are unexpected changes in financial requirements, sovereign debt managers can delay adjusting debt issuance rates during the year, typically through changes in the issuance of T-bills. At the onset of the COVID-19 crisis, sovereign issuers in many

OECD countries (e.g. France, Germany and the United States) expanded their short-term borrowing programmes to manage unexpected surges in financing needs, this was achieved at a low cost in volatile market conditions (OECD, 2021[6]). T-bill issuance is also a complement to running down cash buffers in many circumstances and together these measures can offer substantial operational flexibility to debt managers. After rising rapidly in 2020, T-bill issuance has fallen notably over the course of 2021. The share of short-term instruments in central government marketable debt issuance in the OECD area, fell from 47% in 2020 to 41% in 2021, returning to pre-COVID-19 levels.

Figure 1.7. Maturity composition of central government marketable debt issuance

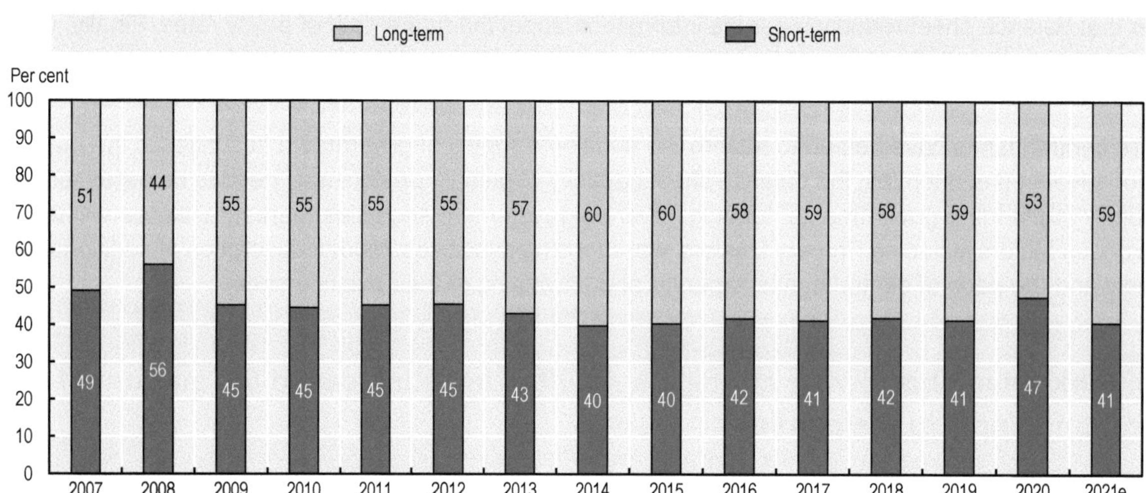

Notes: This is based on standardised gross borrowing.
Source: 2021 Survey on Central Government Marketable Debt and Borrowing; OECD Economic Outlook (December 2021); Refinitiv; national authorities' websites; and OECD calculations.

This strategy, shifting from money market to capital market funding aims to rebuild contingency capacity if significant funding is needed again in short order. There are also country specific factors behind this development. For example, in the United States, part of the decline in T-bills in 2021 was related to the constraints driven by the legislated debt ceiling. The US Treasury paid down T-bills to avoid exceeding the debt limit imposed in August 2021 (US Treasury, 2021[7]).[10]

It should be noted that a few countries including Germany and Mexico issued more short-term debt in 2021 compared to 2020, largely due to increased actual borrowing needs during the year compared to the original funding plans. In addition, relatively higher yields on long-term debt might also reduce the incentive for DMOs to issue at the long end of the yield curve.

1.4.2. Overall borrowing maturities lengthened at relatively low interest rates

As discussed in the previous section, new funding requirements were lower in 2021 relative to 2020 for most OECD countries. This has meant less emphasis on issuing short-dated instruments where domestic demand is more predictable and allowed sovereign issuers to issue more mid- to longer-dated bonds. The previous edition of this publication emphasised the rising rollover ratios and refinancing risk of debt portfolios and recommended sovereign DMOs consider lengthening borrowing maturities. It was noted that the low interest rates environment provides an opportunity for sovereign issuers to issue long maturity bonds to lower portfolio vulnerability from increases in interest rates for future generations. At the same time, any changes in borrowing strategies with respect to maturity composition should carefully consider investor demand, as different government securities have different roles in financial markets (e.g. T-Bills play a key role in money markets).

The 2021 OECD Survey on Primary Market Developments revealed that 21 out of 34 respondents lengthened their borrowing maturity structure relative to 2020, this was on the back of strong investor demand for duration. A number of OECD countries increased the volume of long-dated securities relative to short-term debt which, in turn, increased the weighted average maturity of the borrowing. For example, Canada increased its long-term bond issuance (maturity of 10 years or more) to above 40% of total bond issuance and re-opened its 50-year bond twice in 2021. Similarly, the average weighted maturity of debt issuance of the United Kingdom, skewed towards long-dated debt (maturity of 15 years or more) issuance, rose by around 18 months to 16 years at the end of 2021.

1.5. Increased refinancing needs has created scope for introducing new securities and maturity lines

When sovereign DMOs introduce new securities, they must consider a set of supply and demand side factors. In particular, they assess the strength and sustainability of investor demand, potential impact on existing securities, additional costs due to novelty and liquidity premia, and potential benefits of portfolio diversification and risk reduction, investor diversification and supporting the development of a new market segment (OECD, 2021[6]). Against this background, elevated funding needs after the COVID-19 crisis created additional scope for new maturity lines and new types of securities and allowed countries to introduce these new products without diminishing market liquidity, either in general or for particular parts of their yield curves. Compared to pre-pandemic period, the number of new instruments introduced by OECD area DMOs has increased significantly in recent years. The annual OECD Survey of Primary Market Developments seeks information from DMOs on their issuance of new securities in the form of new maturity lines and new type of instruments. The surveys in 2018, 2019, 2020 and 2021 revealed that, while only 25 new instruments were introduced during the 24 months leading up to the pandemic, this number increased to 46 after the pandemic hit (Figure 1.8).

In 2021, all new instruments except two carried longer-term maturities (i.e. longer than 2-year or more). A few countries extended their yield curves with inaugural issuance. For example, New Zealand extended the nominal curve from 20-years to 30-years, Sweden to 50-years, and Slovenia to 60-years in 2021. Introducing new securities with long-term maturities helps mitigate refinancing risk and diversifies the investor base by generating additional demand from available domestic and international savings pools. At the same time, any new instrument should be assessed prudently, as it would represent value-for-money for the taxpayer, enjoy strong and sustained demand in the long-term and be consistent with governments' wider fiscal objectives. A good example of this is sovereign ESG-labelled bonds, in particular green bonds.

Figure 1.8. Issuance of new securities and maturity lines

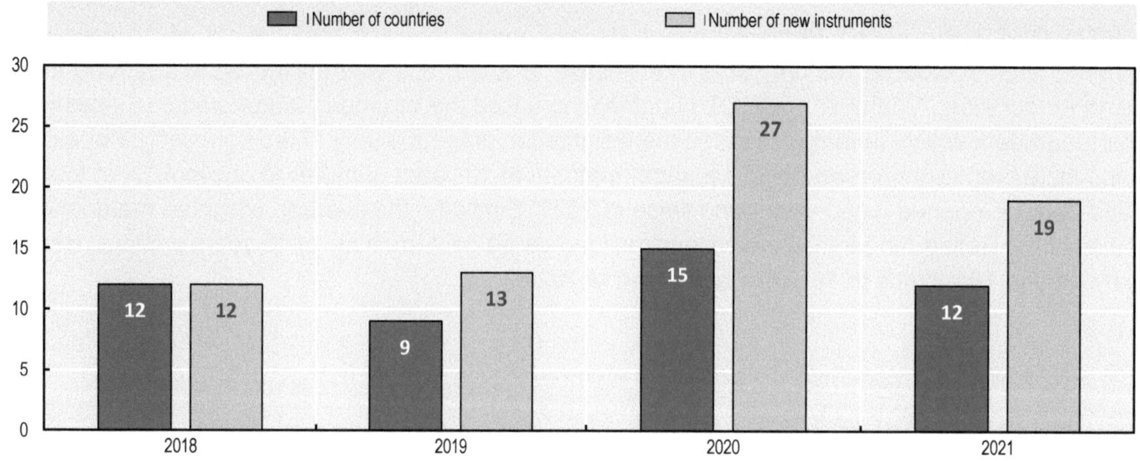

Source: 2018, 2019, 2020 and 2021 OECD Surveys on Primary Market Developments.

1.5.1. Green bonds are becoming an integral part of regular issuance programmes in a number of countries

As a growing number of sovereign DMOs are incorporating ESG factors in public debt management and ESG-labelled sovereign bonds, in particular green bonds, look to become an integral part of regular issuance programmes (Box 1.2). As of December 2021, 18 OECD countries issued green bonds exceeding USD 180 billion, more than half of which were issued following the COVID-19 crisis. In terms of debut issuance, Chile, Luxembourg and Slovenia issued new sustainable bonds, and Columbia, Italy, Spain and the United Kingdom issued green bonds for the first time in 2021. In addition, 16 countries plan to issue a new ESG-labelled bond within the next 12 months, including the inaugural green bond issuances planned by Austria, Canada, Iceland and New Zealand.

In the wake of the pandemic, both the number and volume of ESG-labelled bonds issued in foreign currency have risen. In the OECD area, the share of foreign currency denominated borrowing in total long-term borrowing from the markets increased from 2.1% in 2019 to 2.5% in 2021 driven mainly by ESG-labelled bonds issued by a few countries including Chile and Hungary. For example, in Chile, the share of FX-denominated bonds increased from 17% in 2019 to over 65% in 2021. In these countries, the average term-to-maturity (ATM) has lengthened considerably due to the issuance of FX-denominated bonds. In addition, this strategy of complementing funding programme with international issuance, has helped reduce pressure in local bond markets and reduce financial crowding out risks, in particular in times of elevated funding needs (Priftis and Zimic, 2021[8]).

> ## Box 1.2. Common approaches to incorporating ESG considerations into public debt management
>
> Public debt management (PDM), as an interface between government and financial markets, can play an important role in supporting a government's ESG agenda and in meeting ESG-sensitive investor demand. Common approaches to incorporating ESG factors into public debt management include conveying a government's commitment to improving environmental and social outcomes and issuing ESG-labelled bonds while paying close attention to transparency and long-term financial sustainability. Such practices have been spreading rapidly among OECD countries in recent years in line with increased efforts to address the dual challenges of the COVID-19 pandemic and climate change. The 2021 Survey on Approaches to Incorporating ESG Factors into Public Debt Management revealed that half of the OECD area debt management offices (e.g. Australia, Chile, France and Germany) take into account the national-level ESG strategy either in their investor engagement, communication practices and/or their instrument choice. The trend is set to accelerate as one-fifth of the respondents are planning to implement similar practices in the near future.
>
> Factoring the government's ESG policies into investor relations and general communication strategies, by gathering the relevant information available (similar to a 'one-stop-shop' model), would make it easier for ESG-sensitive investors and rating agencies to assess risks and make investment decisions based on policy commitments. This, in turn, can help DMOs to better understand investors' decision frameworks for asset allocation, promote awareness about governments' ESG policies, identify a relevant green/other ESG bonds framework, and boost ESG credentials for an upcoming labelled bond issue launch. As of 2021, 12 OECD countries reported that they have aligned investor relations with a broader national level ESG strategy and several others are considering doing so. While many respondents noted the extent of incorporating ESG factors into their investor relations is relevant to the issuance of labelled bonds, a few DMOs that do not issue and do not intend to issue such bonds have also adapted their investor engagement to the growing demand for information in this area. The Australian DMO, for example, provides information and data on the Australian Government's Climate Change and emission reduction policies and commitments, information on the government's emerging technology and renewable energy programs as well as links to the relevant departments in a regular investor chart pack. Another prominent example comes from the Finnish Treasury, which launched a digital hub on the country's ESG strategy, thus providing a single-entry point for investors to track where the country is standing in terms of various ESG related indices, government level targets and performance.
>
> Labelled bonds such as green, social, sustainability and sustainability-linked bonds, that have specific sustainability and ESG objectives have gained ground in the government bond markets in recent years, on the back of robust market demand. Eighteen OECD countries have issued ESG-labelled bonds, mostly in the last two years. Alignment with national level ESG strategies and increased demand from investors are the main motivations for starting a sovereign green/ESG bond issuance programme. Respondents also noted the following challenges: i) lack of eligible projects; ii) identification of eligible budget expenditures; iii) setting a framework for green bonds, and; iv) impact reporting including underlying granular data for sector specific metrics. While an emerging field, leading practices to date of sovereign ESG-labelled bonds (e.g. France, Germany, Italy and the Netherlands) share the following common features: i) stake holder engagement through the lifetime of the bonds from selecting eligible projects to monitoring and reporting the projects, ii) commitment to transparency and reporting disclosures with regard to the types of projects in which funds will be invested as well as the areas of spending to be excluded, iii) commitment to sustain liquidity through issuance volume and instrument design.
>
> Source: 2021 Survey on 'Approaches to incorporating ESG factors into public debt management' and discussions in 2021 annual meeting of the OECD WPDM.

1.6. Countries are emerging from the crisis with more debt, while strong growth helps stabilise debt burdens

Public debt sharply increases following wars, economic disasters, financial crises, and other events in which government outlays increase at rates in excess of revenues. In recent history, the 2008-financial crisis and the Euro-area debt crisis that followed pushed up government debt levels significantly and relatively quickly. Between 2007 and 2012, the outstanding volume of central government debt increased by around 70% from around USD 21 trillion to USD 35 trillion in the OECD area. In this period, central government marketable debt-to-GDP ratios increased by around 25 percentage points in total and by 8 percentage points in 2009 alone (Figure 1.9). In the years preceding to the pandemic, debt growth was offset by positive GDP growth-interest-rate differentials, which resulted in a small decline in the debt-GDP ratio for the OECD area (i.e. by 1 percentage point). However, the pandemic hit OECD countries hard in 2020, and led to an unprecedented impact on fiscal balances. While fiscal balances deteriorated by around 10% of GDP, the OECD-area economy contracted by 5.5% in 2020. A combination of rising fiscal deficits and contracting economies pushed government debt-to-GDP ratios by around 16 percentage points, up nearly twice the impact of the 2008 financial crisis.

Figure 1.9. Marketable debt-to-GDP: 2008 financial crisis vs COVID-19 shock

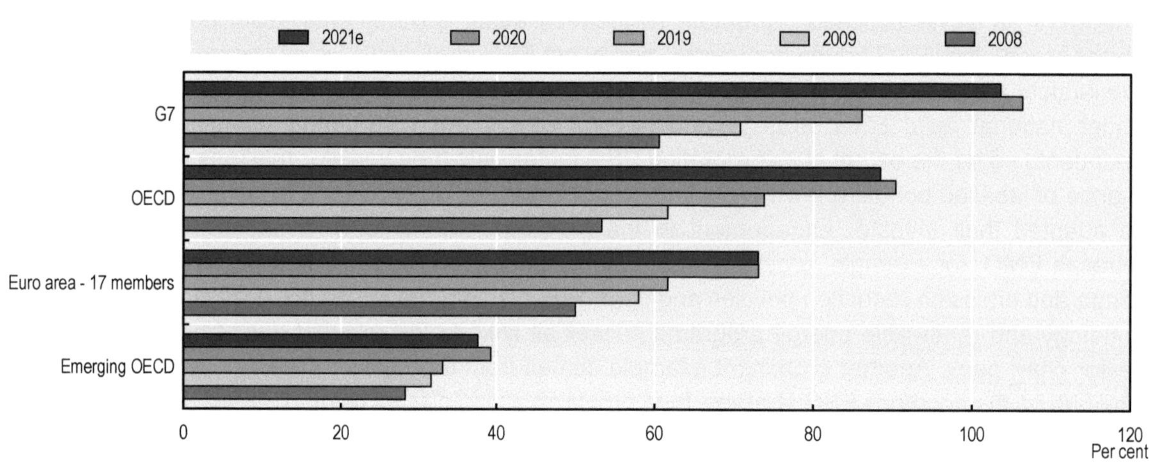

Note: Emerging OECD group consists of Chile, Colombia, Costa Rica, Hungary, Mexico, Poland and Turkey.
Source: 2021 Survey on Central Government Marketable Debt and Borrowing; OECD Economic Outlook (December 2021); IMF World Economic Outlook Database (October 2021); Refinitiv, national authorities' websites and OECD calculations.

In 2021, while government debt continued growing in nominal terms, the central government marketable debt-to-GDP ratio is estimated to have fallen by around 2 percentage points for the OECD area. This decline was due to favourable growth-interest rate differentials generated by fiscal and monetary support provided in the wake of the pandemic and the strong rebound that generally followed economic re-openings. This outcome slightly bettered our 2020 forecast for 2021, largely due to the stronger-than-expected economic recovery. This also highlights that with the right policy mix, debt dynamics can be improved and put back on a sustainable path.

OECD level aggregate figures hide considerable variation across countries. Figure 1.10 illustrates that while debt-to-GDP ratios deteriorated from 2019 to 2020 across the OECD area, the impact of the pandemic on debt ratios was particularly significant for some countries including Canada, Italy, Japan, Spain, the United Kingdom and the United States. Compared to 2020, debt ratios in 2021 improved for the most part in the OECD area, except for a few countries, including Austria, Chile, and New Zealand. This largely reflects the uneven economic recovery across the OECD area and different size of continued fiscal support measures in 2021.

Figure 1.10. Changes in selected central government debt-to-GDP ratios across the OECD (percentage point changes between 2019-20 and 2020-21)

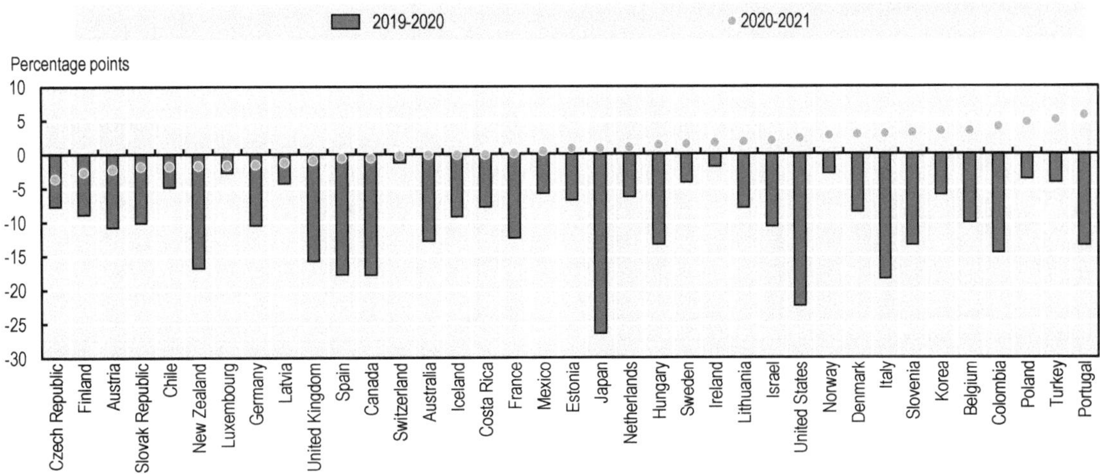

Source: 2021 Survey on Central Government Marketable Debt and Borrowing; OECD Economic Outlook (December 2021); IMF World Economic Outlook Database (October 2021); Refinitiv, national authorities' websites and OECD calculations.

The 2021 survey on the sovereign borrowing outlook projects the outstanding level of central government marketable debt to increase from around USD 50 trillion in 2021 to USD 53 trillion in 2022 (Figure 1.11). This represents a total increase of more than USD 13 trillion in outstanding government securities since the outbreak of the COVID-19 crisis, which is higher than the total debt growth over the decade before the crisis. For the OECD area as a whole, the debt-to-GDP ratio is projected to decline marginally from 90% in 2020 to 88% 2022, largely driven by stabilised borrowing needs and low interest payments.[11] It should also be noted that these projections were made prior to the war in Ukraine, which is expected to hinder the European economies, particularly those that have a common border with either Russia or Ukraine (OECD, 2022[1]).

As countries emerge from COVID-19 with greater debt loads, long-term debt-to-GDP trajectories will very much depend on the interplay between fiscal primary deficits, interest rates and long-term economic growth. In the ongoing recovery phase, when infections have been brought under control, it is important to channel fiscal support toward boosting investment. Encouragingly, in many countries public investment is projected to increase in 2022-23 relative to 2019 levels, though by a relatively modest amount (OECD, 2021[2]). This, in turn, would support debt sustainability by leading to stronger medium- and long-term economic growth and a gradual reduction of debt-to-GDP ratios.

Figure 1.11. Central government marketable debt and fiscal balances

Panel A: Outstanding central government marketable debt in OECD countries, 2007-22 / Panel B: Primary balances in relation to GDP, in selected OECD countries, 2019-22

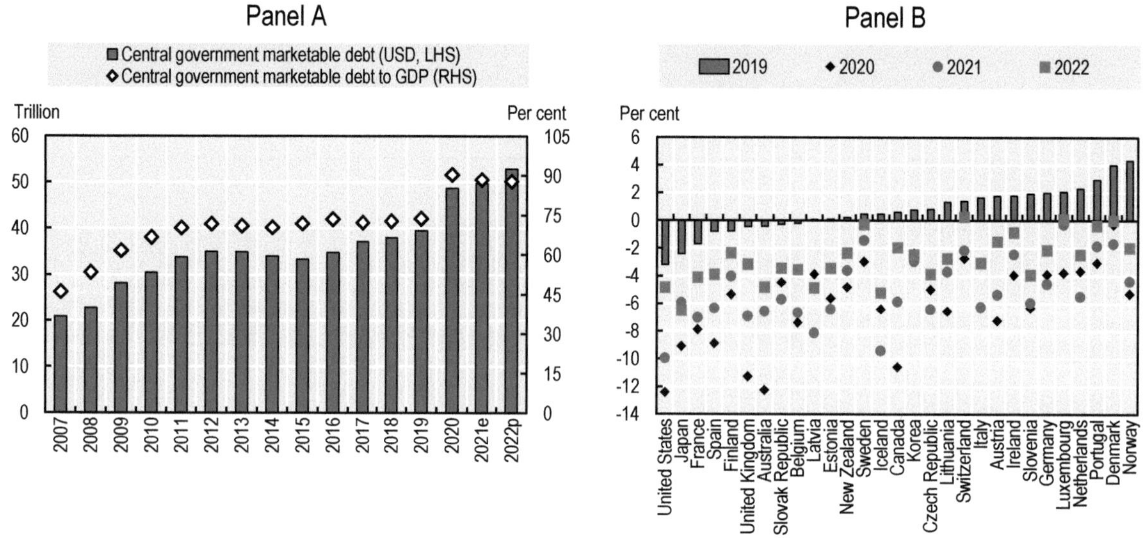

Source: 2021 Survey on Central Government Marketable Debt and Borrowing; OECD Economic Outlook (December 2021); IMF World Economic Outlook Database (October 2021); Refinitiv, national authorities' websites and OECD calculations.

Box 1.3. Definitions and concepts used in the Sovereign Borrowing Outlook Survey

The 2008 financial crisis had important implications for sovereign funding, debt levels and the composition of the debt stock. It brought sovereign debt operations to the forefront and highlighted the need for greater transparency provided by granular data on relevant metrics such as outstanding debt, redemptions and funding plans (OECD Sovereign Borrowing Outlook 2009 and OECD Sovereign Borrowing Outlook 2012). Investors and other stakeholders need to understand the current risk exposure of central government debt, future funding needs and debt strategies. They also require a breakdown of these metrics by instruments, maturity and currency types. To address this information need, the OECD Working Party on Debt Management (WPDM) launched the first survey in 2009 following significant consideration of the possible advantages and disadvantages of the different coverage of entities and instruments and the different ways to value them.

The survey collects gross borrowing requirements, redemptions and outstanding debt amounts. It provides breakdowns of these items by maturity, currency and interest rate types. It uses the core definition of sovereign debt, so-called central government marketable debt, mainly due to its comparability and collectability. This measure, directly linked to central government budget financing, enables the OECD to collect actual historic data and estimates of future government borrowing requirements and funding strategies. It provides detail on outstanding debt by instrument, maturity and currency. This is a narrower definition than the general government definition which is used, for example, by the OECD System of National Accounts (SNA) and consists of central government, state and local governments and social security funds controlled by these units.

In terms of debt instruments, the Borrowing Outlook Surveys and the results in this publication focus on marketable debt, as OECD governments are financed predominantly by marketable debt instruments (i.e. financial securities and instruments that can be bought and sold in the secondary market). It should be noted that most government debt statistics (e.g. OECD SNA, EU Maastricht debt, and IMF Public Sector Debt Statistics) cover marketable and non-marketable debt. An advantage of using this publication's definition is to indicate to investors which instruments are available for trade in the secondary market, and for the issuers to calculate different characteristics of the debt, such as duration or time to maturity.

Change in methodology in aggregating survey data

The original methodology set in 2009 used the assumption of fixed exchange rates (as of 2009 values) to aggregate data across the different national currencies in the OECD area. This assumption was adopted for comparability reasons. The strength of the US dollar over the period, however, has resulted in material differences that complicated interpretation of the results (Figure 1.12). Considering this caveat, the OECD WPDM decided to adopt a flexible rate methodology in reporting the survey results in 2021. To this end, this edition of the Outlook presents the survey data converted all annual figures based on the end of year (31 December) local to USD rate in that year.

Figure 1.12. Central government marketable debt considering different exchange rate assumptions, 2021 estimates.

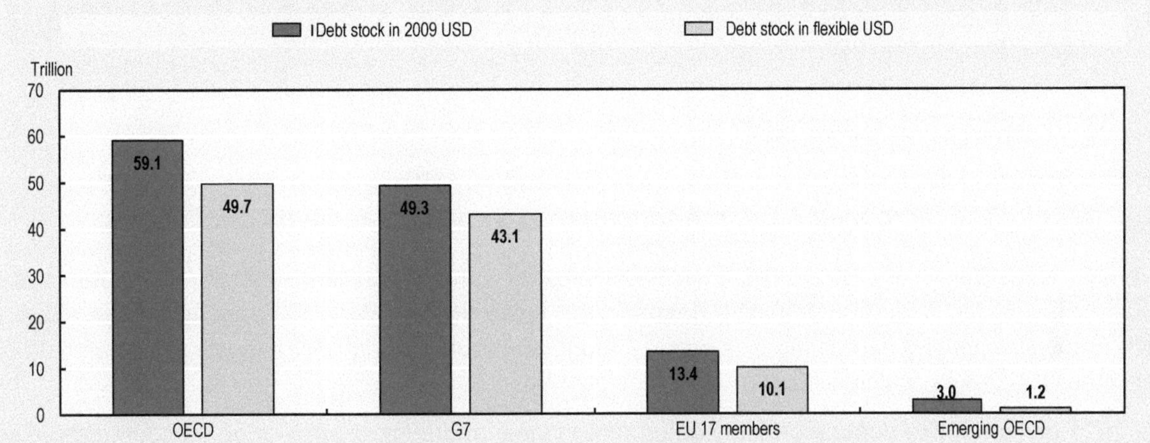

Note: Emerging OECD group consists of Chile, Colombia, Costa Rica, Hungary, Mexico, Poland and Turkey.
Source: 2021 Survey on Central Government Marketable Debt and Borrowing; OECD Economic Outlook (December 2021); IMF World Economic Outlook Database (October 2021); Refinitiv, national authorities' websites and OECD calculations.

1.6.1. Interest cost on government debt declined despite greater debt

Despite the surge in government debt in the wake of the COVID-19 crisis, interest cost on debt continued to fall in most countries due to the low level of interest rates. Figure 1.13 illustrates the percentage of government interest expenditure in GDP from 2007 to 2021. Interest expenditure in relation to GDP in this period fell by more than 50% in 16 countries (including Canada, France, Germany and Sweden) during this period. Even countries with large debt stocks and borrowing needs including Italy, Japan and the United States registered decreases in interest expense-to-GDP ratios. In 2021, only six countries (i.e. Australia, the Czech Republic, Hungary, New Zealand, Norway and the United Kingdom) have seen slight increases compared to 2020.

As economies emerge from the pandemic, interest rates are expected to rise. This means that refinancing maturing debt will occur at higher rates. In this regard, fiscal policies will need to consider the potential for additional interest burdens in future budgets. It should also be noted that a temporary rise in bond yields would only have a limited impact on overall debt servicing costs. Though, any sudden shifts in sentiment and perceptions of sovereign risk not necessarily related to long-term solvency, may lead to a deterioration in credit spreads, and even an interruption of market-based borrowing as seen during the 2010-12 European sovereign debt crisis (OECD, 2019[9]).

Figure 1.13. General government interest expenses in relation to GDP

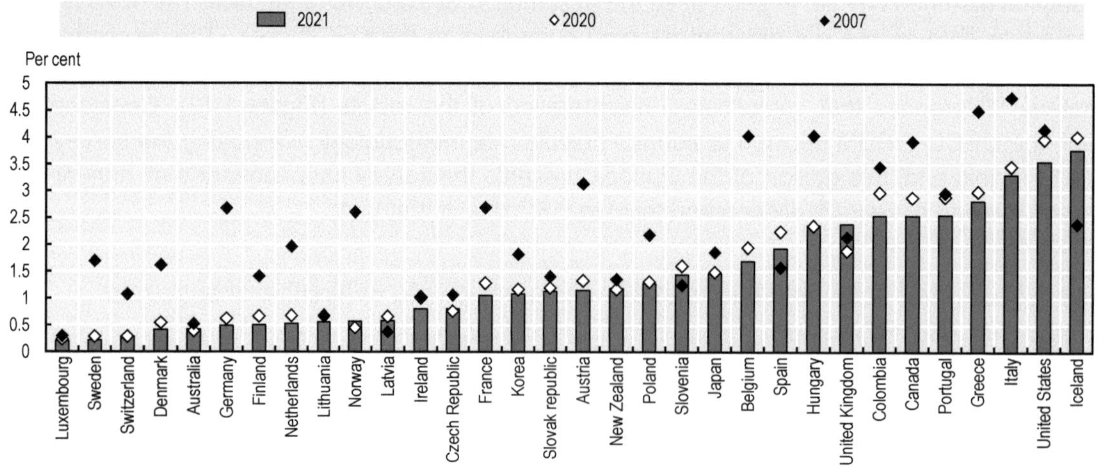

Source: OECD Economic Outlook (December 2021).

1.6.2. Despite the increased ATM, refinancing risk exposure remains challenging

Sovereign issuers in many OECD countries have expanded their short-term borrowing programmes to manage unexpected surges in financing needs in the wake of the COVID-19 pandemic. The share of short-term instruments (i.e. maturity less than 12-months) in outstanding central government marketable debt in the OECD area, which averaged 10% in the past five years, increased to 16% in 2020 (Figure 1.14).

This 2021 edition of this publication highlighted that in view of the rapid pace of debt accumulation and favourable funding conditions, rebalancing of sovereign debt portfolio maturities should be considered to ease near-term redemption pressures and strengthen the resilience of the debt portfolio against refinancing risk. A lengthening of government debt portfolio maturities may also facilitate a smooth exit of expansionary monetary policies and mitigate the budgetary impact of interest rate increases. With a lengthened ATM, this rise will be slowly passed on to debt service costs and help to avoid endogenous debt accumulation.

Figure 1.14. Maturity structure of central government marketable debt

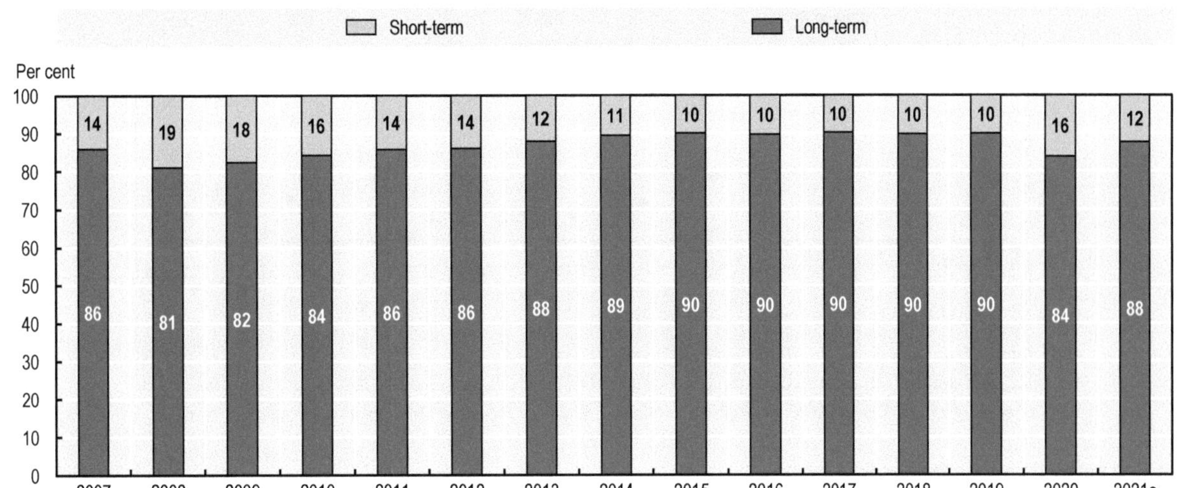

Source: 2021 Survey on Central Government Marketable Debt and Borrowing; OECD Economic Outlook (December 2021); IMF World Economic Outlook Database (October 2021); Refinitiv, national authorities' websites and OECD calculations.

Since 2021, sovereign funding strategies in many countries have been modified to mitigate refinancing risk by lengthening issuance maturities. In the OECD area, the share of long-term instruments in the outstanding government marketable debt increased from 84% to 88% in 2021, but remained lower than pre-pandemic levels. It should be noted that central bank quantitative easing programmes have implications for maturity extension efforts, given that central banks often buy government bonds and fund them with central bank reserves which pay interest at the deposit rate and are characterised as floating rate liabilities. In this respect, an extension of debt maturities has been partially offset by central bank bond purchases in those countries, where national central banks launched large quantitative easing (QE) programmes. Going forward, that impact is expected to diminish as central bank balance sheets get smaller (as bonds mature).

In addition to the maturity structure of debt stock, the ATM of outstanding debt returned to pre-pandemic levels in most countries. From a risk management perspective, the higher ATM and duration figures imply a lower pass-through of interest rate changes to government interest costs and enhanced fiscal resilience. After a cumulative increase of 1.6 years since the 2008 financial crisis, the ATM for the OECD area declined slightly from 7.66 years in 2019 to 7.36 years in 2020. As a result of extended maturities in 2021, the ATM of outstanding debt standing at 7.63 years has almost fully returned to pre-pandemic levels and reached record highs in 16 OECD countries including France, Italy, Portugal, Spain and the United States (Figure 1.15).

Figure 1.15. Average term-to-maturity of outstanding marketable debt in selected OECD countries

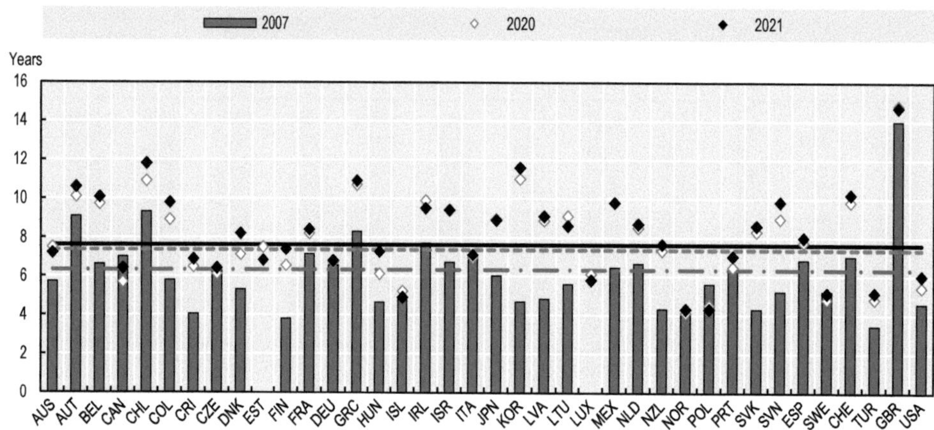

Note: See Annex 1.A for country specific notes.
Source: 2021 Survey on Central Government Marketable Debt and Borrowing.

An important aspect of a governments' medium-term debt strategy is related to the percentage of its debt to be refinanced (i.e. rollover) in the medium-term. Figure 1.16 presents redemption profile of central government marketable debt for the next 12, 24 and 36 months. As of December 2021, total debt maturities for OECD governments over the following 36 months is 42% of the outstanding marketable debt. The rollover ratio for the next 12 months is 22%, which is slightly lower than the previous year's estimates of 25% but remain higher than pre-pandemic levels of 20%. Among the country groups, G7 countries, where economic flexibility and access to deep and liquid financial markets ease market perception of refinancing risks, have the highest ratios.

Figure 1.16. Redemptions of central government marketable debt in OECD country groupings, as a percentage of debt stock

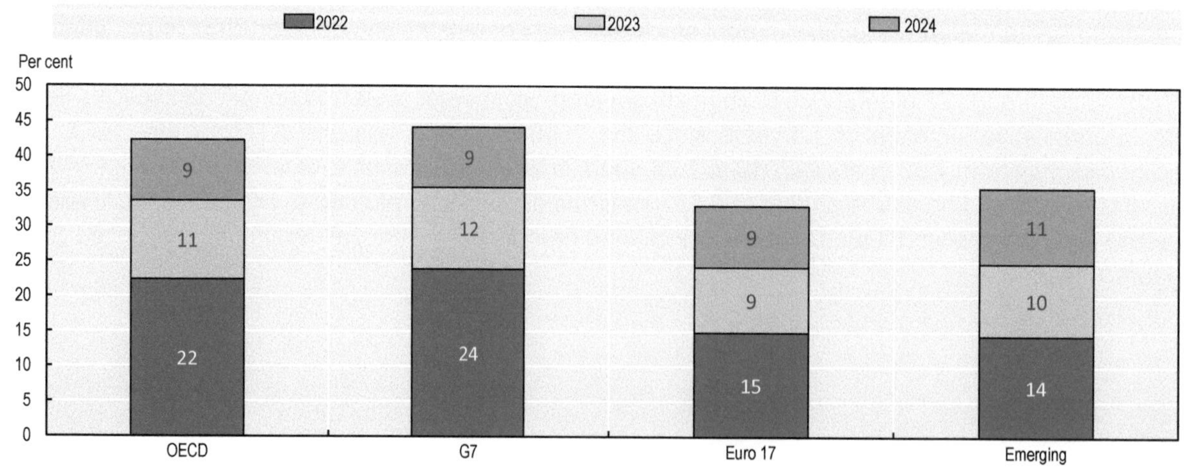

Note: Using the debt comparable application data, calculated on current USD amounts outstanding. Emerging OECD group consists of Chile, Colombia, Costa Rica, Hungary, Mexico, Poland and Turkey.
Source: Refinitiv.

For a given maturity structure, an increasing outstanding amount of debt means increases in the amount of debt to be refinanced. In terms of absolute levels of debt to be repaid or refinanced, the aggregate redemption amount for the OECD area as whole in the next three years has also slightly declined (i.e. around USD 20 trillion) compared to 2020, even though it remains higher than pre-pandemic levels. The high level of the observed debt redemption profiles is expected to persist, largely due to the increasing refinancing burden from the maturing debt, combined with continued budget deficits in most OECD countries. In this regard, OECD DMOs should continue taking a prudent approach towards managing short- and long-term refinancing risks. Such strategies might include smoothing the cash flow profile of upcoming maturities, reducing pressure on the Treasury bill segment, and rebuilding contingency capacity. As shown by the key refinancing risk indicators, many OECD debt managers have already begun to extend issuance structures by increasing the share of long-term debt issuance and consider introducing new maturity lines and new instruments (e.g. Italy, the United Kingdom and the United States). These debt management considerations are taken against the backdrop of rising interest rates and elevated debt to GDP ratios, as they aim to enhance fiscal resilience by seeking to mitigate refinancing risk.

Refinancing risk is particularly important for sovereigns with high debt redemption profiles and/or relatively limited access to deep financial markets. In times of market turbulence, sovereigns with weak fundamentals are more vulnerable to spikes in borrowing rates, while "safe havens", such as Germany and the United States, experience the "flight to safety" phenomenon which can translate into lower borrowing costs and greater demand. The last few decades provide ample evidence of this phenomenon. In view of tightening global liquidity conditions, sovereign DMOs of the countries with weak fundamentals should take a more cautious approach in managing refinancing risk.

1.7. Implications of the pandemic for future debt management

1.7.1. Key debt management lessons from the COVID-19 crisis

An overview of the effectiveness of the borrowing strategies and risk management approaches used during crises is important in terms of applying them to other countries and keeping them available at other times. Members of the OECD's Working Party on Debt Management shared their thoughts and practices on various aspects of debt management in 2021. They underlined that the main difference between 'normal 'times and 'periods of crisis' is that DMOs need to meet rapidly changing borrowing needs, often in more volatile market conditions. In this regard, the COVID-19 crisis was not an exception in terms of greater need for cash management flexibility. The need for cash management flexibility is met with short-term borrowing and contingency buffers, two important tools used effectively by some countries during the 2008 financial crisis. Most OECD countries initially handled the COVID-related funding needs with short-term funding and then gradually adjusted the borrowing towards longer-term funding (e.g. Australia, Canada and the United States).[12] In recent years, several countries, including Germany and Italy, have started (or widened) their repo activity to improve cash management, provide more flexibility in issuance plans and support market liquidity. The 2021 Survey on Primary Market Developments indicates that several DMOs including Austria, France, Portugal and the United States benefited from liquidity (cash) buffers in the wake of the pandemic, which were used primarily to mitigate unexpected variations in borrowing needs during the initial acute phase of the COVID-19 crisis (OECD, 2021[6]).

In addition to maintaining access to short-term funding markets and contingency buffers, the crisis also underlined the importance of having different borrowing methods (auction, syndications, and private placements) in place. For example, syndications are assessed as useful when price making is relatively challenging in difficult market conditions, or when large single volume issuance is required and a syndication will reduce execution risk. The number of countries using private placements and syndications has been at similar levels for many years (i.e. around two-thirds of OECD countries use syndications, and a quarter use private placements).[13] Discussions during the annual meeting of the WPDM revealed that their use has become more frequent or that there have been increases in volumes issued this way in recent years.

Figure 1.17. Key lessons learned from the COVID-19 crisis

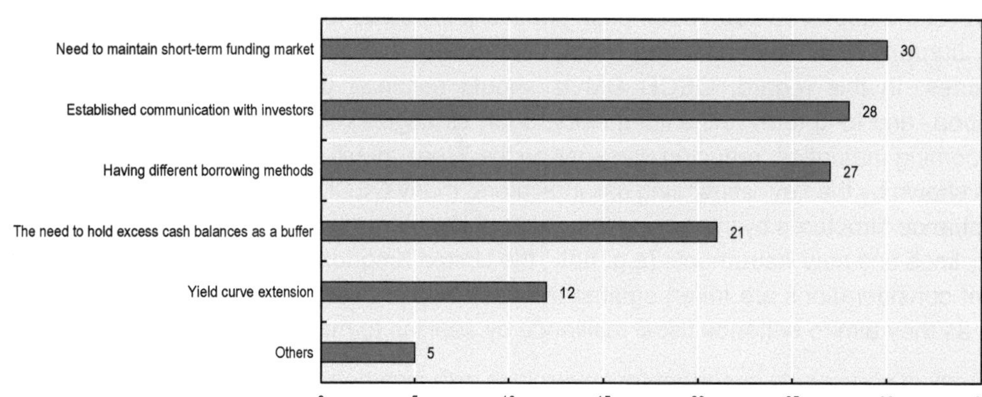

Notes: Other key lessons learned include (i) The benefit of having a broad and diversified market access, including in foreign currency, (ii) Being able to work remotely, (iii) Keep available also other funding options, like international financial institutions and utilise when necessary and if financially favourable borrowing conditions are offered, (iv) Use of liquidity buffers (trust funds), and (v) Existence of a business continuity/recovery plan to fall back to in case of need.
Source: 2021 OECD Survey on Primary Market Developments.

Looking ahead, many countries have large maturities to roll-over and will maintain large auction sizes in 2022 compared to pre-pandemic levels. Taking both into consideration, funding activities have become more sensitive to market developments, while monetary policy is becoming less supportive. Financial conditions have already tightened modestly, which implies that maturing sovereign debt in coming periods will gradually be refinanced at a higher cost. Going forward, downside risks to the outlook include the emergence of new COVID-19 variants, persistent inflation (which could quickly lead to higher and more volatile yields), and mounting geopolitical tensions. The sensitivity of debt servicing costs to interest rate risk might be heightened in case of sudden and sharp rises in market rates. In the short to medium term, rollover risk may emerge as a key policy concern for debt managers, in particular in countries with – perceived – debt sustainability problems, where sudden shifts in sentiment can lead to sharp increases in borrowing costs and even temporary and periodic loss of market access. In the long run, public debt levels are vulnerable to risks to future public finances, including population ageing, climate change, low growth and high levels of inequality. Without credible and transparent fiscal frameworks, these risks can further undermine fiscal balances and raise debt sustainability concerns (Rawdanowicz et al., 2021[10]).

In terms of funding conditions, a number of risk factors could add pressure, including rising inflation expectations and divergent recoveries between advanced and emerging market economies. It should be noted that, in some cases, political and geo-political factors (e.g. elections and the tensions over Ukraine) may contribute to stressed market conditions. Further, as central banks begin to normalise monetary policies, both through higher policy rates and reduced (or ceased) asset purchases, market liquidity may become fragile and affect sovereign funding.

Secondary market liquidity for government bonds, including repos, is an important contributing factor in supporting primary market access and minimising sovereign borrowing costs over time. To ensure the smooth functioning of government securities markets in the coming periods, debt managers should attach greater importance to i) close monitoring of the resilience of market intermediaries; ii) strengthening investor relations and co-ordination among authorities; and, iii) being a regular and transparent issuer.[14] In the event of an illiquidity concern, a security lending facility (SLF) can be used effectively for closing the demand-supply gap for individual securities and preventing settlement fails to a large extent. SLFs are one of the tools typically used by central banks but also offered by several debt management offices in the OECD area.[15]

Lastly, given the uncertainties around fiscal outcomes, debt managers need to remain flexible if borrowing needs change materially and at relatively short notice.

1.7.2. Higher inflation and implications for government debt

Given the muted inflation pressures experienced by most countries over the past decade, inflation was not a concern for investors before the pandemic. Hence, the inflation risk premia on conventional government bonds was relatively low, in line with the expectations of investors who viewed the outlook for inflation as benign. With the global economic recovery and impact of the war in Ukraine, supply-chain bottlenecks and sharp increases in energy prices, short-term inflation is projected to be higher than it was prior to the pandemic in many countries. Inflation in the OECD area surged to 6.6% in the 12 months to December 2021, reaching the highest rate in three decades. After peaking at the turn of 2021-22, the OECD projects annual consumer price inflation to stabilise to around 3% in the OECD area by end-2023 (OECD, 2021[2]). This turnaround is sharp and rising inflation (in outcomes and expectations) has implications for the value of public debt and demand for inflation-linked bonds.

An upward inflation shock reduces the real value of a government's outstanding debt. Overall, the impact of the inflation shock depends on several factors, including the average maturity of the debt portfolio, the share of fixed rate debt, and actual inflation compared to market expectations. The higher the average maturity of debt held by the private sector, and the proportion of fixed rate debt, the higher the impact of inflation on reducing the real value of debt. It is important to highlight that inflation is stochastic, and that investors will take inflation risk into account when pricing and choosing to hold government debt.[16]

A stronger case for inflation-linked bonds

With rising inflation the demand for inflation-linked bonds typically increases, because they offer a direct hedge against inflation. Traditionally, institutional investors, such as pension funds, with liabilities that increase with inflation are natural investors in such securities. Despite the reduction of observed break-even inflation rates before the pandemic, the demand from such investors for inflation-linked bonds remained strong and supported the sustained supply. Inflation indexed debt makes up a meaningful portion of the debt stock for a number of sovereign issuers. For example, the United Kingdom stands out at around 25% inflation-linked debt as a percentage of total central government marketable debt, as defined benefit pension liabilities have embedded inflation indexation, and hence form a persistent demand base.[17] In terms of the volume, the United States is the largest issuer with over USD 1.7 trillion of Treasury Inflation Indexed Securities (TIPS) outstanding.

In the OECD area, the pace of the issuance of inflation indexed bonds has slowed in the wake of the pandemic. The percentage share of inflation indexed debt issuance in total long-term debt issuance declined from 5.7% in 2019 to 4.2% in 2021, as sovereign issuers favoured fixed-rate long term securities in view of cost and risk considerations. As a result, the share of inflation-linked debt in outstanding long-term debt declined slightly from 8.8% to 8.0% between 2019 and 2021. Debt managers tend to exercise considerable flexibility over the amount of gross issuance allocated to inflation linked bonds because of the fact they comprise only a minor part of most long-term debt portfolios.

According to the recent surveys, sovereign issuers observe a growing investor demand for inflation-linked bonds, as inflation risk premia have risen in the current uncertain environment. This reflects a confluence of factors, including the perception that central banks have an increased tolerance for above target inflation, continued fiscal expansion, continued supply chain bottlenecks, and price pressures related to the climate transition. In addition, it was noted that short-dated inflation-linked bonds (e.g. 5-year and 10-year maturities) have attracted increased demand. In response to growing demand, a number of countries have begun to (or are considering) increase their issuance of inflation linked bonds (e.g. Czech Republic, France and the United States). Their percentage share of total borrowing is projected to increase from 4.2% in 2021 to 6.3% in 2022, thus the outstanding volume of inflation-linked bonds is expected to reach

USD 4.5 trillion in 2022. Despite the increase in their issuance, their share in total long-term debt will remain lower than the pre-pandemic period of close to 9%.

1.7.3. *Keeping an eye on digitalisation in bond markets*

Technology in the financial sector is used to help automate existing processes and to increase operational efficiency. Major areas of application include financial advice and marketing services and, to a lesser extent, settlement and payment processes. Digitalisation in capital markets, which has been ongoing for several decades, accelerated in the wake of the pandemic. For instance, the pandemic has enhanced the shift to digital payments, in particular where the financial systems had been less developed (Auer, Cornelli and Frost, 2020[11]). In addition, it has contributed to the speeding up of work on the development of central bank digital currencies (CBDCs) (Auer et al., 2020[12]).

The widespread adoption of new financial technologies has substantial implications for primary and secondary government debt markets. In primary markets, a major application of digitalisation is the auction process. Electronic auction systems play an important role by making it easier for retail investors as well as institutions to bid directly in auctions (e.g. Italy and the United States). Automation of auction procedures increases their efficiency vis-à-vis the use of manual procedures, as it enhances speed, reliability and cost-effectiveness. In 2019, The European Central Bank launched a project called 'European Distribution of Debt Instruments' for consultation. The goal of this project is to provide Euro-area issuers with a single centralised process for debt securities issuance to harmonise issuance process and reduce intermediation costs.

More recently, experiments on issuance of digital bonds have been on the rise. Since their first trials in 2017, a number of bonds were issued as digital records by both private sector and international organisations (e.g. WB and EIB). Essentially, distributed ledger technology allowed the issuer to create, allocate, transfer and redeem a bond without a need for a central securities depositary (CSD) and a custodian. Digitalisation of securities may bring benefits to issuers including a reduction of operational costs and settlement time, and better market transparency. On the other hand, the lack of regulations, protocols and standards for digital securities, which are not yet accepted as financial securities in many countries, entails security concerns.

In the secondary markets, digitalisation has altered the ecosystem of government securities markets. Today, in several OECD countries (e.g. Italy, the United Kingdom and the United States), a considerable amount of trades – especially for on-the-run securities – are made through electronic venues. For example, in the United States, the inter-dealer market for Treasury securities is almost entirely electronic, with a large presence of Principle Trading Firms[18] (PTFs) that employ automated trading technologies. These advances supported market liquidity with quicker, safer and cheaper transactions, but may also cause less heterogeneous behaviour, leading to greater volatility. This underpins the concern expressed by sovereign debt managers about correlated trades in the government securities market. In view of financial stability implications, financial regulatory authorities should closely monitor new market structure developments and may wish to impose new training requirements on investors and traders to address these risks. As well, authorities should build their own internal capacities to better understand and oversee these risks. For example, recent studies on episodes of US Treasury market dysfunction during periods of stress highlight the importance of addressing anonymous trading on electronic interdealer trading through such means as the introduction of central clearing for these trading activities (Duffie, 2020[13]; G30 Working Group on Treasury Market Liquidity, 20221[14]).

Sovereign DMOs are not 'first movers' in terms of financial technology use. That said, before adopting any new technologies, they tend to wait to ensure that the entire market infrastructure, including the associated regulations, is well established and that various risks are mitigated properly. At the same time, they would benefit from diligent observation of digital transformation in financial markets to gain a deeper understanding of emerging risks, costs and opportunities that digitalisation is bringing to both debt issuance and trading processes.

1.7.4. Review of debt management strategies to improve resilience

The 2021 Survey on Primary Market Developments asked about plans to review the long-term funding strategy as a consequence of increased debt levels following the COVID-19 pandemic. More than a third of the respondents are considering reviewing long-term funding strategies because of increased debt levels following the COVID-19 pandemic (see Annex A for more detailed information).

The survey results indicate that a number of countries are considering changes in business continuity plans, investor relations and cash buffer practices. Lengthening maturities and issuance of new securities will also remain high on policy agendas. A review of issuance techniques, communication with central banks as major investors and primary dealership systems are being considered by some debt management offices.

Figure 1.18. Potential implications of the pandemic on public debt management

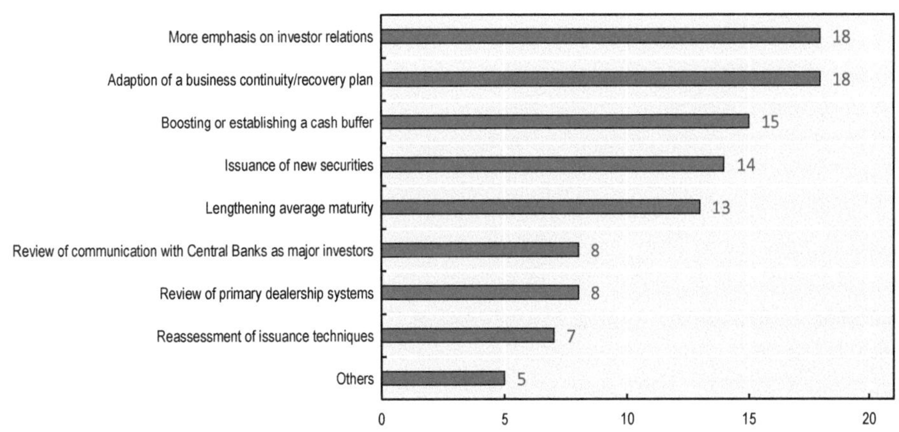

Notes: Other implications were (i) Manage maturity structure of debt issuance and growing share of money market instruments. (ii) Assess whether the debt issuance mix used to raise funding during the pandemic should be modified or rebalanced. (iii) The government will continue to review the Debt Management Strategy (DMS) for opportunities to borrow at longer maturities and lock in historically low interest rates, as well as enhance the predictability of debt servicing costs. (iv) Implementation of the pilot plan for the market maker system. (v) More flexible mechanisms in order to issue more if the market demand conditions allow it.
Source: 2021 OECD Survey on Primary Market Developments.

Adaption of business continuity plan to secure ability to perform critical functions at all times

The COVID-19 pandemic forced Debt Management Offices (DMOs) to switch to remote working very quickly, in line with national-level measures. Although pandemics per se were not amongst the business interruption scenarios in many OECD country DMOs (except Colombia, Ireland, Japan and Switzerland) before the pandemic, all included arrangements to ensure business continuity, which enabled critical functions such as funding and repayment operations to be successfully carried out remotely (OECD, 2021[6]). After three major outbreaks in less than 20 years (i.e. Sars, Mers and COVID-19) and assuming there will be others in the future, DMOs should give consideration to pandemic-related scenarios in their business continuity plans.

Remote working has become an operational risk management tool that is expected to form some part of the post-pandemic world as it provides flexibility in the workplace and allows essential services to continue without disruption. The 2021 Survey on Primary Market Developments revealed that more than half of the respondents plan to carry out at least some of their operations remotely as standard practice. In particular, payments, cash management operations and auctions are listed amongst the items that are considered to be candidates for remote management (Annex A). Managing "key person risk" should be an important component of these revisions. Cross-team training of more staff with critical skills through virtual classes and webinars to avoid "key person risk" (e.g. staff involved in cash market operations, derivative markets and debt repayments) can enhance the emergency response capacity of DMOs.

Cybersecurity is another area that requires constant attention from policy makers. Cyber-attacks on debt management offices may affect the timely delivery of government funding and repayment programmes. A number of sovereign DMOs have observed a change in the number and sophistication of cybersecurity threats to their organisation following the COVID-19 crisis, mainly driven by extensive use of digital tools and remote working practices. Despite the growing threat of cybersecurity events, both the number of incidents and the extent of actual damage have been limited in the OECD area to date, thanks to robust cybersecurity programmes in DMOs. To keep pace with evolving cyber risks, sovereign DMOs should regularly conduct business impact analysis and review incident management plans and enhance the situational awareness of likely cyber threats and vulnerabilities among the staff (OECD, 2021[6]).

More emphasis given to communication and investor relations

The pandemic forced sovereign issuers to change their communication format and strategy with investors, relevant government authorities and the general public. Almost a third of survey respondents noted a change in their market communication strategies since the pandemic (or at least a departure from past practice to accommodate the extenuating circumstances of limited travel and uncertain fiscal forecasts). DMOs have updated investors more frequently through digital communication tools (e.g. email distribution lists, publishing market notices on their websites, virtual meetings and phone calls) with a forward-looking but also more flexible approach. They have provided information through digital tools regarding funding news, changes in funding needs and plans in a cost-effective and timely manner. In addition, senior government officials (e.g. Ministers, treasury secretaries and heads of DMOs) have communicated actively on how they evaluate the developments and address the risks to ensure proper functioning of government securities markets (e.g. Canada). They have also put more emphasis on timely information sharing with fiscal and monetary authorities.

In terms of publications, DMOs are introducing more frequent digital publications in addition to the annual reports and quarterly financing plans. For example, New Zealand launched a regular e-newsletter to update investors regularly on funding activities and projections, and Portugal changed the format of its monthly e-newsletter to make the communication effort more targeted. Another example is the Australian DMO's quarterly 'investor insights' series for wholesale investors, which aims to explain the thinking behind key parts of their operations and topics related to the Australian Government securities market. In terms of the content, ESG-related issues are becoming more visible in investor relations (e.g. Australia, Finland and the Netherlands). In particular, DMOs launching green bond programmes need to adjust their communication package and to weigh more emphasis on government's environmental and social performance and projects more than in the past.

In order to ease access of information, some DMOs have emphasised the translation of key documents to the languages of major foreign investors. For example, the Australian DMO (Australian Office of Financial Management) provides investor presentations in Japanese. Similarly, the Hungarian DMO (AKK) provide green bond presentation in Japanese and Chinese to facilitate access to information by investors from different regions.

DMOs should continue exploring options for new products to add funding capacity. They should consider further diversifying their investor base, which supports increased certainty of access to funding markets over time, contributes to lower and less volatile yields for government securities, and provides flexibility to meet changing financial requirements. With the prospect of expected higher financing requirements in the coming years, a number of countries noted that there is room to introduce new securities and/or additional maturity segments (see Annex A for more detailed information). This should involve consultation with market participants to assess the market's capacity for debt instruments with different maturities and interest rate structures. Regular consultations with market participants are an integral and valued part of the debt management process in most OECD countries. Country practices evolve over time to ensure all market participants have the opportunity to provide input (e.g. US Treasury and UK DMO have conducted and have published market consultations for new maturity lines/products). More recently, the Finnish Treasury launched a new process for selecting bonds to be auctioned, including requesting recommendations.

Investors should be informed of regulatory changes regarding government securities in a timely manner. A recent example is the new regulations on Collective Action Clauses (CACs) for government bonds introduced in the Euro area. The amendments to the Treaty establishing the European Stability Mechanism envisage that all new government securities issued by EU sovereigns with a maturity of more than one year will be issued with single limb CACs as of 2022 (ESDM, 2021[15]). Going forward, principles and regulations around sustainable finance will also be followed more closely both by issuers and investors. For example, impact reporting and external reviewers for green bonds, and the way Credit Rating Agencies (CRAs) incorporate ESG factors into their methodologies for credit ratings and outlooks may subject to regional regulatory changes.

An important part of emergency response activities is to communicate the changes in financing programmes to stakeholders, including the general public. In their role as regular and large issuers in securities markets (and therefore with a potential to impact markets), DMOs should carefully manage changes in borrowing programmes by balancing the need for transparency and predictability while allowing for sufficient room for manoeuvre. Risks to financing programmes especially when they occur prior to an auction, poses a challenge for transparency and predictability and could cause reputational damage if not well managed. To this end, sovereign debt managers should remain vigilant in monitoring market developments and market participants carefully and closely in case of an event risk. Additional communication with market participants may be required to convey changes in borrowing plans.

Uncertainties around economic recovery require strong co-ordination and communication with fiscal and monetary policy authorities. In particular, timely updates of cash flow forecasts are critical for sovereign issuers to identify the volume and immediacy of funding needs. This requires efficient communication channels between cash managers and their counterparts in spending and revenue collection agencies. At a time when market liquidity becomes more sensitive in financial markets, communication with monetary authorities regarding government cash balances and borrowing strategies, in particular with respects to debt redemption projections, and any change in cash buffer targets, could be critical in avoiding unnecessary pressure on market liquidity.

Improving flexibility through cash buffers

The recent survey on Primary Market Developments indicates that several DMOs including Austria, France, Portugal and the United States benefited from liquidity buffers in 2020 and 2021. Since the outlook remains highly uncertain, having emergency funding tools in place continues to be relevant for all sovereign issuers. Sovereign DMOs may benefit from adjusting their contingency funding tools, such as cash buffers for flexibility.

Almost all countries in the OECD area maintain a liquidity buffer (i.e. 35 countries). In the wake of the pandemic, almost all countries increased their target level of cash buffers. In 2021, cash management practices became more mixed as some countries emerged from the crisis faster than others. While some countries have not made any changes to target levels, some reduced compared to 2020 levels on the back of declining borrowing needs and uncertainties. For example, some DMOs including Australia, Finland,

France, Portugal and the Netherlands increased their cash buffer following the crisis and then decreased it in 2021, as funding circumstances and market uncertainty eased.

Looking forward, it is important to maintain flexibility to be able to make – at least minor – adjustments to account for stressed market conditions, for example around the dates of major events announced after the issuance calendar (i.e. event risk). Sovereign issuers should consider national and major central banks' monetary policy announcements, elections and major economic data releases when designing cash buffers, in addition to redemption profiles and large fiscal outlays. For example, some countries including Austria, France and Sweden will hold presidential elections while several others run legislative elections in 2022. Political developments are often assessed to have only a temporary impact on sovereign yields, with limited effects on sovereign borrowing programmes (OECD, 2018[5]). However, in the period leading up to election dates, with increased tensions, investors might become more concerned with uncertainties and reluctant to participate in funding activities. Lastly, for the Euro area, country mismatches between timing and size of the payments for and recipients from pandemic related NGEU programmes should also be factored in when setting targets for cash buffers.

Against the backdrop of a less favourable funding environment, debt managers should remain vigilant, and closely monitor the resilience of market intermediaries, and co-ordinate with the relevant authorities to quickly address possible stressed market conditions. Authorities may benefit from tools such as security lending facilities and contingency buffers to be able to absorb possible stress in markets and adjust the auction sizes over the year.

References

Agur, I. et al. (January 13, 2022), *Monetary Finance: Do Not Touch, or Handle with Care?*, IMF, https://www.imf.org/en/Publications/Departmental-Papers-Policy-Papers/Issues/2022/01/11/Monetary-Finance-Do-Not-Touch-or-Handle-with-Care-464862. [24]

AOFM (2019), "Bond issuance methods - Tenders vs Syndications", *AOFM Investor Insights*, https://www.aofm.gov.au/investors/wholesale-investors/investor-insights/bond-issuance-methods-tenders-versus-syndications. [17]

AOFM (January 2022), "Australian Government Climate Change: commitments, policies and programs", *Investor chart*, https://www.aofm.gov.au/publications/investor-chart-pack. [28]

Auer, R., G. Cornelli and J. Frost (2020), *Covid-19, cash and the future of payments*, BIS, https://www.bis.org/publ/bisbull03.htm. [11]

Auer, R. et al. (2020), *Rise of the central bank digital currencies*, BIS, https://www.bis.org/publ/work976.htm. [12]

Bartsch, E. et al. (n.d.), "It's all in the mix: how can monetary and fiscal policies work or fail together?", *Geneva Report on the World Economy* No 23. [19]

BIS (December 2021), *BIS Quarterly Review*, Bank for International Settlements, https://www.bis.org/publ/qtrpdf/r_qt2112.htm. [4]

Duffie, D. (2020), *Still the world's safe haven? Redesigning the U.S. Treasury market after the COVID-19 crisis*, Brookings Institution, https://www.brookings.edu/research/still-the-worlds-safe-haven/. [13]

ESDM (2021), *Press Release on Introduce of 2022 Collective Action Clauses*, https://europa.eu/efc/system/files/2021-12/ESDM%20press%20release%20introduction%202022%20collective%20action%20clauses%20-%20revised.pdf. [15]

Finland, State Treasury of (2021), *Sustainability and Finnish Government Bonds*, https://www.treasuryfinland.fi/investor-relations/sustainability-and-finnish-government-bonds/. [21]

Fleming, M. (2020), "Treasury Market Liquidity and the Federal Reserve during the COVID-19 Pandemic", *Liberty Street Economics*, https://libertystreeteconomics.newyorkfed.org/2020/05/treasury-market-liquidity-and-the-federal-reserve-during-the-covid-19-pandemic.html. [18]

G30 Working Group on Treasury Market Liquidity (20221), *U.S.Treasury Markets: Steps Toward Increased Resilience*, Group of Thirty, https://group30.org/publications/detail/4950. [14]

Hilscher, J., A. Raviv and R. Reis (July 2014), *Inflating away the public debt? An empirical assessment*, NBER, https://www.nber.org/system/files/working_papers/w20339/w20339.pdf. [23]

Hurcan, Y., F. Koc and E. Balibek (2020), "How to Set Up A Cash Buffer: A Practical Guide to Developing and Implementing a Cash Buffer Policy", *IMF How-To Note No. 2020/004*, https://www.elibrary.imf.org/view/journals/061/2020/004/061.2020.issue-004-en.xml. [27]

Ministry of Finance of Japan (January 2022), "Monthly newsletter: Japanese Government Bonds", https://www.mof.go.jp/english/policy/jgbs/publication/newsletter/jgb2022_01e.pdf. [25]

OECD (2022), "Interim Report March 2022: Economic and Social Impacts and Policy Implications of the War in Ukraine", *OECD Economic Outlook*, https://doi.org/10.1787/4181d61b-en. [1]

OECD (2021), *OECD Economic Outlook, Volume 2021 Issue 2*, OECD Publishing, Paris, https://doi.org/10.1787/66c5ac2c-en. [2]

OECD (2021), *OECD Sovereign Borrowing Outlook 2021*, OECD Publishing, Paris, https://dx.doi.org/10.1787/48828791-en. [6]

OECD (2020), *OECD Pension Outlook*, OECD Publishing, Paris, https://doi.org/10.1787/67ede41b-en. [26]

OECD (2019), *OECD Sovereign Borrowing Outlook 2019*, OECD Publishing, Paris, https://dx.doi.org/10.1787/aa7aad38-en. [9]

OECD (2018), *OECD Sovereign Borrowing Outlook*, OECD Publishing, Paris, https://doi.org/10.1787/23060476. [5]

Pfeiffer, P., V. Janos and I. Jan (July 2021), "Quantifying Spillovers of Next Generation EU Investment", *Discussion Paper No 144*, https://ec.europa.eu/info/sites/default/files/economy-finance/dp144_en.pdf. [3]

Priftis, R. and S. Zimic (2021), "Sources of Borrowing and Fiscal Multipliers", *The Economic Journal*, Vol. Volume 131/Issue 633, pp. Pages 498–519, https://doi.org/10.1093/ej/ueaa051. [8]

Rawdanowicz, Ł. et al. (2021), "Constraints and demands on public finances: Considerations of resilient fiscal policy", *OECD Economics Department Working Papers*, No. 1694, OECD Publishing, Paris, https://dx.doi.org/10.1787/602500be-en.   [10]

Reinhart, C. and M. Sbrancia (2011), *The liquidation of government debt*, NBER, https://doi.org/10.3386/w16893.   [22]

UK DMO (2020), "Response to an enquiry by Chairman of the Treasury Select Committee", https://committees.parliament.uk/publications/4108/documents/40708/default/.   [16]

US Treasury (2021), *Minutes of the Meeting of the Treasury Borrowing Advisory Committee of the Securities Industry and Financial Markets Association*, https://home.treasury.gov/policy-issues/financing-the-government/quarterly-refunding/most-recent-quarterly-refunding-documents.   [7]

Zhou, J. and P. Mauro (2020), "r-g<0: Can We Sleep More Soundly?", *IMF Working Paper* WP/20/52, https://www.imf.org/en/Publications/WP/Issues/2020/03/13/r-minus-g-negative-Can-We-Sleep-More-Soundly-49068.   [20]

Annex 1.A. Methods and sources

Definitions and concepts used in the Sovereign Borrowing Outlook Survey

The Borrowing Outlook survey collects gross borrowing requirements, redemption and outstanding debt amounts with breakdown of these items by maturity, currency and interest rate types. It uses core definition of sovereign debt, so-called central government marketable debt, mainly due to its comparability and collectability. This measure, directly linked to the central government budget financing, enabled the OECD to collect not only for realisations but also for estimates of government borrowing requirements, funding strategies as well as outstanding debt with instruments, maturity and currency types.

Coverage of institutions: Central Government

The coverage of institutions by debt statistics varies from public sector to central government. Public sector stands as broadest institutional coverage, as it includes local governments, state funds financial and non-financial public corporations as well as central government debt. General government definition, which is used by for example by OECD System of National Accounts (SNA), consists of central government, state and local governments and social security funds controlled by these units. Central government covers all departments, offices, establishments and other bodies classified under general government, which are agencies or instrument of the central authority of a country, except separately organised social security funds or extra-budgetary funds. In terms of layers of coverage of institutions, central government stands out as the core definition. Debt of central government is raised, managed and retired by the national DMOs on behalf of the central government. Hence, advantage of this relatively narrow definition of debt is that it enables countries to provide comparable figures, in particular for the estimations.

Coverage of types of debt: Marketable debt

In terms of instruments, liabilities can be in the form of debt securities, loans, insurance, pensions and standardised guarantee schemes, currency and deposits, and other accounts payable. Debt items can be classified as marketable and non-marketable debt. While marketable debt is defined as financial securities and instruments that can be bought and sold in the secondary market, non-marketable debt is not transferable. For example, bonds and bills issued in capital markets are marketable debt; multilateral and bilateral loans from the official sector are non-marketable debt.

The Borrowing Outlook survey focuses on marketable debt instruments, while most government debt statistics (e.g. OECD SNA, EU Maastricht debt, and IMF Public Sector Debt Statistics) cover both marketable and non-marketable debt items. OECD governments are financed predominantly by marketable debt instruments. This is a central definition for every analysis concerning various issues around debt management including borrowing conditions, portfolio composition, investor preferences and market liquidity. An advantage of using this definition is to indicate to investors which instruments are available for trade in the secondary market and which are not. Another reason is for the issuer to calculate different characteristics of the debt, such as duration or time to maturity, which in the case of non-marketable debt would present a difficult issue.

Terminology

- *Standardised Gross borrowing requirement* (GBR) for a year is equal to net borrowing requirement during that year plus the redemptions on the capital market at the beginning of the same year. Also, the (estimated) cash balance may affect the funding needs. In other words, the size of GBR in calendar year amounts to how much the DMO needs to issue in nominal terms so as to fully pay back maturing debt plus the net cash borrowing requirement through any issuance mechanism.

- *Net* borrowing *requirement (NBR)* is the amount to be raised for current budget deficit. While refinancing of redemptions is a matter of rolling over the same exposure as before, NBR refers to new exposure in the market.

- *The* funding *strategy* involves the choice of i) money market instruments for financing short-term GBR and ii) capital market instruments for funding long-term GBR. The strategy entails information on how borrowing needs are going to be financed using different instruments such as long-term, short-term, nominal, variable-rate, indexed bonds and FX-denominated debt.

- Gross *debt* corresponds to the outstanding debt issuance at the end of calendar years. This measure does not take the valuation effects from inflation and exchange rate movements, thus it is equal to the total nominal amount that needs to be paid back to the holders of the debt.

- Redemptions refers to the total amount of the principal repayments of the corresponding debt including the principal payments paid through buy-back operations in a calendar year.

Regional aggregates

- Total OECD area denotes the following 38 countries: Australia, Austria, Belgium, Canada, Chile, Colombia, Costa Rica, the Czech Republic, Denmark, Estonia, Finland, France, Germany, Greece, Hungary, Iceland, Ireland, Israel, Italy, Japan, Korea, Latvia, Lithuania, Luxembourg, Mexico, the Netherlands, New Zealand, Norway, Poland, Portugal, the Slovak Republic, Slovenia, Spain, Sweden, Switzerland, Turkey, the United Kingdom and the United States.

- The G7 includes seven countries: Canada, France, Germany, Italy, Japan, United Kingdom and the United States.

- The OECD Euro area includes 17 Member countries: Austria, Belgium, Estonia, Finland, France, Germany, Greece, Ireland, Italy, Latvia, Lithuania, Luxembourg, the Netherlands, Portugal, the Slovak Republic, Slovenia and Spain.

- In this publication, from a public debt management perspective, the Emerging OECD group (i.e. OECD emerging-market economies) is defined as including seven countries: Chile, Colombia, Costa Rica, Hungary, Mexico, Poland and Turkey.

- The Euro (EUR) is the official currency of 19 out of 28 EU Member countries. These countries are collectively known as the Euro area. The Euro area countries are Austria, Belgium, Cyprus, Estonia, Finland, France, Germany, Greece, Ireland, Italy, Latvia, Lithuania, Luxembourg, Malta, the Netherlands, Portugal, the Slovak Republic, Slovenia and Spain.

Calculations and data sources

- Estimates that are presented as a percentage of GDP, for consistency reasons, use GDP estimates from the last Economic Outlook in the previous year (so December 2021 for this publication) and are calculated using nominal GDP data.

- Debt is measured as the face value of current outstanding central government debt. Face value, the undiscounted amount of principal to be repaid, does not change except when there is a new issue of an existing instrument. This coincides with the original promise (and therefore contractual obligation) of the issuer. DMOs often use face value when they report how much nominal debt will mature in future periods. One important reason for using face value is that it is the standard market practice for quoting and trading specific volumes of a particular instrument.

- Currencies are converted into US dollars using flexible exchange rates using data sourced from Refinitiv. The effects of using alternative exchange rate assumptions (in particular, fixing the exchange rate versus using flexible exchange rates) are illustrated in Box 1.2 of this chapter and in Figures 1.3 and 1.4 of the OECD *Sovereign Borrowing Outlook 2016*.

- All figures refer to calendar years unless specified otherwise.

- Aggregate figures for gross borrowing requirements (GBR), net borrowing requirements (NBR), central government marketable debt, redemptions, and debt maturing are compiled from answers to the Borrowing Survey. The OECD Secretariat inserted its own estimates/projections in cases of missing information for 2020 and/or 2021, using publicly available official information on redemptions and central government budget balances. Where government plans have been announced, but not incorporated into financing plans as of end November, they are not included in the projections presented in this publication. Also the latest December estimates of government net lending in the OECD Economic Outlook database are used in estimating some missing data.

- Both the 2021 OECD Survey on Primary Market Developments and the 2021 OECD Survey on Liquidity in Secondary Government Bond Markets were carried out in October 2021 and this date should be kept in mind when looking at responses to questions that ask for information about the previous or the next 12 months.

- Yield group debt calculations in Figure 1.5 are based on all issuances and re-openings of fixed-rate bonds (i.e. data excludes: short-term instruments, indexed linked, floating rate instruments and strips) and for comparability reasons only bonds issued in EUR, USD, Japanese Yen, Canadian dollars and British pounds were chosen. Data is sourced from Refinitiv.

Average term-to-maturity (ATM)

The following notes were provided by countries in relation to their calculations of average term-to-maturity.

Annex Table 1.A.1. Average term-to-maturity country comments

Country	Note
Australia	Weighted ATM calculation includes Treasury Bonds, Treasury Indexed Bonds and Treasury Notes. Security weightings are based on the face value of each instrument.
Chile	All marketable debt in Chile corresponds to Bonds. All calculation as of 31 December of each year. Some of them consider amortisation with maturity 1 January of the following year
Colombia	The ATM of Colombia debt stock corresponds to domestic bonds (TES), foreign bonds and, multilateral and bilateral loans.
Costa Rica	It is important to consider that ATM includes: all the Internal debt and only Eurobonds to External debt.
Czech Republic	Marketable central government debt excludes savings government bonds (retail bonds).
Denmark	Excludes effects from swaps and other derivatives.
Estonia	Includes central government marketable debt only, excludes other levels of government.
France	Excludes swap effects
Germany	Calculation excluding holdings in own stock. Inflation-linked securities weighted with 0.75.
Greece	The mentioned data refer to Long Term marketable debt securities (more than 1 year original maturity) and exclude Treasury Bills.
Hungary	Data excludes retail securities, locally issued FX bonds, loans and since 2020 also excludes the non-marketable bonds issued to municipalities. Data includes cross-currency swaps.
Iceland	Excludes swap effects.
Ireland	The estimated ATM for Ireland reflects bonds, Euro Commercial paper and Irish Treasury Bills. Inflation linked bonds and some ultra-long maturity notes issued since 2016 are excluded on the basis that they were issued as private placements. These products account for less than 2% of Gross National Debt outstanding at end-2021.
Israel	ATM data excludes retail bonds and non-tradable bonds for pension funds and insurance companies

Country	Note
Italy	No security has been excluded; swap effects are excluded. For 2021 Please note that loans SURE/NGEU (which would raise the 2021 ATM figure to 7.2), are not included.
Japan	MOF announces ATM, based on Fiscal Year, not Calendar Year. Figures from 2007 to 2020 exclude saving bonds. Figures of 2021 are estimated and include saving bonds.
Mexico	The values previously reported for the ATM in 2019 (10.0), 2020 (10.3), 2021 (10.4) and 2022 (10.3) contained the amount of gross debt of the central government and not just the market debt. Our calculation of the ATM considers all outstanding market debt of the central government (short-term and long-term).
Netherlands	The information in the table is based on the data of T-bill and Bonds.
New Zealand	The calculation is based on all NZ Government marketable securities including Nominal Bonds, Inflation-Indexed Bonds, and Treasury Bills as at end Dec. The calculation excludes the non-market securities held by NZ Reserve bank and Earthquake Commission. However, it includes securities held by the NZ Reserve bank that were purchased under their Large Scale Asset Purchase programme and Government Bond repurchases.
Norway	Includes all outstanding Treasury bills and government bonds
Portugal	Excludes securities issued for collateral purposes.
Spain	Central Government Treasury Bills, Bonds and Obligations (nominal, inflation linked and assumed) and foreign currency debt.
Sweden	Marketable debt securities include: Government bonds; Inflation-linked bonds; Green bonds; Public bonds in foreign currencies; Treasury bills; Commercial paper and; foreign currencies
Switzerland	Outstanding marketable debt, excluding: - own tranches not yet issued - securities for cash management purposes - swap effects
Turkey	Weighted ATM figures reflect central government marketable debt.
United Kingdom	Treasury bills for cash management purposes, DMO's gilt holdings and undated gilts are excluded from the calculation of the weighted ATM.

Source: 2021 Survey on Central Government Marketable Debt and Borrowing.

Notes

[1] For example, the OECD Interim Outlook of March 2022 estimates that well targeted government fiscal measures of around 0.5 percentage points of GDP could substantially mitigate the economic impact of the crisis without substantially adding to inflation.

[2] Maintaining a cash buffer, as a risk management tool for government cash and debt management, is a common practice in the OECD area where 29 of the 38 countries have a cash buffer policy. Countries have often resorted to pre-funding (that is, borrowing more than is required by the fiscal deficit) to accumulate the funds needed. In the wake of pandemic, most OECD DMOs built up their cash buffers to mitigate cash flow volatility and funding risk (OECD, 2021[6]).

[3] As of 31 December 2021, EU Member countries received EUR 46.4 billion in grants and EUR 18.0 billion in loans. The combined share of Italy and Spain reached almost 70% of total disbursement (Source: https://ec.europa.eu/economy_finance/recovery-and-resilience-scoreboard/index.html?lang=en).

[4] Fitch downgraded Mexico from BBB to BBB- in April 2020, Chile from A to A- in October 2020 and changed the rating outlook for Turkey from 'stable' to 'negative' in December 2021; S&P downgraded Chile from A+ to A in March 2021; and, Moody's downgraded Mexico from A3 to Baa1 in April 2020 and Turkey from B1 to B2 in September 2020.

[5] Long-term borrowing strategies are associated with higher borrowing costs in a positive yield curve environment. Term premia reflects the amount investors expect to be compensated for lending for longer periods. It is the difference between the yield on a long-term bond and the yield on a shorter-term bond.

[6] The 2021 OECD Survey on Primary Market Developments asked extent to which countries are concerned about the adequacy of investor demand. Respondents were offered a choice between one and five, with one being "very concerned" and five being "not concerned". In order from box one to box five, the number of responses in each box was: 3, 5, 5, 11 and 13.

[7] Primary dealers (PDs) are financial institutions (i.e. banks or securities firms) that are entitled to buy government securities in primary markets with the intention of reselling them to others, thus acting as a market maker of government securities.

[8] In its April meeting, the US federal Reserve announced that its plan to reduce its balance sheet over time in a predictable manner primarily by adjusting the amounts reinvested of principal payments received from securities held in the System Open Market Account (SOMA). Beginning on June 1 2022, principal payments from securities held in the SOMA will be reinvested to the extent that they exceed monthly caps. For Treasury securities, the cap will initially be set at USD 30 billion per month and after three months will increase to USD 60 billion per month. The decline in holdings of Treasury securities under this monthly cap will include Treasury coupon securities and, to the extent that coupon maturities are less than the monthly cap, Treasury bills.

[9] T-Bills are considered as 'shock absorbers' by sovereign debt managers. From the demand side, investors generally desire the safest, most liquid assets in times of crisis, in particular T-Bills. From the supply side, crisis circumstances often bring uncertainties regarding the size and duration of revenue shortfalls and expenses related to government support measures. Issuing short-term instruments helps to manage uncertainties linked to the financing requirement, some of which may be temporary. Considered together, both factors make this strategy consistent with the DMO's goal of funding government at the lowest cost over time (OECD, 2021[6]).

[10] In the United States, the percentage of debt maturing in the next 12 months jumped from 27% in 2019 to 35% in 2020 as a result of increased T-Bill financing in 2020. T-Bills as a share of total debt are essentially back to pre-COVID-19 levels excluding the Federal Reserve's T-Bill holding where the share remains elevated compared to pre-COVID-19 levels. This is because the Fed is reducing the stock of non-T-Bill privately held Treasury securities relative to that of T-Bills.

[11] In some countries the debt ratio is expected to remain broadly stable (e.g. Australia, Iceland and Costa Rica) or continue rising (e.g. Chile, the Czech Republic, and Finland).

[12] It is also important note that a few countries, including Italy and Portugal, did not follow the suit to avoid potential deterioration of rollover risks.

[13] Syndication is mostly used for i) international bond issues; ii) the first-time issuance of new instruments; iii) long(er)-dated bonds and/or the sale of first tranches of benchmark issues, and iv) targeting and directly placing securities among specific investor groups (Annex A).

[14] Debt management offices in OECD countries are pursuing a high degree of transparency and predictability that facilitate and encourage liquid markets. Broad and deep primary and secondary markets, in turn, are instrumental in lowering the cost of borrowing for the government.

[15] Security Lending Facilities support market participants to continuously quote prices which reduces the risk of shortages, avoids settlement problems and enhances liquidity in government debt markets (OECD, 2019[9]).

[16] De-anchoring of inflation expectations could lead to an increase in real rates as investors require compensation against the inflation risk.

[17] Demand from pension funds for inflation linkers partially depends on the pension system. For example, in the United Kingdom and Canada where demand for the linkers is strong, pension funds are – still – dominantly based on a defined benefit system.

[18] A principal trading firm (PTF) is a firm that invests, hedges, or speculates for its own account.

2 ESG practices and challenges from a public debt management perspective

Awareness of environmental and social issues has been rising in recent years. The growing integration of ESG factors by investors, corporates and governments has implications for sovereign debt management as it has the potential to noticeably affect investment decisions, investment tools and country credit assessments over time. Public debt management, as an interface between governments and financial markets, can play an important role in supporting government ESG agendas by conveying to investors government commitments to improve environmental and social outcomes and by financing such activities through the issuance of ESG-labelled bonds.

Against this background, this chapter takes the perspective of a public debt manager and discusses approaches to incorporating ESG factors into public debt management. Using survey-based data, it identifies common practices, challenges as well as the key features of emerging leading practices.

2.1. Introduction

Governments, corporates and investors all around the world are increasing their efforts to integrate Environmental, Social and Governance (ESG) factors into their policies and practices to help reduce the carbon intensity of their economies, make them more climate-resilient and reduce social inequalities. This increased ESG focus affects, in turn, government securities markets through investor decisions, investment tools and country credit assessments. In response, public debt management offices are paying greater attention to, and increasingly adapting, their investor engagement, communication practices, and debt instruments to fully benefit from these developments.

This chapter takes the perspective of a sovereign debt manager and discusses the ways in which developments in sustainable finance affect public debt and its management, and country approaches to integrating ESG factors into debt management. It uses survey-based data to identify common practices, challenges and key features of emerging good practices, and market data to analyse the key trends in ESG-labelled sovereign bond markets.

Key findings

- The environmental, social, and governance (ESG)-related risks and opportunities and their consideration by investors, credit rating agencies, regulators and governments have implications for public debt and its management through fiscal balances, investment decisions, sovereign creditworthiness and the cost of borrowing. Public debt management, as an interface between governments and financial markets, can play an important role in supporting government ESG agendas, mainly through communication and issuance strategies.

- A growing number of debt management offices are becoming more proactive and transparent in providing information on government initiatives and actions to promote ESG issues. Country practices highlight the importance of leveraging the existing information within government institutions, carrying out investor consultation, ensuring the reliability of data and consistency of definitions with the relevant international standards, and developing institutional technical capacity on sustainable finance.

- While still in the early stages of development, the ESG-labelled sovereign bond market grew significantly in recent years. ESG-labelled bond issuance has grown more than threefold since 2019 and exceeded USD 240 billion as of March 2022 and the number of issuers exceeded 30 countries. The yields on sovereign ESG-labelled bonds appear to reflect sovereign creditworthiness, as well as of the high level demand for these bonds in the markets.

- The key motivation for issuing an ESG-labelled bond is to align with government ESG policy agendas, followed by catalysing the development of the local sustainable bond market and meeting high levels of investor demand, hence diversifying the investor base.

- ESG-labelled bond issuance does, however, raise several challenges for sovereign debt management offices as it requires expertise and information that is not typically found in debt management offices. Further standardisation of ESG products in terms of minimum reporting requirements, and a clear and consistent definition of 'green spending', would help facilitate the issuance process and build a robust and liquid ESG bond market.

- To date, the leading practices of sovereign ESG-labelled bonds share common features such as stakeholder engagement, including cross-department collaboration and communication with market participants, commitment to transparency and reporting disclosures and to sustaining liquidity through issuance volume and instrument design.

- Labelled bonds offer an opportunity for emerging market sovereign issuers to attract international investors by meeting their interest in transparency and ESG issues. However, if issued in foreign currency and left unhedged, this could create further vulnerability for issuers due to the increased currency risk associated with issuing foreign-currency debt.

2.2. Sustainable finance and public debt

Awareness of environmental and social issues (e.g. shifting demographics, education, health, housing, poverty, inequality, etc.) has been rising in recent years, with governance issues having greater consideration and understanding for a longer time. Increasing numbers of investors around the world, including central banks, are paying greater attention to sustainable activities, and seeking to integrate ESG factors into their investment portfolios and risk assessment practices. In parallel, a number of alternative investment products with ecological and social benefits have emerged. Many governments have increased their efforts towards the ESG agenda in recent years, as they aim to meet their Paris climate agreement commitments and UN Sustainable Development Goals. They have included environmental, sustainability, and socio-economic equity objectives in their policy packages to help reduce the carbon intensity of their economies, make them more climate-resilient and reduce social inequalities. The integration of ESG factors by investors and governments has implications for sovereign debt management since they have the potential to affect investment decisions, fiscal sustainability and country credit assessments over time.

2.2.1. ESG considerations are high on government agendas

With the Paris Agreement and the United Nations 2030 Agenda for Sustainable Development of 2015, ESG-related policies have made their way up in the governmental agenda all around the world.[1] Since then, according to the United Nations (UN), more than 130 countries have set, or are considering, a target of reducing emissions to net zero by mid-century (United Nations, 2021[1]). This group of countries includes both advanced and emerging-market economies. The 2019 mobilisation to a "Decade of Action", where governments pledged to mobilise financing to meet the UN Sustainable Development Goals (SDGs), will effectively require governments to pick up the pace towards acting on their ESG agenda.[2] Moreover, adopting such a perspective is of central importance in the context of economic recovery from the COVID-19 crisis, as stimulus packages could be designed to achieve a profound shift to more sustainable, inclusive, and resilient economic growth.[3] Such 'build back better' approach requires governments to support and fund investments that lead to a sustained economic recovery, which in turn raises government budget revenues. In this context, growth for build back better policies supports long-term fiscal sustainability.[4] Furthermore, the OECD recognises that governments need to focus on reviving hard-hit economies by boosting growth, income and employment while supporting cleaner, more inclusive and sustainable economies (OECD, 2020[2]). With the Glasgow Climate Pact, governments agreed to revisit and strengthen their commitment to achieving a number of climate related targets, and to establishing a new mechanism and standards for international carbon markets in 2021 (UN, 2021[3]).[5]

Against the background of this policy momentum, government implementation efforts towards green and sustainable growth have been increasingly underpinned by long-term strategies with interim stage objectives, instruments and measures that call for active involvement and co-ordination of a number of different national authorities.[6] Clearly, governments are in a unique position to make regulations to combat climate change (e.g. in controlling carbon emissions). The scaling up of environmental and social commitments nationally has also brought with it implications for the role of central budget offices, treasuries and debt management offices (DMOs) that are not responsible for policies on social and environmental policy. For example, a number of OECD governments have adopted green budgeting which aims to integrate climate and environmental perspectives into budgetary processes and decision making, to support the progress of climate and environmental policies (OECD, 2020[4]). [7] In this context, national climate change or environmental strategies and plans help to guide taxation and spending decisions that can support the achievement of national objectives.

Given that governmental budgets are already constrained in many countries, additional funding for green budgetary purposes will likely require additional borrowing, in particular in the short-term. This need for additional resources can be met through issuance of conventional bonds as part of general borrowing requirements, or through issuance of labelled bonds such as green bonds. As discussed in Section 2.3.2, in addition to fund social and green spending, ESG-labelled sovereign bonds are issued to support the growth of a local ESG bond market, and to demonstrate government commitments to social, sustainable, low-carbon growth strategies.

2.2.2. Soaring demand for ESG investing fuels new approaches to credit risk assessments and instrument developments

Historically, the evolution of financial markets has been driven by the need to mitigate various challenges and grasp opportunities, and ESG related innovations are no exception to this. A growing number of institutional investors and funds incorporate various ESG investing approaches, to better align between societal values and long-term financial value. For example, pension funds have been increasingly considering ESG risk factors in their portfolio selection and management, as ESG-related issues might present risks and opportunities for their investee assets.

While the definition of sustainable investment varies between countries and over time, and most of the sustainable investing data rely on survey-based approaches, they all indicate a steep rise in ESG-sensitive investing, in particular since the COVID-19 pandemic. For instance, a forthcoming OECD report on climate change and corporate governance estimates that assets under management of the investment funds that label themselves as ESG or sustainable fund increased from about USD 800 billion in 2019 to USD 1.7 trillion in 2021 (OECD, 2022[5]). This surge in ESG investing is commonly attributed to the following factors: i) A more holistic approach to risk management by including ESG considerations into the risk mitigation process ii) A wider awareness about social, environmental and human rights issues and risks for the world; iii) An increasing engagement of the younger population who are relatively more sensitive to environmental and social consequences of their choices, in investment, and iv) Development of new regulations and values.

From an investment strategy perspective, the traditional approach to investing into sovereign debt usually takes into account the macroeconomic outlook of the issuer in order to assess whether sovereign debt risk factors could materialise. To assess these risks, investors have long focused – through sovereign credit ratings – on internal political issues, demography trajectories and the standards of governance as well as on economic indicators, such as the rate of economic growth, levels of external debts and exposure of domestic banks. Hence, except for governance indicators, ESG factors have not been particularly visible in conventional sovereign credit ratings. With a holistic approach, sustainability is increasingly recognised as an important parameter influencing the overall economic performance of a country. By tackling climate risks, improving social cohesion, and supporting good governance, a state can support better economic performance in the long run, and in turn strengthen its creditworthiness. For instance, a recent study by Kahn et al. (2019[6]) finds that persistent changes in climate have a long-term negative impact on economic growth in both advanced and emerging, as well as hot and cold, countries. At the same time, ESG instruments are associated with higher levels of transparency, due to reporting and disclosure, and thus integrating ESG considerations in allocation decisions, provides investors with an enhanced framework to analyse sovereigns from a credit perspective. While no one-size-fits-all investment strategy exists, and the decision of investors to adopt an ESG perspective depends on a variety of factors, different international bodies (among which the OECD, the World Bank, and the Global Sustainable Investment Alliance) have provided a spectrum of investment approaches that seems to apply to the majority of institutional investors (Box 2.1).

Box 2.1. ESG considerations in investment approaches

Investor appetite towards sustainable investing has been steadily increasing in the last few years, reflecting the fact that investors are paying greater attention to the social and environmental consequences of the decisions that governments make. Sustainable investing strategies in sovereign debt can be summarised as follows:

- Traditional investment strategies aim at maximising financial market returns. In such a context there is little to no space for ESG considerations and practices.
- Negative screening strategies exclude certain countries from portfolios, based on activities considered not investable (e.g. excessive reliance of the national economy on non-renewable sources of energy).
- Positive screening strategies aim to add desirable asset characteristics to a portfolio, by including issuers who are compliant with international norms and standards.
- Sustainability-themed strategies aim to select categories of assets who contribute to sustainable development.
- Impact investing strategies aim at achieving a positive environmental and/or social impact, while safeguarding long-term financial sustainability.
- ESG integration strategies explicitly include ESG factors into financial analysis.
- Responsible ownership strategies aim to influence sovereigns' behaviour, by engaging in stewardship policies with the issuer (OECD, 2019[7]) (World Bank, 2020[8]).

The rise in sustainable investing has implications for sovereign credit assessments, as investors consider the ESG performance of the government, and are not obliged to invest in labelled bonds. In this context, ESG ratings and ESG risk scores have gained consideration as tools to assess the environmental and social impact, as well as to establish environmental, social and governance risks, of specific investment choices. ESG ratings take a perspective of material quantification of the sovereign credit risks linked to environmental, social and governance factors. Therefore, by providing information on the exposure to and management of a country's ESG risk factors, they are mainly used to assess its sustainability and creditworthiness. On the other hand, ESG scores take a perspective of evaluation of the impact of specific investments, and they aim to gauge a country's ESG relative performance. Recent studies in this area suggest that the agencies that assign ESG ratings to both bonds and their issuers use different methodologies and are not completely transparent, which may lead to misperceptions about a country's overall sustainability performance.

Source: OECD (2019[7]), *Social Impact Investment 2019: The Impact Imperative for Sustainable Development*, https://doi.org/10.1787/9789264311299-en; World Bank (2020[8]) *Engaging with Investors on Environmental, Social, and Governance (ESG) Issues: A World Bank Guide for Sovereign Debt Managers*, https://thedocs.worldbank.org/en/doc/375981604591250621-0340022020/original/WorldBankESGGuide2020FINAL.11.5.2020.pdf.

Labelled bonds, which aim to provide investors with sustainable, transparent and high-quality investment opportunities, are becoming an important part of financial markets as they grow not only in size but also in terms of the variety of instruments. Annual green, social and sustainability bond issuance reached over USD 1.1 trillion in 2021, recorded a 45% increase compared to 2020 (CBI, 2021[9]). Despite the record growth, the issuance of ESG bonds is still a modest amount compared to the USD 18 trillion of government borrowing by OECD countries as well as USD 5.9 trillion in corporate bond borrowing in the same year. While corporate sector issuance dominates the ESG debt market, sovereign issuance has been growing rapidly in recent years as discussed in Section 2.3.2.

Going forward, ESG debt market is expected to grow further on the back of increasing funding needs of both private sector and public sector issuers for social projects, climate mitigation and adaptation projects in line with national targets and robust investor demand. Issuers may also be inclined to use labelled bond programs as a means of signalling commitments to ESG aims. The appetite of investors for ESG-labelled bonds on the other hand appears to be motivated by several reasons. First, investors are increasingly influenced by societal values and are characterised by the desire to improve the alignment of financial products with societal and moral considerations. Second, under some circumstances, ESG investing can help improve risk management and lead to returns that are comparable to returns from traditional financial investments. For instance, evidence from primary studies on corporate stocks suggests that socially responsible investing has a positive impact on returns, particularly for portfolios that score well on environmental and diversity dimensions (Galema, Plantinga and Scholtens, 2008[10]). On the other hand, studies on fixed income market resulted in mixed findings: A literature review of over 240 research papers issued between 2016 and 2020 finds that, for fixed income instruments, 33% of the reviewed studies showed a better performance of portfolios with an ESG focus, while 54% found either neutral (performance comparable to traditional portfolios) or mixed effects, and 14% found negative effects (Whelan et al., 2021[11]). Third, significant progress made in regulations and guidelines with respect to ESG labelling, taxonomy and transparency obligations across different jurisdiction has contributed to attract ESG sensitive investors and to the development of the ESG bond market (Box 2.2).

Box 2.2. Guidelines for ESG-labelled debt

In recent years, sustainable finance has made significant progress from a regulatory and statutory standpoint, as both regulators and market participants sought greater market transparency and more certainty around the long-term sustainability of various types of investments, at a time when ESG considerations were increasingly being incorporated into investment approaches and strategies. The scope of regulations and guidelines is to facilitate investment by giving investors' confidence and assurance through the clear definition of which investments and financial instruments can be considered sustainable or green, and to allow the easier implementation of policy action by easing the tracking of sustainable finance flows (OECD, 2020[12]). Beside national governments and jurisdictions (where examples include China, France, Japan and the Netherlands), both market associations, such as the International Capital Market Association (ICMA), and supranationals, such as the European Union, have contributed to policy and regulatory making. [8]

The ICMA plays an important role in the development of sustainable finance by serving as Secretariat for a set of voluntary frameworks known as Principles, which are used as a reference by participants in both international bond markets and sustainable finance markets more broadly. The Principles lay forth best procedures for issuing bonds with social and/or environmental goals, through guidelines and recommendations that enhance transparency and disclosure, thus ensuring market integrity (ICMA, 2022[13]).[9] In particular, four macro-categories, one for each bond label, are published under the governance of the ICMA's Principles: i) the Green Bond Principles, which were first issued in 2014; ii) the Social Bond Principles (SBP); iii) the Sustainability Bond Guidelines (SBG); and iv) the Sustainability-Linked Bond Principles (SLBP). The Green Bond Principles, the SBP and the SBG are all based on four components that determine whether labelled debt instruments are aligned with the relative framework, namely use of proceeds; process for project evaluation and selection; management of proceeds, and reporting. The SLPB, instead, have five core components, that range from the selection of Key Performance Indicators to the process of verification (ICMA, 2021[14]; 2021[15]; 2021[16]; 2020[17]).

On the other hand, the European Union has worked towards the enhancement of the European sustainable finance framework, with the hope of channelling private financial flows into sustainable investment and relevant economic activities and of catalysing mobilisation of capital towards sustainable investment. To do so, in 2018 the European Commission adopted an Action Plan on "Financing Sustainable Growth", which was built on the introduction of: i) a classification system for sustainable activities; ii) a disclosure framework for financial and non-financial companies; and iii) a set of standards and benchmarks for sustainable investment solutions (European Commission, 2018[18]). The first block is also known as "EU Taxonomy", a statutory classification system that can be used by financial institutions and investors to establish the sustainability of investments, by evaluating whether a particular economic activity contributes to a series of environmental objectives. In particular, the Taxonomy establishes six environmental objectives, which are climate change mitigation; climate change adaptation; sustainable use and protection of water and marine resources; transition to a circular economy, pollution prevention and control; and protection and restoration of biodiversity and ecosystems (European Commission, 2020[19]). The second core block is a mandatory disclosure regime for financial and non-financial companies of the impact of their activities on the environment and the society, to allow financial market participants to have the necessary information to pursue the objective of sustainable investment. The last block is the introduction of a set of benchmarks, standards and labels to facilitate financial markets participants to align their investment strategies with climate and environmental goals. In particular, under this block the Commission is legislating on a voluntary standard for European green bonds (European Commission, 2021[20]). Going forward, the Commission is expected to expand and to develop this framework as part of the European Green Deal (European Commission, 2021[21]).

2.2.3. The implications of ESG considerations for public debt and its management

The ESG-related risks and opportunities and their consideration by investors, credit rating agencies, regulators and governments, along with related innovations in the financial markets have implications for public debt and its management. This includes the potential for impacts on the fiscal balances, sovereign creditworthiness and cost of borrowing as well as on the role of public debt management in supporting governments' efforts in achieving the climate goals in the Paris Agreement and the SDG goals by communicating ESG analysis and data and supporting ESG segment of the financial markets.

The first set of effects entail the impact of environmental and social risks on a country's fiscal sustainability, which, all other things being equal, is the ability of a government to sustain its current spending, tax and other policies in the long run without threatening government solvency or defaulting on any of its debt. Any persistent increase in public expenditures and fall in tax revenues would lead to increased public deficits and debt.[10] For example, the health and rebuilding costs of more frequent and severe natural disasters would increase budget expenses. Similarly, the transformation of economies, particularly in the energy sector, is likely to trigger infrastructure costs to the budget, while at the same time energy exporting countries may, over time, suffer from lack of demand for fossil fuels, putting pressure on budget revenues. This fiscal impact ultimately depends on a country's exposure to the effects of such risks, ability to reduce vulnerability (readiness) and mitigation capacity.

Measurement and reporting of the fiscal impact require conceptual considerations, a comprehensive data, and quantitative and qualitative analyses. While important, these factors can be challenging (OECD, 2021[22]). For example, quantitative estimates of the economic impact of demographic developments and their impact on expenditure on health, social security, education and other demography-related items can be a challenge due to lack of robust projections as well as interconnectedness between the parameters. Similarly, integration of climate related physical and transition risks in public debt sustainability analysis requires different assumptions on the path for greenhouse emissions and magnitude and the persistence of the budgetary consequences of policies aimed at mitigating climate change.[11] In this context, data availability is a key challenge for ESG-related analysis (e.g. stress test analysis, scenario analyses as well as scoring and rating analyses). Once the data and methods develop to a point where long-term macro-fiscal implications of climate and social risks can be incorporated in sovereign credit risk analyses properly, sustainability can be expected to become a key macroeconomic variable. While the existing literature on this topic is limited, a few primary studies suggest that climate change vulnerability has adverse effects on sovereign credit ratings, and that countries with greater climate change resilience benefit from higher credit ratings (Cevik and Jalles, 2020[23]).

Assessment of potential fiscal costs will help countries to outline realistic budget targets, develop fiscal strategies and avoid budget risks. Underestimation of structural budget challenges, on the other hand, would risk fiscal credibility and debt sustainability. Already, fiscal impact analyses, for especially climate change scenarios, have been reported by a number of countries either in the form of standalone reports or an annex to budget laws. For example, the UK published the Fiscal Risks Report in 2019 (UK Office for Budget Responsibility, 2019[24]) and Switzerland published the Report on the Long-Term Sustainability of Public Finances in 2016 (FDF, 2016[25]). Australia presented results of climate change impact on level and cost of debt analyses in an annex of the long-term emissions reductions plan of its net-zero by 2050 goals in 2021 (Australian Government, 2021[26]). The European Commission presents the possible impacts on debt trajectories for its member countries in the Debt Sustainability Monitor in 2020 (European Commission, 2021[27]).

The fiscal impact of environmental and social risks has the potential to bear consequences for sovereign creditworthiness and cost of borrowing. The literature in this area is just developing, and therefore the results of primary studies should be interpreted with caution. Nevertheless, some of the empirical analyses present evidence on the link between climate change, social risks and sovereign risk. For instance, Cevik and Tovar Valles (2020[28]), investigating the impact of climate change vulnerability and resilience on sovereign bond yields and spreads in 98 advanced and developing countries over the period 1995-2017, find that exposure to climate risks increases both credit spreads and yields for long-term bonds, in particular for emerging economies (where a 1 percentage point increase in climate exposure increases credit spreads by more than 15 bps in the long-run). Importantly, their findings highlight that the ability of policy makers to enhance climate resilience through mitigation and adaptation strategies can significantly reduce the costs of borrowing in the long-run. Klusak et al. (2021[29]) are able to simulate the effect of climate change on sovereign credit ratings for a sample of 108 countries and find evidence that climate-induced downgrades could be as early as 2030 under a business-as-usual scenario, while the effect would almost be eliminated under a more stringent climate policy. In addition, they are able to assess the material costs of climate change on interest payments, finding that it could increase the annual interest payments on sovereign debt by a range that goes from USD 22 to 33 billion for more positive climate scenarios to USD 137 to 205 billion under high emission scenarios. Finally, the empirical analysis of a sample of 20 OECD countries shows that sovereign bond markets price country ESG factors: countries with good ESG performances are associated with lower default risks and lower yield spreads, suggesting that more sustainable countries are less risky and face lower borrowing costs (Capelle-Blancard et al., 2019[30]). These results therefore have implications for public debt management, which aims to meet the government's financing needs and payment requirements in the medium-to-long run at the lowest possible cost.

The increasing interest in ESG analysis by investors, researchers and rating agencies raises investor's demand for greater transparency on this topic. As an interface between a government and its investor base, the ability of DMOs to collect and disseminate information on ESG-related projects and other data, and communicate the national ESG strategy to investors will contribute in shaping the set of financing tools that are available for the central government. In this context, authorities (e.g. debt management offices and budgetary authorities) would benefit from incorporating ESG-related risk scenarios in public debt sustainability analyses, which in turn would necessitate enhancement of risk management capacities and practices. The ability of sovereign debt managers to engage with primary dealers and to monitor secondary markets developments in relation to ESG issues, as well as their ability to adjust their communication strategies to meet the requirements of sensitive investors will contribute to enlarge the investor base and to attract ESG-dedicated investors. At the same time, knowing the composition of the investor base, as well as their geographical location and investment behaviours – for instance, whether domestic institutional pension funds prevail over foreign hedge funds – will reduce the volatility of the debt and will help tilt ESG issuance strategies towards long-term, buy-and-hold investors.

Finally, an important implication of ESG related developments for public debt management is related to the issuance of ESG-labelled sovereign bonds, which supports the development of a domestic market for labelled bonds. From a debt management perspective, the issuance of labelled bonds can help attract those investors who are seeking to support sustainability goals; enhancing the financing capacity, and diversifying funding sources. However, sovereign ESG-labelled bonds bring about new risk management challenges as to selection and effective prioritisation of prospective projects, co-ordination among the various line ministries, legislative changes, special monitoring, reporting and disclosure requirements as well as marketing activities. In addition, labelled bonds, if issued in a foreign currency and not hedged, can be a source of currency risk for issuers. As discussed in Section 2.3.2, this challenge is particularly relevant for EMEs, who may wish to benefit from ESG-labelled bonds to access international capital markets.

In addition to carrying their traditional operational work of managing conventional debt instruments and issuance strategies, DMOs (or other government departments) will have to develop not only new competencies in terms of assessing risks related to climate change and developing and launching new instruments, but also new communication strategies to be able to explain to the investor base the national ESG strategy and the agenda, as well as the commitments, of the government in terms of addressing climate and social risks. Moreover, they will need to be able to co-ordinate with relevant line ministries and to make their part in the development of the broader national strategy. Much of these additional activities have to be sustained regularly, requiring staffing in debt management offices (DMOs). In addition, there is a need to improve knowledge of environmental and social issues, which are not within the DMOs' area of expertise. Meeting with capacity building needs could be challenging for small debt management offices with limited resources.

2.3. Incorporation of ESG-considerations in public debt management

Sovereign DMOs can adopt different approaches to incorporating ESG factors into public debt management. This might include i) being more proactive and transparent in providing information to investors, rating agencies and broader public on government initiatives and actions to promote ESG issues; ii) adding ESG-related risk scenarios into debt analysis, and medium- and long-term debt sustainability analyses, and; iii) issuing ESG-labelled bonds.

The development of a strategy for integrating ESG factors in PDM requires an assessment of the potential areas of application (e.g. communication with investors and credit rating agencies, impact analyses on cost of sovereign debt, issuance of labelled bonds) as well as adopting suitable and sound frameworks in terms of roles and responsibilities within and across relevant agencies. To identify DMOs' view, the challenges encountered and innovative practices concerning different approaches, the OECD conducted a survey on the "Approaches to incorporating Environmental, Social and Governance (ESG) factors into public debt management including issuance of sovereign green bonds" to all OECD member countries in 2021. Following that, a similar survey was extended to a selected number of non-OECD countries in early 2022. This section draws mainly on responses received to these surveys and reflects on countries' views on different approaches and potential challenges with regard to the integration of ESG factors in PDM practices in terms of communication and transparency practices, as well as debt analysis.

2.3.1. Factoring government's ESG policies into investor relations and general communication strategy

As discussed in Section 2.2, the ability of debt management offices to communicate the national environmental and social efforts and to engage consistently with their investor base can play an important role in addressing ESG disclosures by increasing transparency and disclosing relevant information/metrics for ESG ratings and accessing market insights. Already, a number of DMOs are factoring government's ESG policies into investor relations and general communication strategy. The survey results from the OECD countries show that 34% of the responding countries are already taking into account the national-level ESG strategy in their investor relations, and 40% more are either planning to or studying whether to take into account the national-level ESG strategy in their investor engagement. It should be noted that only a few OECD countries including Japan and the United States reported that they do not foresee to take into account ESG factors in their engagement with investors. The responses from non-OECD countries indicated that more than half of the respondents have a strategy to incorporate ESG factors into public debt management and that about one-third of the respondent countries do not have such strategy.[12]

In terms of the motivations, DMOs commonly highlight that the main aim of the expansion of communication topics towards the ESG-issues is to supplement general information already available to investors and other relevant parties with information from other sources (like a 'one-stop-shop') and to use interaction with investors to better understand their decision frameworks for asset allocation (Figure 2.1 and Figure 2.2). Two-way communication with investors enables DMOs to better understand investors' information requests, their assessment of country's ESG standing and demand for the ESG-labelled bonds. In countries where the DMO opts not to proceed with thematic issuances, being able to communicate the ESG characteristics of conventional debt instruments still remains important. The aim is to add value to international ESG comparisons by emphasising government' sustainability priorities and give useful insight to the investors from a national perspective. DMOs also benefit from engagement to influence investor assessments of its country's ESG performance in favour of increasing or holding allocations into its bonds, and boost country's ESG credentials. DMOs of non-member countries also cited 'alignment with international market best practices' among one of the main motivations.

Figure 2.1. Main motivation to incorporate ESG related factors into investor relations information- responses from the OECD area DMOs

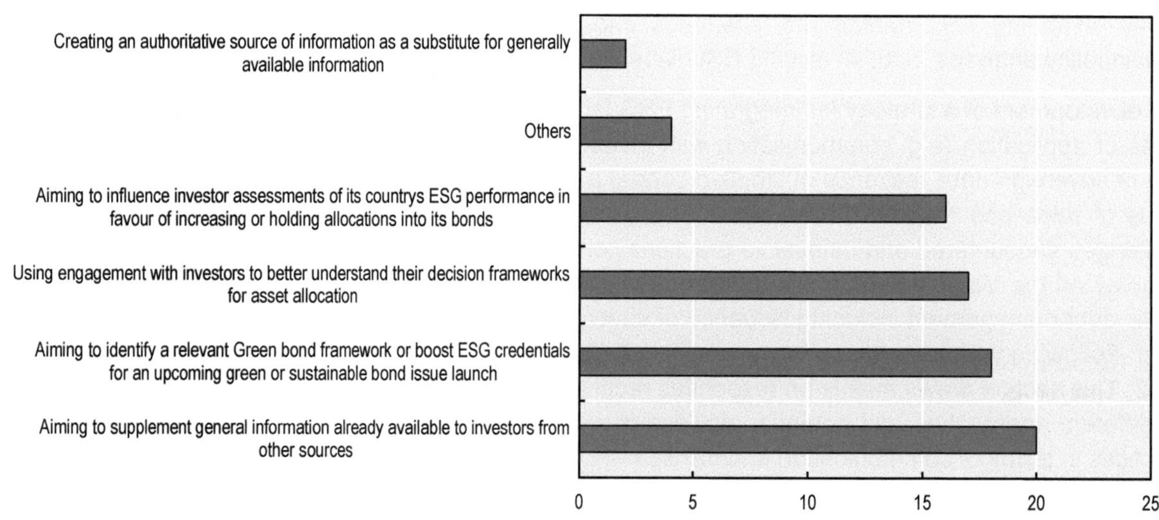

Source: 2021 survey on Approaches to incorporating Environmental, Social and Governance (ESG) factors into public debt management including issuance of sovereign green bonds.

Figure 2.2. Main motivation to incorporate ESG related factors into investor relations information- responses from the non-OECD DMOs

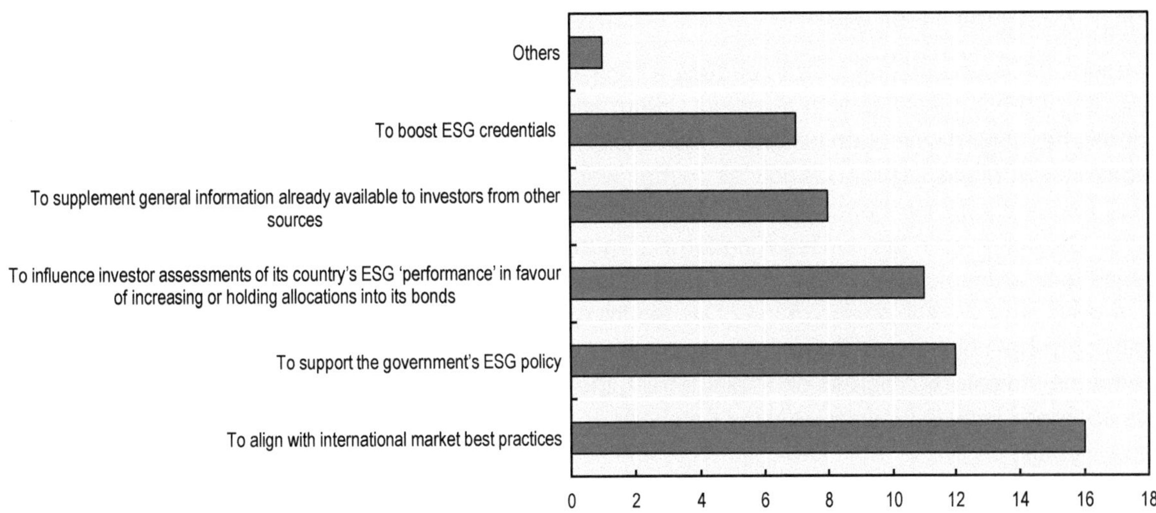

Source: 2022 survey on Approaches to incorporating Environmental, Social and Governance (ESG) factors into public debt management including issuance of sovereign ESG-labelled bonds by the OECD Public Debt Management Unit.

Figure 2.3. Information shared to investors by OECD and non-OECD DMOs

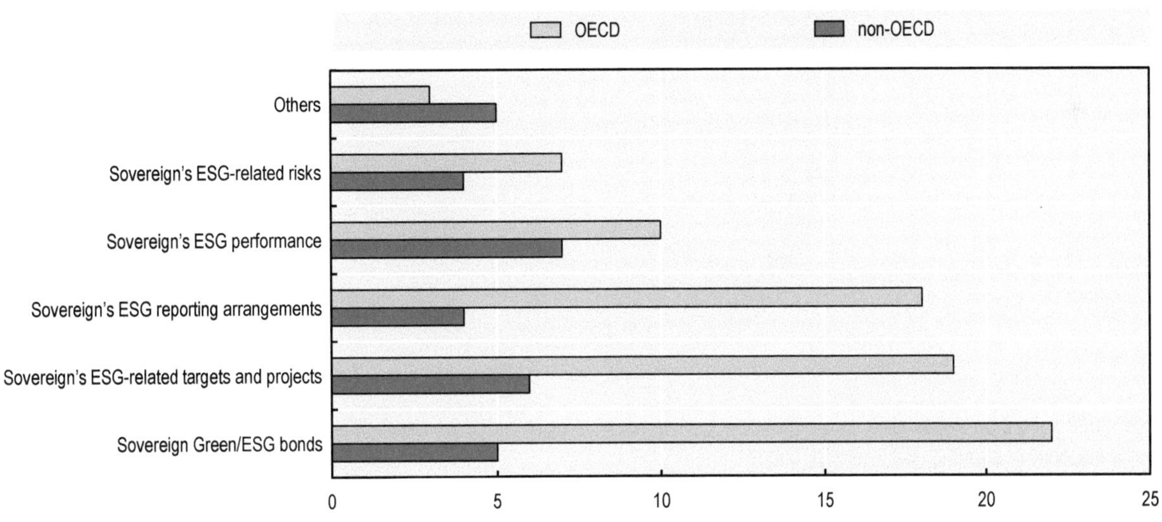

Note: Sovereign's ESG performance intended as a country's rank with respect to its environmental performance, OECD's better life index, UN Sustainable goals, World Bank Governance Indicators and reporting arrangements intended as reporting on allocation of proceeds and/or impact reporting. The "Others" category mostly included countries reporting that they were at the beginning of the process, and that no information was shared.
Source: 2021 survey on Approaches to incorporating ESG factors into public debt management including issuance of sovereign green bonds and 2022 survey on Approaches to incorporating ESG factors into public debt management including issuance of sovereign ESG-labelled bonds.

In terms of the topics, DMOs often share information on the ESG aspects on labelled bonds including reporting on allocation of proceeds and/or impact of spending on green projects, and government's ESG-related targets and projects. The survey results indicated that some DMOs, rather than communicating to their investor base the whole spectrum of ESG issues and strategies, focus exclusively on its environmental dimension in the context of their thematic issuances (Figure 2.3). This is, for instance, the case of the German DMO, which currently takes the national-level ESG strategy into account in its investor engagement in the context of their green bond issuance, and its currently analysing the possibility to pursue this on a more general level, and of Colombia, which provides investors with relevant information on the National Development Plan (NDP).

Sovereign DMOs use various tools to engage with investors, rating agencies and broader public including regular and ad-hoc meetings with investors, information presented on websites and annual reports. The pandemic has forced sovereign issuers to shift rapidly towards digital communication tools such as email distribution lists, publishing market notices on their websites, and virtual meetings. ESG-related information is most frequently disseminated through investor presentations, e-newsletters and meetings (e.g. Chile, France, Germany and the United Kingdom) (Figure 2.4). Some countries also launched dedicated websites to share various reports and analyses on sustainability performances. Information in the form of data, reports, analyses on a wide range of issues from progress on climate change mitigation plans, social equality and well-being, ageing population, as well as country's ranking in OECD's Better Life Index, WB's Governance Indicators, progress on implementing the UN SDGs are shared through websites. Examples of this approach include Finnish Treasury's website on 'Sustainability and Finnish Government Bonds' and Benin's website on Sustainable Development Goals targeted by Benin.[13]

Figure 2.4. Common tools for disseminating ESG-related information by non-OECD DMOs

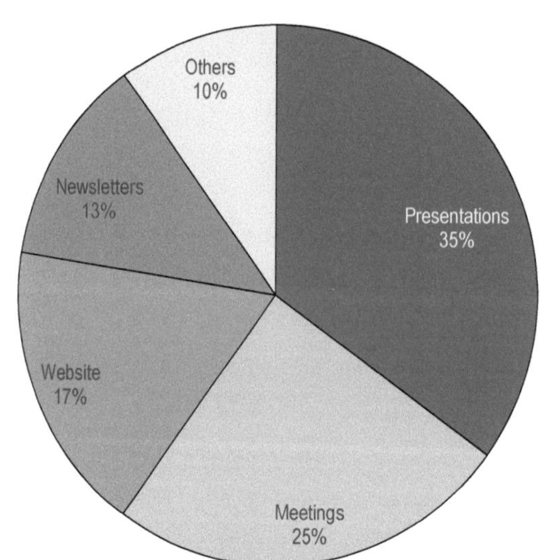

Source: 2022 survey on Approaches to incorporating Environmental, Social and Governance (ESG) factors into public debt management including issuance of sovereign ESG-labelled bonds.

Major challenges draw on issuers' ESG-related communication practices as follows:

- Identification of relevant information for investors and credit rating agencies
- Co-ordination among the relevant public institutions, difficulty in accessing existing data
- Lack of relevant data and analysis
- Insufficient staff resources
- Insufficient technical capacity

The main challenges with communicating ESG-related issues source from the fact that DMOs may not have the necessary expertise and information related to ESG policies nor have any influence/say on the policies that are implemented. Often, DMO staff in EMs lack the necessary knowledge to address question related to ESG-policies that are posed by investors, and can't quality check the reliability of the information

(Figure 2.5). In this context, the perception of greenwashing could pose a challenge in sovereign sustainable finance.[14]

The survey results highlight the importance of strengthening the co-ordination between DMOs and the respective line ministries to ensure access to all the necessary information in a timely and efficient manner. In addition, raising awareness among the DMO staff about the ESG risks, country's vulnerability and the way these risks are addressed by the national government is stated as an important factor for improving communication. DMOs of EMEs particularly highlighted the need for capacity building activities with respect to issuance of labelled bonds; how to analyse fiscal impact of environmental and social risks, and; how to improve ESG related communications strategy.

Figure 2.5. ESG awareness among non-OECD DMOs

Panel A: Did DMO staff receive training on ESG related topics?

Panel B: To what extent is the DMO aware of ESG risks and the way these risks are addressed by the national government?

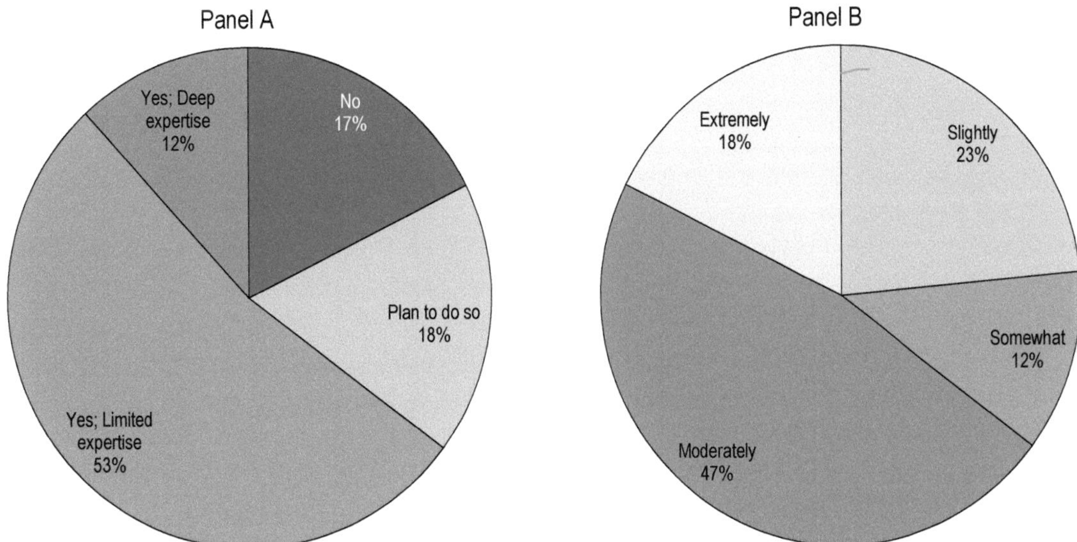

Note: In Panel A the Yes options were "Yes, limited expertise/knowledge in the DMO" and "Yes, deep expertise/knowledge among several staff" In Panel B, no country selected the "Not at all aware" option.
Source: 2022 survey on Approaches to incorporating Environmental, Social and Governance (ESG) factors into public debt management including issuance of sovereign ESG-labelled bonds.

Figure 2.6. Key areas for capacity building

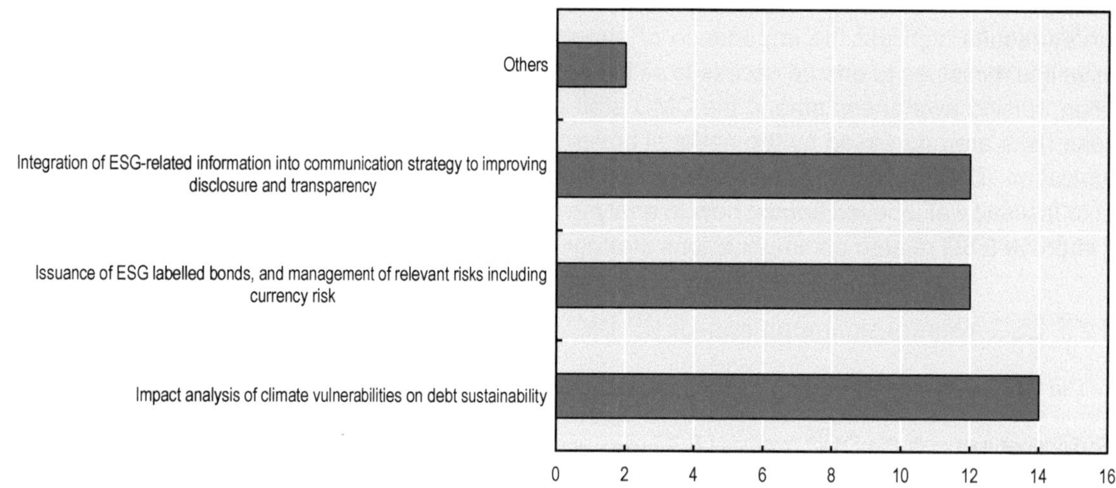

Source: 2022 survey on Approaches to incorporating Environmental, Social and Governance (ESG) factors into public debt management including issuance of sovereign ESG-labelled bonds.

Common features of leading practices

Drawing on the key points from the implementation experiences of OECD countries, which are still evolving, this section proposes common features of leading practices on integrating ESG factors in PDM practices in terms of communication and transparency practices. These features focus on the coverage, debt management offices in the surveyed countries, and are intended to support the ongoing development and implementation of incorporation of ESG factors into public debt management.

- *Leverage existing information collected by the relevant ministries/agencies*: ESG covers a wide set of cross cutting issues from demographics to greenhouse emission targets, most of which do not fall under DMOs area of responsibilities. At the same time, the reliability and timeliness of the ESG information shared is very important in terms of credibility and reliability of sovereigns. Hence, it is important to establish a robust co-ordination mechanism for co-ordinating with the relevant national authorities such as ministries/agencies of environment, energy, health and housing such as through high-level committees, and avoid a duplication of resources.

- *Consider the preferences of both foreign and domestic investors regarding areas and metrics as well as tools of ESG communication:* Expansion of communication of relevant ESG issues requires an assessment of the potential ESG related targets and indicators (e.g. how country is ranked or rated vis-à-vis international standards, progress reports etc.), and communication tools (e.g. newsletters, websites, investor presentations, regular and ad-hoc meetings including overseas roadshows). DMOs should prioritise areas, and metrics considering investors and other relevant parties' interest as well as government commitments with respect to ESG issues.

- *Ensure reliability and quality of data and consistency of definitions with the relevant international guidelines/standards on sustainable finance:* As environmentally and socially responsible investment is a new segment of the financial markets, relevant taxonomy and definitions are still at development stage. At the same time, ESG-sensitive investors' confidence in data and other analysis is key for its long-term development. In this regard, sovereign debt management offices should attach great importance to the accountability and transparency principles when interpreting the relevant taxonomy, disseminating the information collected from other sources, and ensure consistency of definitions with the existing international guidelines/standards on sustainable finance. Failing to adhere to these principles would lead to 'greenwashing' concerns and deteriorate development of sustainable finance and credibility of government.

- *Enhance institutional capacity with respects to number and knowledge of staff:* Given that DMOs do not have the competence in ESG-related policies and/or activities, capacity development is key for the collection, analysis and dissemination of ESG related information. Authorities should adopt suitable and sound frameworks in terms of roles and responsibilities within and across relevant agencies, and support the responsible staff in the development of ESG expertise. They can benefit from using their networks and contacts within the financial market community and beyond to understand best practice, emerging trends, investor preferences.

2.3.2. Launch of ESG-labelled sovereign bond programmes

In recent years, a number of sovereign debt management offices have expanded their borrowing instruments with ESG-labelled debt securities. From a debt management perspective, issuing a new instrument helps to enhance the financing capacity of sovereigns and to diversify their funding sources. In addition, sovereign ESG-labelled bonds feature broader benefits to the overall economy and the financial market by supporting governments' efforts in financing green and social projects and promoting the development of a domestic market for labelled bonds (OECD, 2022[31]). On the demand side, the number of investors who are committed to responsible investment and integrating ESG factors into their investment processes is increasing quite rapidly (e.g. Norwegian Global Fund, Denmark's ATP Pension Fund, Swedish National Pension Fund and The California State Teachers' Retirement System etc.) which, in turn, supports portfolio investments in ESG-labelled securities.

The labelled bond market has seen rapid growth in issuance across four primary categories: green bonds, social bonds, sustainability bonds, and sustainability-linked bonds (Box 2.3). Since 2016, when Poland was the first sovereign to issue a green bond, sovereign ESG bond issuance in both advanced and emerging market economies has grown exponentially, reaching more than USD 240 billion at the end of March 2022. The survey results from OECD debt management offices indicate that more than one-third of respondents is planning or studying whether to incorporate ESG factors into its issuance decisions, with more than a quarter of countries currently doing so.

The responses to the OECD surveys suggest that the motivations behind such momentum are varied and dependent on the national context. Of 30 respondents, 25 emphasised that the key motivation for issuing an ESG-labelled bond was that of aligning with the existing ESG policy agenda as a way to finance the government's environmental and social strategy.[15] Country experiences suggest that the issuance of labelled bonds brings about a positive market story with supportive news flows, which in turn help issuer countries to communicate their sustainability strategies. For some of the respondents an important motivation is that of meeting the increased investors' demand (15 out of 30 respondents) and that of strengthening the development of sustainable finance (12 respondents out of 30). Another key driver, as highlighted by 13 of the respondents, was that of diversification of the investor base, which remains important for many issuers, in particular for the EM issuers. For instance, Slovenia allocated 48% of its EUR 1 billion green bond to ESG-focused investors, while this percentage stands between 50% and 80% for both Benin and Indonesia and at 77% for Mexico's specific SDG bond issuance. Nevertheless, this investor diversification benefit exists as well for advanced economies: for instance, Italy and Spain allocated respectively more than half and more than two thirds of their initial ESG issuances to sensitive investors.

The findings of the survey with regard to motivations imply that the pricing advantage ('greenium') is not one of the main determinants of ESG-labelled sovereign bond issuance. While securing funding at a lower cost surely is an additional benefit that sovereign debt managers take into account in their issuance strategies, the results of the OECD surveys suggest that this is not the main reason why they do so.

Against this background, this section first present issuance trends in sovereign ESG bond market, then discuss issuers' experience and views on the motivations behind and the challenges with labelled bond issuance. Following that it proposes a set of common features of leading practices in ESG-labelled bond issuance and provides a brief discussion about the outlook for labelled bonds.

Box 2.3. Overview of ESG-labelled borrowing instruments

Specific bond labels are defined and distinguished by the ICMA's Principles, but national regulations or standards might apply as well. The main difference between green, social and sustainability instruments and sustainability-linked instruments is that the former are project-based, while the latter are target-based. Project-based instruments are those whose proceeds are earmarked to specific projects: green, social and sustainable instruments are a form of financial instruments whose proceeds are exclusively earmarked to fund green projects, social projects or a combination of the two. Green projects include activities that deliver benefits to efforts related to climate change mitigation or adaptation; natural resource depletion; loss of biodiversity; air, water or soil pollution. Social projects include the promotion of sustainable social infrastructures, essential services and of socio-economic improvement, as well as the generation of employment and the alleviation of unemployment. Finally, proceeds from sustainability bonds must finance a combination of green and social projects, with the aim of promoting the social co-benefits associated with green, and the green co-benefits associated with social, benefits. On the other hand, target-based instruments are those whose financial and/or structural characteristics can vary depending on whether the issuer achieves predefined ESG objectives, but whose proceeds can be used for general purposes.

Project-based and target-based instruments also differ in terms of reporting requirements and external review processes. The structure of sustainability-linked bonds implies that the issuer makes an explicit and formal commitment towards future improvements in the predefined ESG objectives. As such, this commitment will be included in the instrument documentation and will rest on the selection of key performance indicators (KPIs) and of sustainable performance targets (SPTs), which are used to gauge the issuer's performance in terms of KPIs. Hence, issuers of sustainability-linked instruments must mandatorily seek independent and external verification by a qualified external third party of the performance of each KPI with respect to the related SPTs. In addition, they should provide a reporting document with up-to-date information on the performance of KPIs with respect to the baselines and a verification assurance report that outlines the performance against SPTs and the related impact on the bond's financial and/or structural characteristics; as well as a set of information that enables investors to analyse the performance of the issuer with respect to SPTs. Reporting documents and external reviews are not mandatory for issuers of project-based instruments. However, they are strongly recommended, given that a commitment to transparency helps investors to better assess the impact of each project. In practice, the issuance of project-based bonds has in most cases been accompanied by the publication of allocation reports and by third party reviews, suggesting that this has become a standard practice among debt management offices.

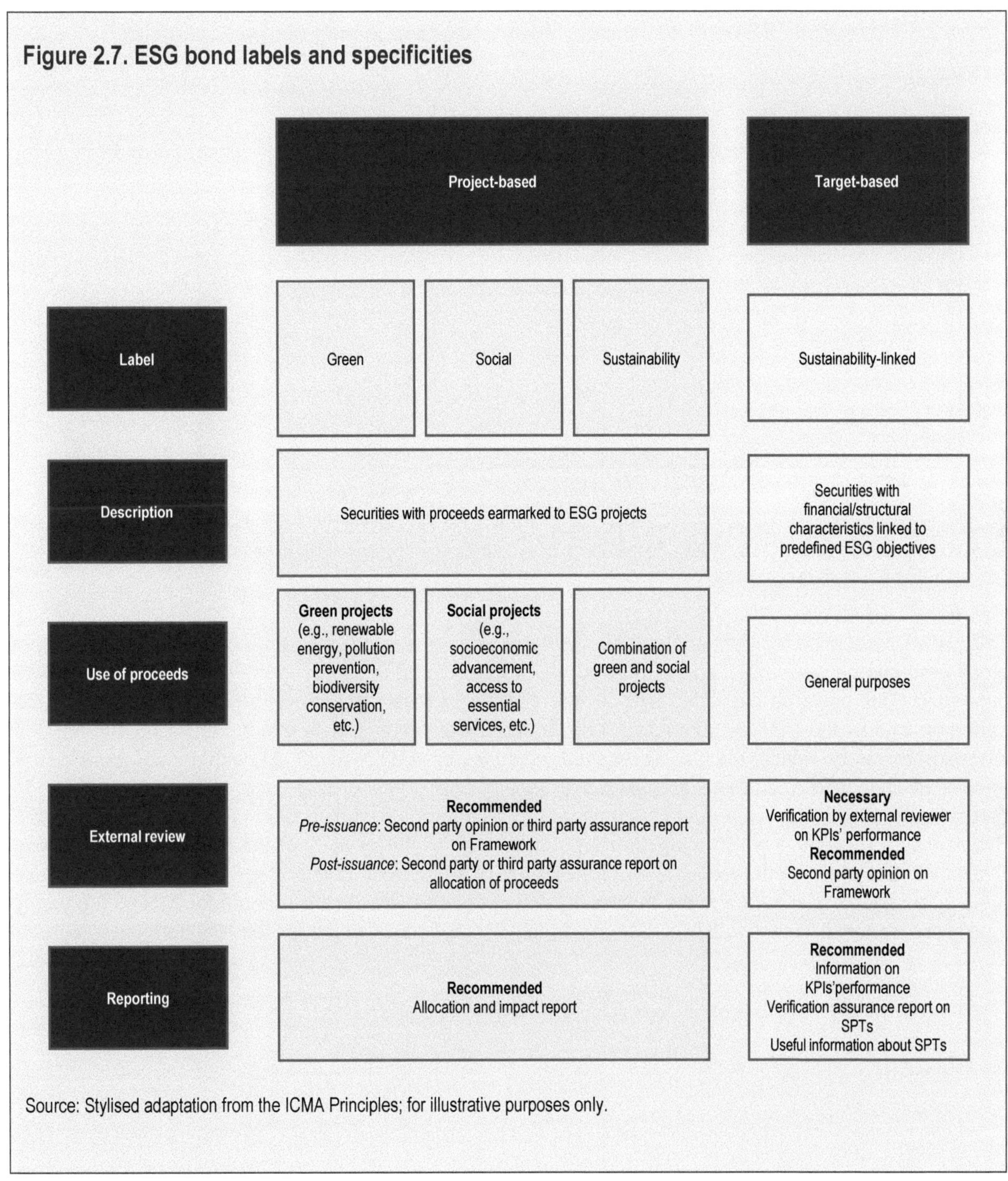

Figure 2.7. ESG bond labels and specificities

Source: Stylised adaptation from the ICMA Principles; for illustrative purposes only.

Trends in issuance of sovereign ESG-labelled bonds

Although the number of issuers is evenly spread across advanced and emerging market economies, large ESG-thematic financing programs are most common among advanced economies, which account for around 75% of the total ESG-labelled bond issuance. Nevertheless, issuers from emerging market economies have gained importance from 2018 onwards and some of them fare particularly well in terms of volume. As a result, the share of gross annual ESG-labelled bond issuance by EMEs has increased from 14% in 2018 to 43% in the first quarter 2022. While the issuance trend has been upward for all issuers, between 2019 and 2021 the sovereign ESG bond market has grown faster across emerging market economies than advanced economies by around 30%.

Figure 2.8. Sovereign ESG bond issuance by advanced and emerging market economies

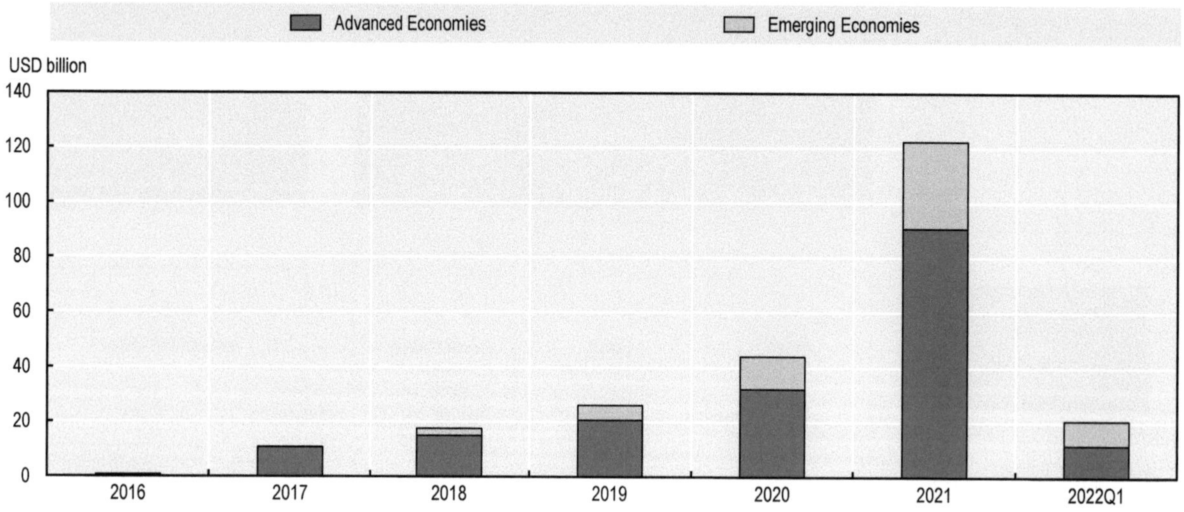

Note: Calculations include ESG-labelled bonds (with green, social, sustainability, and sustainability-linked labels) issued by sovereigns in the period from 1 December 2016 to 31 March 2022. Further details on the analytical methodology can be found in Annex 2.A.
Source: OECD calculations based on data from Refinitiv.

This growing issuance momentum has been sustained over the last five years, with a tenfold increase in gross amounts between 2017 and 2021, and has accelerated particularly in the wake of the COVID-19 pandemic. This could be explained by both the sudden increase in borrowing needs prompted by the pandemic and by the financial community's newfound understanding of its role in promoting a green and long-term recovery. Hence, the market reached record levels in 2020 and 2021, with annual issuances of around USD 44 and 122 billion, and year-over-year growth rates of 69% and 178%, respectively. In particular, 2020 has seen nine debut issuances – by countries including Germany, Indonesia, Mexico, Sweden and Thailand – which altogether amount to approximately 42% of the yearly gross issuance. Similarly 2021, which alone accounts for more than 50% of the total outstanding amount over the whole period, has seen the entrance to the market of 11 first-time issuers, which account for 31% of the yearly total gross issuance, including Benin, Colombia, Italy, Peru, Spain and the United Kingdom.

Figure 2.9. ESG sovereign bond issuance before and after the pandemic

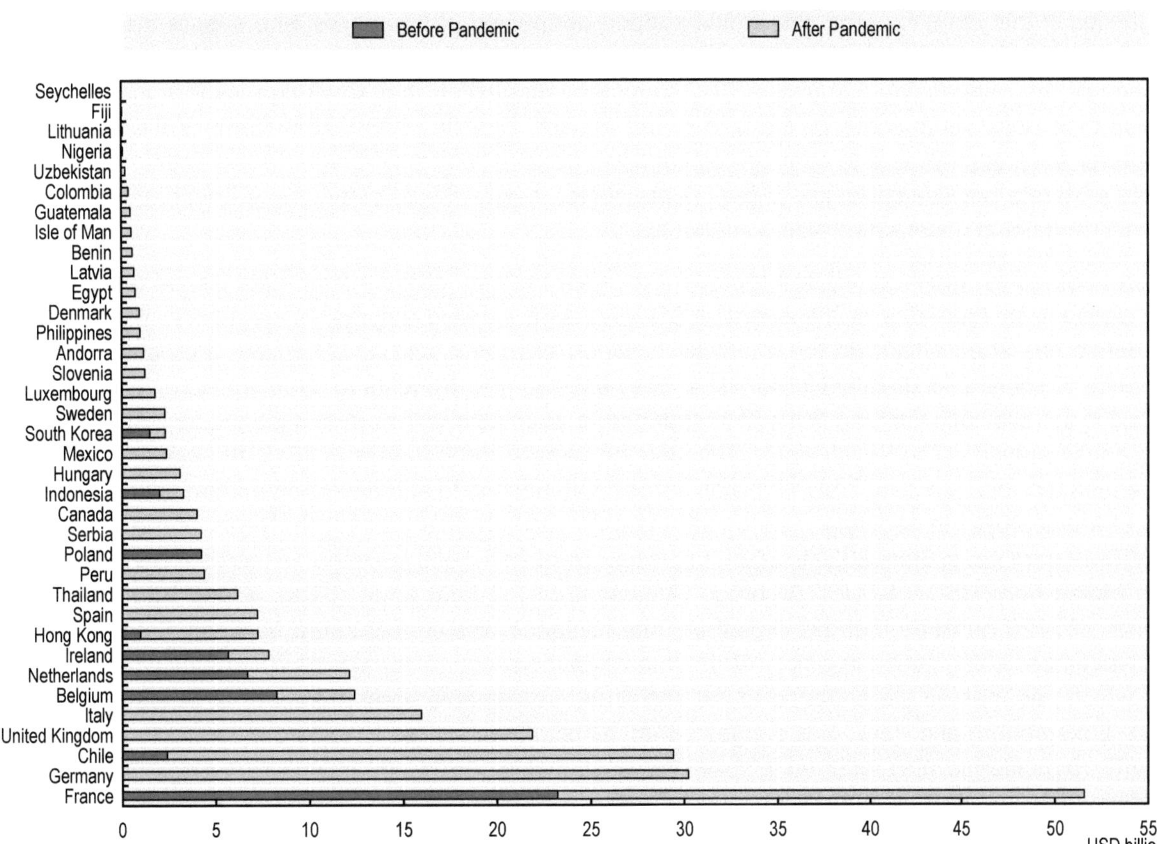

Note: The "After Pandemic" category contains all issuances made in 2020 and 2021. Issuance in the first quarter of 2020 amounted to 4% (USD 7.5 billion) of the total post pandemic issuance approximately, and was mostly concentrated in February and March, when COVID-19 cases started surging.
Source: OECD calculations based on data from Refinitiv.

The five largest issuers (Chile, France, Germany, Italy and the United Kingdom) make up for a little over 60% of the total amount issued, while the remaining 31 countries only account for less than 40% of the market. Among the 36 issuers, France is by far the most active issuer of green bonds with a little over USD 50 billion already on the market, almost double than any other sovereign. Germany, Italy and the United Kingdom are the next largest advanced economies issuers, with issuances of around USD 30, 16 and 22 billion respectively. Among these issuers, Chile is both the largest issuer among EMEs and the only sovereign to have issued all categories of thematic bonds (Box 2.4).

The recent OECD surveys revealed that the issuance momentum is expected to continue in coming years, both among OECD members, where perspective debut issuers include Austria, Greece, Iceland, and in a wide range of emerging market economies, where perspective debut issuers for the next 12 months include the United Arab Emirates and Uruguay. In addition, a few countries, such as Brazil, are in the initial process of setting up the ESG framework to issue thematic bonds.

Issuance strategies and annual borrowing programs of large issuers of labelled bonds (e.g. Chile, France, Germany, Italy and the United Kingdom) suggest that there is a willingness to fully integrate ESG-thematic issuance in annual issuance strategies. This also applies to emerging market economies, where several countries, in particular Asian and Latin American countries, have already allocated an important part of their annual strategy to environmental and social borrowing (i.e. Indonesia and Thailand). While the market is still in its early development stage, most of the large thematic bond issuers are committed in terms of mainstreaming ESG issuance in their annual strategy and sustaining the liquidity of debt securities on both primary and secondary markets. If these commitments were to translate into a regularity of thematic issuances in the years to come, this would support deepening of the market and ensure the entrance of new issuers, influenced by leading examples. To date, cumulative sovereign volumes account for a small fraction of the outstanding cumulative ESG volumes, suggesting that sovereign issuers are yet to fully exploit their potential to scale up the size of the market. Despite recent developments there remains a scope for sovereign issuers to channel capital flows to social and environmental expenditures. Doing so would generate positive spillovers to the private sector, especially by setting up a benchmark for private issuers, and could generate crowding in effects.

In terms of labels, green bonds still represent the vast majority of the instruments issued on the market and account for four-fifths of the overall ESG sovereign labelled volume. Nonetheless, the COVID-19 pandemic has shed a light on the interlinks between economic and social crises, thus galvanising the issuance of social and sustainable bonds, as they allowed governments to raise financing for project that helped in the alleviation of the effects of the pandemic, such as health care and job preservation spending. As a consequence, since Seychelles' first sovereign social bond issuance in 2018, the market has jumped more than ten-fold, reaching USD 49 billion across both advanced and emerging market economies at the end of March 2022. In particular, this trend was particularly marked during the years of the onset of the COVID-19 pandemic. From 2020 to 2021, the issuance of social and sustainable thematic bonds has more than tripled from USD 9 to USD 30 billion. Almost all of the total amount was issued from the second quarter of 2020 onwards, but the largest volume issuance was concentrated between September 2020 and November 2021, period in which the volume issuance accounts for almost 70% of the whole issuance and which has marked the entrance to the social and sustainable bond market of large issuers such as Chile, Luxembourg and Peru. This suggests that, as countries started to exit from the acute phase of the COVID-19 pandemic, they recurred to social and sustainable borrowing to fund future expenditures aiming at preventing new health and social crises of such a magnitude. This increasing trend is expected to continue in 2022. In the first quarter the share of social and sustainable bonds accounted for 43% of the total ESG issuance, driven in particular by Chile, which has issued sustainable bonds for USD 4 billion in January 2022 as well as the first sovereign sustainability-linked bond, for an amount of USD 2 billion, in March 2022 (Box 2.4).

Figure 2.10. Sovereign ESG issuance by type

Panel A: Total issuance by label type.

Panel B: Yearly evolution of the ESG sovereign bond market

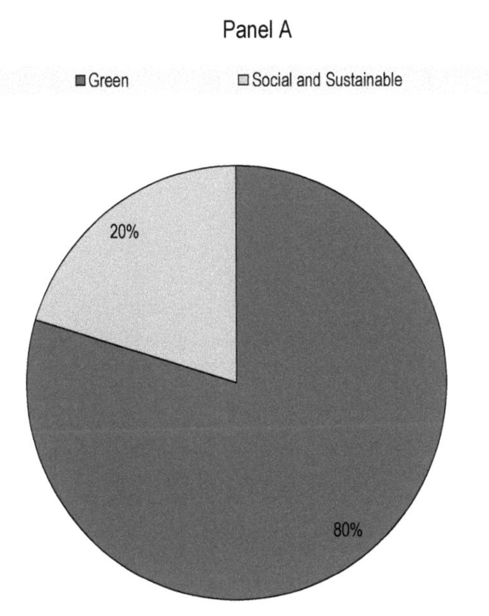

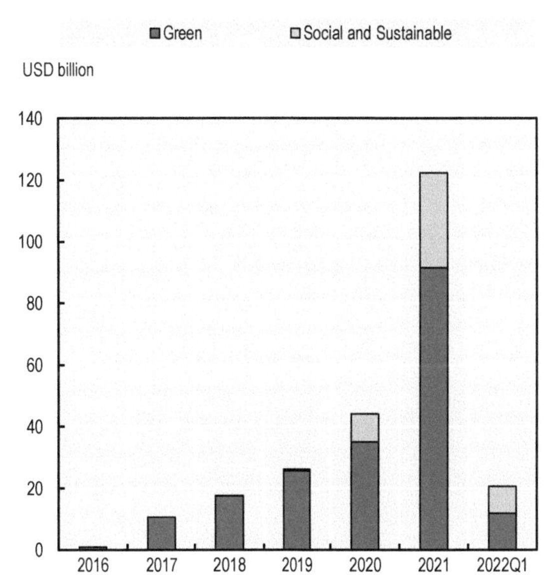

Source: OECD calculation based on Refinitiv data.

Box 2.4. Sustainable Bonds: The case of Chile

In order to contribute to Chile's climatic and social challenges, necessary to achieve sustainable development, the Ministry of Finance has incorporated since 2019, in its usual policy of sovereign debt plan, the issuance of thematic instruments. These instruments commit public spending on projects that contribute substantially to the economic, social, and environmental development objectives of the country and aligns incentives for the market to advance sustainable practices.

In 2019, the Ministry of Finance published its Green Bond Framework to subsequently extend it to the current framework for Sustainable Bond Framework in 2020, which includes the guidelines for the issuance of green, social, and sustainable bonds (that funds green and social projects). After the publication of its Sustainability-linked bond (SLB) framework, in March 2022 Chile issued the first sovereign SLB, achieving a new milestone in the development of sustainable financial instruments. To make a document with credible standards and recognised by the market, it must be verified by an independent third party. In the case of Chile, these Frameworks are aligned with ICMA's principles and received a favourable opinion from Vigeo Eiris and Sustainalytics, in the case of Sustainable Bond Framework and SLB Framework, respectively. On the other hand, the green portfolios are certified under CBI standards.

The Sustainable Bond Framework aims to provide clear guidelines on the type of projects that would be financed through these instruments, the reports that will be published ex post, and the project selection and exclusion system. Once the financial conditions of the bond have been settled and the portfolio of projects to be financed has been communicated transparently, a fundamental step is the ex-post annual report on the progress in the disbursement of the projects, the eligibility of these according to the standards established in the framework and the environmental and/or social impact of the projects.

On the other hand, the SLB Framework aims to provide transparency on the selected key performance indicators (KPIs) as well as the sustainability performance targets (SPTs) as well as the verification and subsequent reports.

At the end of March 2022, 28.7% of the Treasury's total debt stock corresponds to thematic bonds. This is equivalent to a total USD 33 billion in thematic bonds, of which USD 17.8 billion correspond to social bonds, USD 7.7 billion to green bonds, USD 5.5 billion to sustainable bonds and USD 2 billion to SLB. In 2021, 66% of the total issuances were in ESG related bonds. During the issuances of these instruments, among the main financial highlights of these transactions are a greenium of approximately 10 basis points in the first green bond issues in euros; an average oversubscription of 3.5 times and an expansion in the investor base, reaching a peak participation of investors with ESG mandates of 71% in the transaction in euros in 2019.

Among the main challenges that arise in the issuance of these instruments are the preparation of the project portfolio, along with the elaboration of the Framework, and the reporting system, as well as the coordination of the various actors involved in both project management and resource disbursement.

A fundamental initial step in the process of issuing thematic bonds has been the strengthening of the capacities of the DMO on different climate and ESG concepts, to later explain them to investors specialised in ESG investing. In line with the latter, the DMO have added a specific section in its website with Q&A about the main elements of its thematic bonds and an explanatory video of the Framework. Thus, the permanent updating of the information channels is fundamental.

Although the construction of the portfolio of both social and green projects as well as the preparation of ex-post reports suppose an extra effort, the benefits of obtaining better conditions of financing and an expansion of the investor base, together with the visibility of the State's efforts, have been essential to insist on this type of issuance. For the future, Chile expects to increase the ESG composition in its stock of debt, combining traditional ESG bonds associated to certain projects, with other SLBs, issued under the SLB Framework.

Given that the majority of ESG sovereign bond issuers are European countries, the main currency of issuance is the Euro, which alone accounts for almost 70% of the total issuance. The share of dollar denominated ESG sovereign bonds is 14% of the total issuance and the British Pound accounts for a little less than 10% of the total issuance. Other currencies, including the Canadian Dollar, Krona, Peso, Yen, and Yuan make up for the remaining 8% of the total issuance. These peculiarities are of particular importance for emerging market economies: among the total EME issuance, the share of foreign currency denominated debt stands at around three-fourths of the whole issuance over the period between 2016 and March 2022. Labelled bonds offer an opportunity for these issuers, in particular for those with large financing needs and shallow domestic debt markets, to attract international investors by meeting their interest in transparency and ESG issues. In this context, ESG-labelled instruments could entail further vulnerabilities for these issuers due to currency risks, considering that it often remains unhedged. Among the EME issuers that responded to the OECD survey on ESG considerations in PDM, only Indonesia has hedged bond related cash flows against such currency risks. Other countries, instead, do not envisage to do so or, as is the case for the Seychelles. It should be noted that the lack of hedging of foreign currency ESG-labelled bonds adds vulnerabilities and reduces transparency in terms of fiscal trajectory.

Figure 2.11. Currency composition

Panel A: Breakdown by currency. Panel B: Emerging market economies sovereign ESG debt by foreign and domestic currency

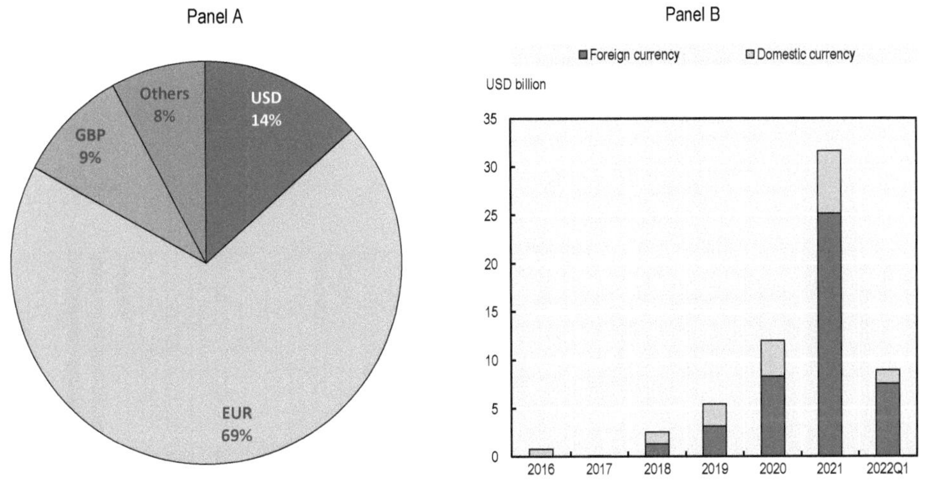

Note: The "Other currencies" category includes Canadian Dollar, Chilean Peso, Chinese Yuan, Colombian Peso, Danish Krone, Fijian Dollar, Hungarian Forint, Indonesian Rupiah, Japanese Yen, Nigerian Naira, Swedish Krona, Thai Baht, and Uzbekistani Sum.
Source: OECD calculation based on data from Refinitiv.

The cost of ESG-labelled sovereign bonds is generally in line with that of comparable conventional bonds, in some cases lower than that of a similar maturity conventional bond. In the primary market, between 2016 and March 2022, 13% of the total ESG-labelled bonds were issued with negative yield, 67% with a yield lower than 2%; 16% of the issued debt had a yield between 2% and 4%, and 4% of the total debt had a yield that was higher than 4% (Figure 2.12). This yield composition is a reflection of the creditworthiness of issuers and is particularly driven by the fact that volumes issued by highly rated countries are significantly larger than volumes issued by countries whose credit ratings are lower. In line with cost trajectories for conventional securities, issuers classified as investment grade face the lower issuance costs. Luxembourg, the sovereign that as benefitted from the lower issuance cost, has an AAA rating.[16] Similarly, countries whose labelled debt was issued with a yield lower than 1%, such as Belgium, France, Germany and the United Kingdom, benefit from an investment grade status and have high credit ratings. When the sample of countries is restricted to EMEs, the issuers that have issued securities with a yield lower than 1% are those whose credit ratings fare better in comparison. For example, both Chile, which has had multiple issuances with a yield smaller than 1%, the lowest being 0.39%, and Poland, which has been able to issue a bond with a 0.63% yield, had an A- rating. On the other hand, countries that have faced the highest borrowing costs (with yields larger than 4%) are all classified as non-investment grade. This is the case of Benin (5.2% yield and B+ rating), Colombia (yields ranging between 7.5% and 7.9% and BB+ rating), Fiji (6.3% yield and B+ rating), Guatemala (5.375% yield and BB- rating), Seychelles (6.5% yield approximately and B+), and Uzbekistan (14% yield and BB-). Egypt, the largest volume issuer in this group, with a total issuance of USD 750 million, still faced a 5.25% yield, in line with its B+ rating. Hence, yields of labelled securities are influenced by the issuer's creditworthiness, rather than being a direct consequence of the ESG nature of such securities.

Nevertheless, the responses to the OECD surveys suggest that while cost of labelled securities are in line with conventional one, the former tend to exhibit a moderate 'greenium' – the negative spread between yields on conventional and green bonds of a similar maturity. The existing literature on the greenium is mixed. On the one hand, some researchers find a statistically significant greenium on certain types of stocks and portfolios (Alessi, Ossola and Panzica, 2020[32]).On the other hand, a study by the IMF finds that no significant greenium at issuance exists for sovereign green and non-green securities (IMF, 2019[33]). This premium might simply be a consequence of supply and demand dynamics. Survey results highlight, as a potential reason underpinning the greenium, a relative scarcity effect induced by a demand higher than the supply of ESG-labelled instruments on the market. Hence, when ESG-labelled securities on the market will be less scarce, the yield differential between conventional and sustainable securities may not persist.

Figure 2.12. Volume share of fixed-rate ESG-labelled bond issuance by yield category

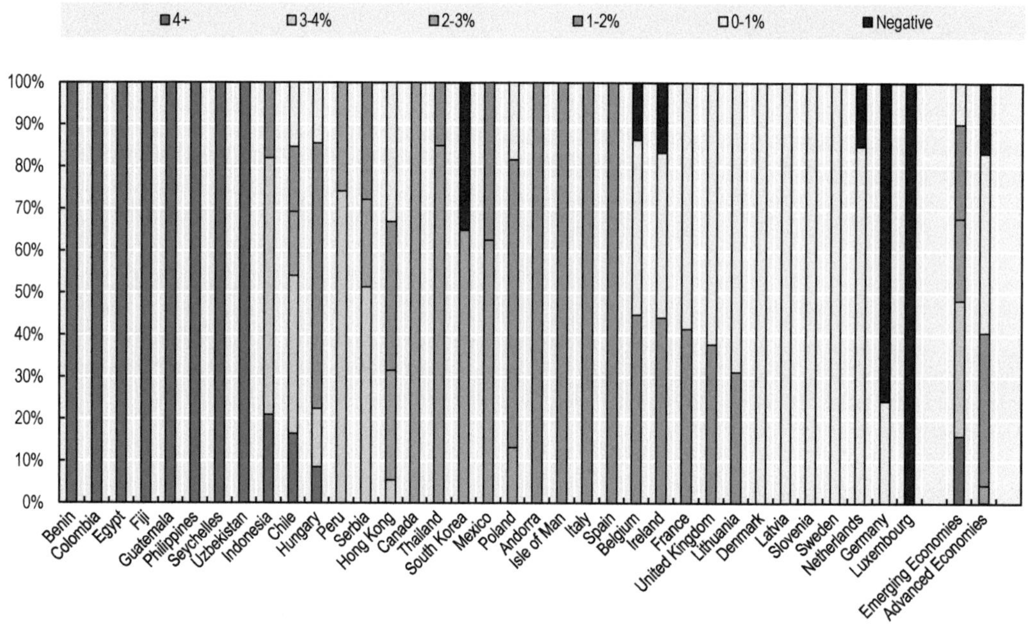

Note: Fixed-rate bond issuances and re-opens categorised by yield at issuance.
Source: OECD calculations based on data from Refinitiv.

In terms of maturity structure and size, sovereign labelled bonds vary significantly. The maturity of ESG sovereign debt varies from country to country, ranging from two years for Indonesia's Green Sukuks to 50 years for bonds issued by both Chile and Peru and the average time to maturity of the total debt stock is slightly over 13 years, which highlights the long-term dimension of environmental and social spending and funding.

Key challenges in issuing sovereign ESG-labelled bonds

Lack of – or limited – eligible government expenditures can be a potential barrier to sovereign green and social bond issuance as issuing a new instrument requires a long-term commitment to create and maintain liquidity, and to lower issuance cost. Responses to the survey also highlight that low levels of liquidity and limited trading activity in secondary markets are sources of concern for many sovereign issuers. It should be noted that governmental budgets are constrained and governments in many countries face competing pressures when prioritising the use of resources. Against this backdrop, the survey results revealed that issuers with limited funding requirements prefer to allocate their scarce activities in nominal bonds to secure their liquid sovereign curve. Some issuers do not view earmarked project bonds as a perfect match to fund the general government budget deficit. As well, issuing a green bond may create a fragmentation in sovereign issuance structures and increase funding costs due to illiquidity premium. In response to such difficulties, sovereign issuers may consider issuing sustainability bonds, which include both social and green expenditures and sustainability-linked bonds which consider issuer's strategy towards achieving predefined sustainability objectives within a set timeline, and their proceeds do not need to be allocated to specific projects.

Issuance process of an ESG-labelled bond is different from that of a conventional bond as it requires a number of ex-ante reviews and ex-post reporting as well as additional marketing activities. The issuance process for ESG bonds is far more onerous than it is for conventional bonds First of all, a governing framework that includes detailed information on eligible expenditures (or Key Performance Indicators for SLBs), management of proceeds, allocation and impact reporting and external reviews, needs to be published. Setting up such a framework requires co-ordination with other relevant government departments whose budgets include eligible expenditures, consultation with investors, and communication with external reviewers. The survey results indicate that sovereign issuers find evaluation and selection of eligible expenditures challenging, due for example to a lack of a clear and consistent definition of 'green spending'.

In addition to preparation, implementation of the framework throughout the bond's lifetime entails various operational and financial costs that can deter many sovereign issuers with limited resources and capacity from issuing ESG-labelled bonds. For example, labelled bonds often require issuers to perform distinctive monitoring and reporting activities in order to respect internationally recognised guidelines and adhere to best market practices. Country practices highlight the complexity with interpreting taxonomies and measuring the environmental and social value generated by the underlying projects for a clear impact reporting. Such difficulties could be even more acute in countries with limited public debt expertise and capacity. Some countries benefit from services of advisory/consultant companies to produce frameworks, reviews and reports in addition to third-party verification of frameworks and impact reports. This in turn affects not only operational cost but also financial cost of the bond issuance to the sovereign issuers.

In view of challenges with regard to the issuing process and the capacity gap, potential EM issuers may benefit from other countries' experiences as well as international financial organisations such as the World Bank Group and UNDP regarding different aspects of the labelled bonds including preparation of the most suitable policy framework, leveraging media interest, market intelligence and project screening activities.

Common features of leading practices

The considerable market demand for ESG-labelled bonds, especially among institutional investors committed to this market segment, makes them a potentially helpful tool for public debt management operations. In the current context of high levels of debt servicing combined with significant borrowing needs required to rebuild out of the COVID-19 pandemic in a more sustainable and resilient way, issuance of labelled bonds present opportunities. This can be particularly helpful for EME issuers by facilitating their access to international capital markets. At the same time, it is important to meet with investors' demand for and consistency with standards of clarity in the use of proceeds, quality in impact reporting and benchmark size issuance for successful growth of this asset class. In this regard, sovereign issuers could strengthen the sustainable finance market development only by implementing sound practices in ESG-thematic public debt management in terms of transparency and liquidity. Moreover, failure to adhere to commitments would harm investors' confidence and deter the development of this newly emerging asset class.

Despite the relative novelty of such an approach to sovereign borrowing, some common features of leading practices on issuance of ESG-labelled bonds have already been emerged. They are as follows:

Strong interaction and collaboration with stakeholders throughout the life of the bond

The issuance of an ESG-labelled sovereign bond requires important efforts in terms of cross-collaboration between different ministries over its entire period of existence, from the initial structuring decisions to the final repayment at maturity. Receiving a clear mandate from the national government is a critical first step for debt management agencies since it ensures co-ordination amongst participating line ministries. A standard step for labelled bond process is to establish a framework, which aims to determine eligible sectors and establish a monitoring and reporting practice. This has been the case across sovereign issuers: it is, for instance, the case of the United Kingdom where the Chancellor of the Exchequer announced the national plan to issue Green Gilts in 2020. This then ensured the UK DMO and Treasury with the necessary authority to promptly publish the national Green Framework in June 2021 and to issue the first green bond in September 2021 (HM Treasury, 2021[34]).

Moreover, the issuance of labelled bonds requires the policy collaboration between the DMO and the Ministry of Finance, given its budgetary responsibilities, and with other line ministries (i.e. agriculture, transport, infrastructure, environment, energy, etc.) in order to identify eligible expenditures and their size. This is critical because translating theoretical environmental goals into practical initiatives necessitates knowledge and a domain of competence that neither the Ministry of Finance nor the DMO alone possess. After the issuance of the bond on the market, collaboration between different stakeholders remains necessary, as various parties involved will have to contribute to the preparation of the required reports on the allocation and impact of bond proceeds. Coordination issues can be addressed by either establishing contact points at each institution or establishing a committee involving government ministries / agencies that are involved. The survey results revealed that a number of sovereign DMOs established an intergovernmental committee to support the establishment of an ESG-labelled bond programme. This includes, for example Canada's Interdepartmental Green Bond Committee, consisting of representatives from multiple departments that are involved in implementing the government's climate and environment plan.[17] Another prominent example is Germany, where an Inter-Ministerial Working Group, was established to oversee and validate key decisions about the Green German Federal securities. Under the responsibility of the Federal Ministry of Finance, this Working Group pools the expertise needed for a thorough and robust selection and evaluation of Eligible Green Expenditures. [18]

This collaboration can be expanded to supranational organisations, which can provide effective technical assistance with the issuance process. For instance, Seychelles benefited from the assistance of the World Bank with the structuring and placement on international markets of its USD 15 million blue bond (a bond whose proceeds are earmarked for marine and oceanic projects) issued in 2018 (World Bank, 2019[35]).

In addition, sovereign issuers should conduct investor consultations to inform their decision-making process and analysis. Such consultation with primary dealers and broader market participants about potential demand for different types of ESG-labelled bonds, as well as other design features such as preference about maturity segment and issuance methods could be valuable for successful management of the issuance process.

Commitment to transparency and reporting disclosures

The process of issuing a sovereign labelled-bonds typically involves a budget tagging exercise and commitments to report on the allocation of proceeds and their impact, which greatly increases transparency and accountability on public spending. This greater transparency should also encourage greater investor demand, in particular for EM issuers, since it helps strengthening trust between investors and issuers.

Investors attach great importance to the environmental and social efficiency of their investments, as well as the financial stability and risk resilience features, and a cursory reporting process can seriously affect the success of future issuances. The quality of pre- and post-issuance reporting metrics and external independent review and verification provides transparency, ensures accountability and underpins the credibility of labelled bonds. Sovereign issuers must adhere strongly to the principles of transparency and reporting established by international guidelines. France sets a good example of high commitment to transparency with its commitment to deliver ex-ante and ex-post reporting as well as evaluation reports for green bonds (also referred to as Green OATs 'Obligation Assimilable du Trésor') (Box 2.5).

> ## Box 2.5. France's commitment to transparency
>
> In its 2021 Budget, the French Government introduced a "Green budget" – a new classification of its budgetary and fiscal expenditures based on their environmental impact – as a way to improve its reporting of the impact of public finance initiatives on the ecological transition (OECD, 2021[36]).
>
> Furthermore, the French DMO (Agence France Trésor, AFT) developed a comprehensive framework based on the "Green Bond Principles" and the "Transition Energétique et Ecologique pour le Climat" (TEEC) label in order to issue green bonds. This framework includes key features both in terms of project selection and reporting. An inter-ministerial working group managed by the Ministry of Finance and the Ministry of Environment, and overseen by the Prime Minister, conducts the screening for the evaluation and selection of projects. Then, a 'Green OAT Evaluation Council', made up of independent scientists and economists, evaluates ex-post the environmental performance of France's Eligible Green Expenditures.
>
> In terms of reporting, until the funds are fully allocated, two yearly reports will be released for investors: (i) a report on the use of proceeds and (ii) a report on the performance of 'Eligible Green Expenditure'. In addition, under the supervision of the Green OAT Evaluation Council, the ex-post environmental effect of 'Eligible Green Expenditure' will be examined in a special report at regular intervals. This contributes to maintaining a high level of transparency in both the selection of projects and in the allocation of proceeds, as well as in holding the government accountable for how green bonds are used, ultimately contributing to setting high standards in green bond market (Agence France Trésor, 2021[37]).

Commitment to sustain liquidity through issuance volume and instrument design

While ESG-labelled sovereign bonds benefit from a considerable investor appetite, some peculiarities of thematic market segments can negatively affect their liquidity. Usually, an instrument is said to be liquid if transactions in it can happen rapidly without reducing its price to a significant degree.

Given that the only difference of green bonds is that their proceeds are earmarked to specific social and environmental projects, their potential to be sold on secondary markets is comparable to conventional bonds. However, on the buy side, there may be some concerns about the liquidity of labelled bonds. First, the stock of instruments accessible for investment remains limited. While ESG sovereign markets have expanded in size and diversity, they still account for a small fraction of the sovereign bond market and outstanding amounts of thematic bonds remain modest in comparison to conventional ones. Furthermore, sovereign ESG-labelled bonds are largely oversubscribed on the primary market. While this could mean that it would be easy for investors to offload their bonds if the demand for such instrument remains robust, it also means that the accessibility of ESG bonds in the secondary market will remain limited. Second, thematic bonds investors are mostly buy-and-hold institutional investors and/or ethical investors, who hold their purchases until maturity. While this could mean that, in times of crisis, green bonds will experience more stability, it also means that the amount of free float available in the market is limited.

Ensuring the liquidity of sovereign ESG markets is crucial for debt management offices. If the liquidity of labelled government securities was reduced, the price discovery process in the secondary market would be impaired and it would translate into higher yields through a liquidity premium in primary markets (OECD, 2018[38]). Ultimately, this would increase the costs of funding green and social projects for sovereigns. Given that even small changes in the interest rate paid on a sovereign bond can result in significant additional costs or savings and that sovereigns have an interest to catalyse ESG investments at a low cost to finance the environmental and social transition, DMOs have a great responsibility to maintain well-functioning social and sustainable markets.

There are several market practices that can help to ensure the liquidity of environmental and sustainable debt securities. An important contributor to market liquidity is the size of issuances, as it determines the amount that is available for trading. Usually, sovereign debt managers pursue a benchmark bond issuance policy to reach a significant issue size for a bond, which in turn allows them to benefit from a liquidity premium. As a rule of thumb, larger securities tend to be more liquid because they allow for a reduction of transaction and information costs. As information about the security is broadly disseminated among investors (because of a large pool of investors that own it or that have analysed its features), it will remain in dealers' inventories for a shorter period of time. For ESG-labelled bonds this is achieved by making sure that the size of the inaugural issuance is comparable to that of conventional issues. To date, the largest inaugural sovereign ESG issues are the GBP 10 billion Green Gilt issued by the United Kingdom in September 2021 and the EUR 8.5 billion green BTP issued by Italy in March 2021. For small issuers, however, ensuring liquidity of an ESG-labelled bond through issuance of large volumes can be a challenge given their limited financing needs.

Re-opening existing issues, in which DMOs place additional quantities of previously issued bonds on the market, is another popular approach employed by sovereign debt managers to support the liquidity of thematic bonds. Depending on whether they want to issue these additional amounts via auction, DMOs have two main policy tools for primary market operations. They can reopen the issue through an auction. Using this process, re-openings have a different price and issue date than the initial issue of the security. This enables issuers to build larger supply in existing lines in markets and to limit fragmentation which impedes market liquidity. In addition, tap issues can also be used to provide additional amounts, where bonds are issued at their original face value, maturity and coupon rate.

France has achieved its large issuance volume of more than USD 50 billion – which makes it the largest sovereign issuer in the world – by regularly taping its two Green OATs (issued in September 2017 and in March 2021). In particular, the outstanding amount of the 2017 Green OAT has been more than quadrupled from the original EUR 7 billion at issuance to the approximately EUR 31 billion that are currently outstanding, while the amount of the 2021 issuance has been doubled to EUR 14 billion. Specifically, in order to comply with common practices on thematic bond issuance, the proceeds from tap issues are also matched to Green Eligible Expenditures, as the cumulative amount of such expenditures has risen over the years (Agence France Trésor, 2021[39]). Other countries, such as Chile, Hungary and Thailand, have chosen to reopen or tap their existing bonds, as a way to raise their total liability on ESG markets.

In addition to actual issuance, issuers can indicate their commitment to issuing further amounts as well as to building out a yield curve in the coming years. For example, the German Finance Agency is committed to the green market, which means that green bond issuance will be a regular component of its issuance programme in the future, and it additionally intends to establish a benchmark green curve for other issuers. Similarly, the UK Debt Management Office has committed to issuing at least GBP 15 billion of green gilts in financial year 2021-22, as well as to building out a green curve in the coming years.

Lastly, market-oriented bond innovations can be used to ensure liquidity in ESG securities, which are usually smaller in size than conventional bonds. For example, the German Finance Agency successfully introduced a twin bond framework in 2020, which was also followed by Denmark in 2022. Under this twin bond framework, any new green German bond will always be issued alongside an existing conventional bond, which sets a good example in terms of: i) introducing an empirically accurate measure of the "greenium" – the spread between yields on conventional and green bonds of a similar maturity –; and ii) ensuring the liquidity on the market by allowing investors to switch between the conventional and the green bond (Box 2.6).

Box 2.6. The German Twin Bonds

Germany, the largest economy in Europe, has taken an innovative stance on its green debt issuance process, by choosing to enter the market under a "twin" bond structure. This means that all green German Federal securities will have a conventional traditional Federal security on the side, with which they will share some characteristics. In particular, the twins will have the same characteristics in terms of coupon, interest payment dates and rhythm, and maturity date – which results in an identical tenor for both securities. Nonetheless, they will present differences in terms of i) issuance volumes, with the conventional twins that will be placed at a larger volume than their green counterparts; ii) pricing dates, with the conventional twin that is issued earlier than the green security; and iii) ISIN codes, so that the two securities are separate in nature and can be held or traded separately from each other. The maturity segments for the green issues will be predefined by the standard tenor of the medium and long-term federal securities, with the German DMO that plans to target 2-, 5-, 10-, and 30-years maturities, with the aim of building a green yield curve in the medium term, and to fully integrate green issuance in its issuance schedule.

Two major reasons motivated the selection of this instrument design. The first aim of the German DMO was that of having access to an accurate measure of the "greenium", the yield difference that investor are willing to pay to hold green bonds. The second reason was to ensure the liquidity of green Federal securities on both primary and secondary markets. In order to execute this twin concept on the primary market, the German DMO takes several steps in terms of issuance timing. As a matter of fact, the conventional twins is always issued first, usually by an auction process (which is the established procedure for German Federal Government securities). When the associated Green Federal security is born on the market (which can happen either via auction or syndication), an analogous stock of the conventional bond is issued into the own stock of the Federal Government at the same time. On the other hand, with regards to the secondary market the German Finance agency intends to ensure the secondary market tradability and to sustain the liquidity of the green twins. In particular the twin instrument design and the German DMO's additional amount of own holdings in the conventional bond in its portfolio facilitate combined and debt neutral sale and purchase transactions between both bonds, the so-called switch trades that allow investors to exchange the green twin with the conventional one at any time. Moreover, the German finance Agency can also recur to outright purchase/sale and securities lending programmes, as well as getting into repurchase agreements. This commitment should result in a liquid green curve and, consequently, in a pricing reference for other euro-denominated green bonds.

The aim of the German Government was that of setting an example in the green bond markets, especially in Europe. Germany's traditional debt is regarded as the safest in Europe and serves as a risk-free benchmark. This function might possibly be reproduced in the green sector as well. In the meantime, its example has started to gain following in Europe. On the 19th of January 2022 Denmark has had its debut issuance of 5 a billion Danish crowns (EUR 762 million) green bond, paired to its benchmark 10-year benchmark bond, 0.00 percent 2031. Investor in Danish green bonds will only be able to switch from the green twin to the corresponding conventional twin. Exchanges from the conventional to the green twin will not be possible.

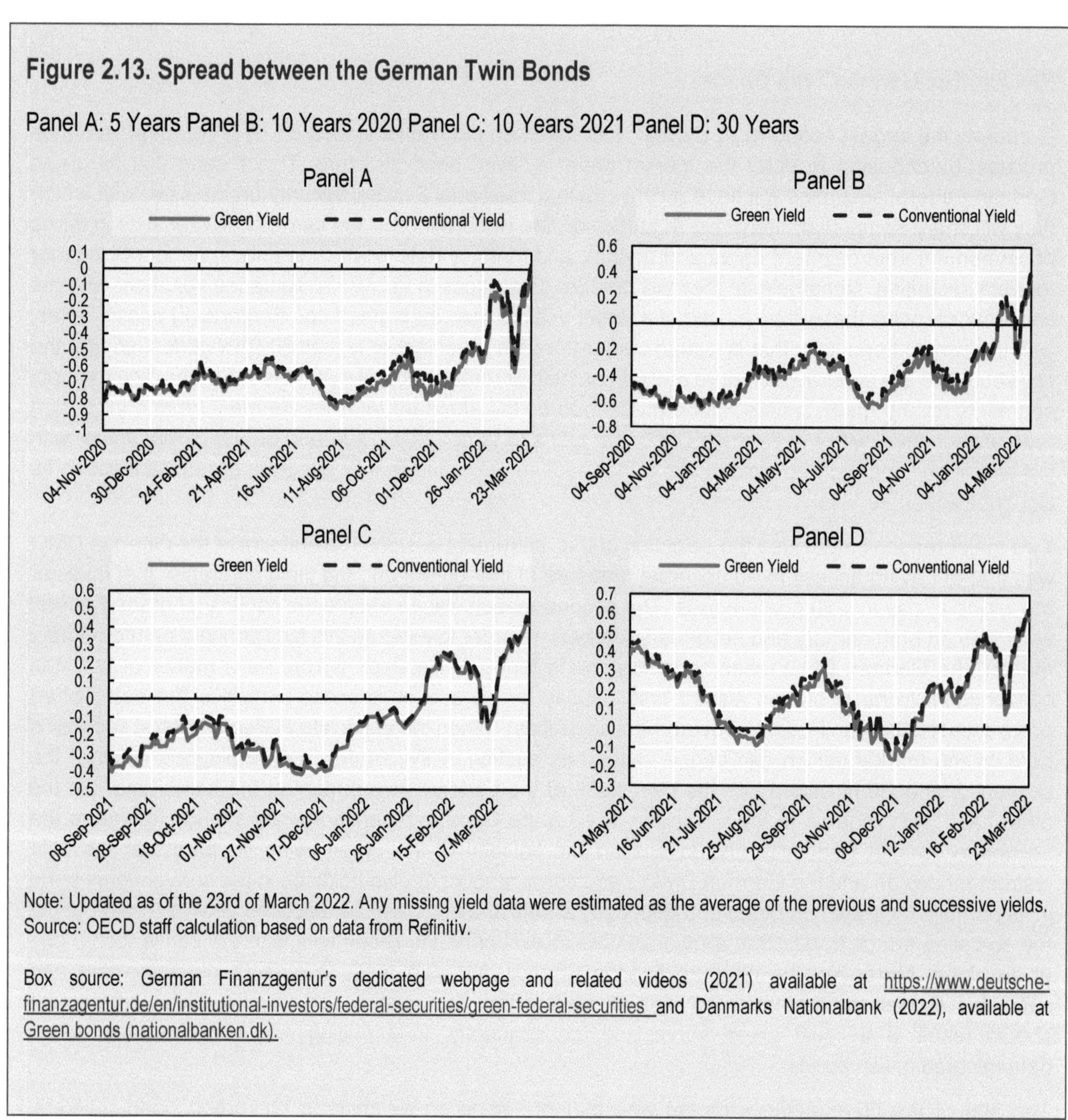

Figure 2.13. Spread between the German Twin Bonds

Panel A: 5 Years Panel B: 10 Years 2020 Panel C: 10 Years 2021 Panel D: 30 Years

Note: Updated as of the 23rd of March 2022. Any missing yield data were estimated as the average of the previous and successive yields. Source: OECD staff calculation based on data from Refinitiv.

Box source: German Finanzagentur's dedicated webpage and related videos (2021) available at https://www.deutsche-finanzagentur.de/en/institutional-investors/federal-securities/green-federal-securities and Danmarks Nationalbank (2022), available at Green bonds (nationalbanken.dk).

The outlook for ESG-labelled bonds

Building on the recent years' momentum, ESG-labelled bonds have great potential to grow further and become a distinct asset class. The outlook depends on various factors concerning investors' demand and issuers' supply. The survey results suggest that sovereign issuers expect sustained growing investor demand for sustainable investing, and that investors are becoming more sophisticated (e.g. demanding quality impact analysis and more quantitative comparable data). To the extent that these demands are met, this can support maturity across different sustainable finance products and assets. However, there are some pitfalls to watch out for and issues to be considered carefully both for the robust growth of sustainable finance market segment, and efficient management of public debt.

Going forward, it is important to address the implementation challenges that sovereign issuers are currently experiencing with regard to relevant resources and expertise within debt management office, availability of eligible projects in budgets, co-ordination among the relevant ministries and agencies, as well as scaling up the quality and supervision of impact and other reporting. In this context, growing commitments of governments towards building a better and more sustainable future, and wider implementation of OECD's green budgeting principles, would help addressing the challenges related to availability and identification of eligible projects in budgets. It should also be noted that given the complexities and additional financial and operational costs of labelled bonds due to idiosyncratic requirements (e.g. payments to external services), a decrease in operational and additional financial costs in the future will further encourage the number of sovereign issuers and bonds. In this context, further standardisation of ESG products would not only help facilitate the issuance process, but also build a robust and liquid ESG bond market. Amongst the most important areas for standardisation will be: (i) minimum reporting requirements; (ii) a clear and consistent definition of what constitutes 'green spending'; and (iii) an agreed mechanism to deal with issuers that do not allocate funds raised in accordance with these standards.

Investors' confidence is pre-requisite for sustaining demand and achieving low cost of borrowing for any issuer. This is particularly relevant for ESG-sensitive investors. The process of issuing a labelled bond encourages issuers to disclose information about sustainable practices, helping investors evaluate the ESG performance of the project. On the other hand, greenwashing, which can occur throughout the budgetary process and through the bonds lifetime potentially damages the issuer's reputation and could cause a loss of credibility, which can have a significant detrimental impact on access to sustainable finance sources. Therefore, paramount importance should be given to compliance with regulatory landscape in respect of ESG disclosures and recommends; providing investors with quality, comparable and digestible data; avoiding potential misinformation, and double counting of expenditures. In this regard, public debt managers' role in communicating information about government's sustainable practices, helping investors evaluate the ESG credentials of the overall country is pertinent. ESG-related capacity challenges in public debt management offices as well as budget office and other relevant line-ministries, oversight institutions and the preparers of the financial statements of government should be addressed.

Foreign-currency denominated labelled bonds, which have attracted both investors and issuers in EMEs, should be handled with care. This can pose a challenge for debt management offices that lack the technical capacities to properly assess and manage the currency risk exposure of a debt portfolio. If not managed properly, increasing share of foreign-currency denominated debt can be a source of external vulnerability for issuers. Sovereign debt management offices should consider currency risk attached and look into hedging options while benefiting from growing demand for labelled bonds from international investors.

In terms of cost effectiveness, as supply of sovereign ESG-labelled bonds increases and meet the investor demand in the future, 'greenium' on sovereign bonds may fall or completely disappear. The survey results highlight that sovereign debt managers observe that issuer credentials – including sustainability credentials – are more important for cost of borrowing than the choice of specific financing instruments. This in turn raises an important question for policy makers as to what extent project-based bond issuance is making a real difference in climate and social change that could not be achieved by other means. Having said that, other motivations for issuing labelled bonds such as catalysing the development of local sustainable bond market, and meeting growing demand from ESG-sensitive investors are expected to remain relevant in the future.

References

Agence France Trésor (2021), *Green OAT: Announcement of the Amount of Green Eligible Expenditures For 2021*, https://www.aft.gouv.fr/en/publications/communiques-presse/20210125-green-oat-eligible-green-expenditure. [39]

Agence France Trésor (2021), *Green OATs*, https://www.aft.gouv.fr/en/green-oat. [37]

Alessi, L., E. Ossola and R. Panzica (2020), *The Greenium matters: greenhouse gas emissions, environmental disclosures, and stock prices*, Publications Office of the European Union, Luxembourg, https://doi.org/10.2760/49586. [32]

Australian Government (2021), *Australia's Long-term Emissions Reduction Plan*, Commonwealth of Australia 2021, https://www.industry.gov.au/sites/default/files/October%202021/document/australias-long-term-emissions-reduction-plan.pdf. [26]

Capelle-Blancard, G. et al. (2019), "Sovereign bond yield spreads and sustainability: An empirical analysis of OECD countries", *Journal of Banking & Finance*, Vol. 98, pp. 156-169, https://doi.org/10.1016/j.jbankfin.2018.11.011. [30]

CBI (2021), *Sustainable Debt: GLobal State of the Market*, https://www.climatebonds.net/files/reports/climate_bonds_initiative_sustainable_debt_global_state_of_the_market_2021.pdf. [9]

Cevik, S. and J. Jalles (2020), "Feeling the Heat: Climate Shocks and Credit Ratings" WP No. 2020/286, https://www.imf.org/en/Publications/WP/Issues/2020/12/18/Feeling-the-Heat-Climate-Shocks-and-Credit-Ratings-49945. [23]

Cevik, S. and J. Jalles (2020), *This Changes Everything: Climate Shocks and Sovereign Bonds*, p. 24, https://www.imf.org/en/Publications/WP/Issues/2020/06/05/This-Changes-Everything-Climate-Shocks-and-Sovereign-Bonds-49476. [28]

European Commission (2021), "Communication from the Commission to the European Parliament, the Council, the European Economic and Social Committee and the Committee of the Regions. Strategy for Financing the Transition to a Sustainable Economy", *COM(2021) 390 final*, https://eur-lex.europa.eu/legal-content/EN/ALL/?uri=CELEX:52021DC0390. [21]

European Commission (2021), *Debt Sustainability Monitor 2020*, Publications Office of the European Union, https://ec.europa.eu/info/sites/default/files/economy-finance/ip143_en.pdf. [27]

European Commission (2021), "Proposal for a Regulation of the European Parliament and of the Council on European green bonds", *COM/2021/391 final*, https://eur-lex.europa.eu/legal-content/EN/ALL/?uri=CELEX:52021PC0391. [20]

European Commission (2020), "Regulation (EU) 2020/852 of the European Parliament and of the Council of 18 June 2020 on the establishment of a framework to facilitate sustainable investment, and amending Regulation (EU) 2019/2088", *Official Journal, L 198*, https://eur-lex.europa.eu/legal-content/EN/TXT/?uri=CELEX:32020R0852. [19]

European Commission (2018), *Action Plan: Financing Sustainable Growth*, https://eur-lex.europa.eu/legal-content/EN/TXT/PDF/?uri=CELEX:52018DC0097&from=EN. [18]

FDF (2016), *Report on the Long-Term Sustainability of Public Finances in Switzerland*, Federal Department of Finance. [25]

Galema, R., A. Plantinga and B. Scholtens (2008), "The stocks at stake: Return and risk in socially responsible investment", *Journal of Banking & Finance*, Vol. 32/12, pp. 2646-2654, https://doi.org/10.1016/j.jbankfin.2008.06.002. [10]

HM Treasury (2021), *UK Government Green Financing*, https://www.gov.uk/government/publications/uk-government-green-financing. [34]

ICMA (2022), *Sustainable Finance*, https://www.icmagroup.org/sustainable-finance/. [13]

ICMA (2021), *Green Bond Principles*, https://www.icmagroup.org/assets/documents/Sustainable-finance/2021-updates/Green-Bond-Principles-June-2021-140621.pdf. [14]

ICMA (2021), *Social Bond Principles*, https://www.icmagroup.org/assets/documents/Sustainable-finance/2021-updates/Social-Bond-Principles-June-2021-140621.pdf. [15]

ICMA (2021), *Sustainability Bond Guidelines*, https://www.icmagroup.org/assets/documents/Sustainable-finance/2021-updates/Sustainability-Bond-Guidelines-June-2021-140621.pdf. [16]

ICMA (2020), *Sustainability-Linked Bond Principles*, https://www.icmagroup.org/assets/documents/Regulatory/Green-Bonds/June-2020/Sustainability-Linked-Bond-Principles-June-2020-171120.pdf. [17]

IEA (2022), *Oil Market Report - March 2022*, IEA, Paris, https://www.iea.org/reports/oil-market-report-march-2022. [40]

IMF (2019), *Global Financial Stability Report: Lower for Longer*, https://www.imf.org/en/Publications/GFSR/Issues/2019/10/01/global-financial-stability-report-october-2019. [33]

Kahn, M. et al. (2019), "Long-Term Macroeconomic Effects of Climate Change: A Cross-Country Analysis" NBER Working Paper No. 26167, https://doi.org/10.3386/w26167. [6]

Klusak, P. et al. (2021), "Rising temperatures, falling ratings: The effect of climate change on sovereign creditworthiness", *SSRN Electronic Journal*, https://doi.org/10.2139/ssrn.3811958. [29]

OECD (2022), *Climate Change and Corporate Governance*, Corporate Governance, OECD Publishing, Paris, https://doi.org/10.1787/272d85c3-en. [5]

OECD (2022), *OECD Sovereign Borrowing Outlook 2022*, OECD Publishing, Paris, https://doi.org/10.1787/b2d85ea7-en. [31]

OECD (2021), *Climate Change and Long-term Fiscal Sustainability*, OECD Publishing, https://www.oecd.org/gov/budgeting/scoping-paper-on-fiscal-sustainability-and-climate-change.pdf. [22]

OECD (2021), *Government at a Glance 2021*, OECD Publishing, Paris, https://doi.org/10.1787/1c258f55-en. [41]

OECD (2021), *Green Budget Tagging: Introductory Guidance & Principles*, OECD Publishing, Paris, https://doi.org/10.1787/fe7bfcc4-en. [36]

OECD (2020), *Developing Sustainable Finance Definitions and Taxonomies*, Green Finance and Investment, OECD Publishing, Paris, https://doi.org/10.1787/134a2dbe-en. [12]

OECD (2020), *OECD Green Budgeting Framework Highlights*, http://www.oecd.org/environment/green-budgeting/OECD-Green-Budgeting-Framework-Highlights.pdf. [4]

OECD (2020), *The 2020 OECD Ministerial Council Statement recognised the need for governments to focus on restarting hard-hit economies by boosting growth, income and employment while promoting cleaner, more inclusive and sustainable economies*, http://www.oecd.org/coronavirus/policy-responses/a-debt-standstill-for-the-poorest-countries-how-much-is-at-stake-462eabd8/. [2]

OECD (2019), *Social Impact Investment 2019: The Impact Imperative for Sustainable Development*, OECD Publishing, Paris, https://doi.org/10.1787/9789264311299-en. [7]

OECD (2018), *OECD Sovereign Borrowing Outlook 2018*, OECD Publishing, Paris, https://doi.org/10.1787/sov_b_outlk-2018-en. [38]

UK Office for Budget Responsibility (2019), *Fiscal risks report - July 2019*, https://obr.uk//docs/dlm_uploads/Fiscalrisksreport2019.pdf. [24]

UN (2021), *The Glasgow Climate Pact – Key Outcomes from COP26*, https://ukcop26.org/wp-content/uploads/2021/11/COP26-Presidency-Outcomes-The-Climate-Pact.pdf. [3]

United Nations (2021), *United Nation | Climate Action*, https://www.un.org/en/climatechange/net-zero-coalition. [1]

Whelan, T. et al. (2021), *ESG and Financial Performance: Uncovering the Relationship by Aggregating Evidence from 1,000 Plus Studies Published between 2015 – 2020*, https://www.stern.nyu.edu/sites/default/files/assets/documents/NYU-RAM_ESG-Paper_2021.pdf (accessed on April 2022). [11]

World Bank (2020), *Engaging with Investors on Environmental, Social, and Governance (ESG) Issues: A World Bank Guide for Sovereign Debt Managers*, https://thedocs.worldbank.org/en/doc/375981604591250621-0340022020/original/WorldBankESGGuide2020FINAL.11.5.2020.pdf. [8]

World Bank (2019), *Seychelles: Introducing the World's First Sovereign Blue Bond - Mobilizing Private Sector Investment to Support the Ocean Economy*, https://thedocs.worldbank.org/en/doc/242151559930961454-0340022019/original/CasestudyBlueBondSeychellesfinal6.7.2019.pdf. [35]

Annex 2.A. Methodology for data collection and classification

Primary sovereign bond market data and country groupings

Primary sovereign bond market data are based on original OECD calculations using data obtained from Refinitiv that provides international security-level data on new issues of sovereign bonds. The ESG data set covers ESG-labelled bonds issued by sovereigns in the period from 1 December 2016 to 31 March 2022 and includes long-term debt only. Long-term debt is defined as any security with a maturity longer than 365 days. Securities with maturity less than 365 days issued by sovereigns are excluded from the dataset. The database provides a detailed set of information for each bond issue, including the proceeds, maturity date, interest rate and interest rate structure.

Refinitiv provides bond type information for most of its government securities entries. ESG-labelled securities are those classified under ESG in the database. In addition, Refinitiv provides a categorical indicator variable to specify whether an ESG issue is a green bond. Hence, to further subset the data according to the specific bond label ("Green" and "Social and Sustainable"), securities that were classified as being ESG-labelled but not green were considered to be part of the "Social and Sustainable" category.

The definition of emerging markets used in this report is consistent with the IMF's classification of Emerging and Developing Economies used in its World Economic Outlook. The regional definitions are also those used by the IMF, while the income categories used (high income, low income, lower middle income, upper middle income) are defined by the World Bank according to GNI per capita levels.

A number of bonds have been subject to reopening. For these bonds the initial data only provide the total amount (original issuance plus reopening). To retrieve the issuance amount for such reopened bonds, specific data on the outstanding amount on each reopening date for the concerned bonds have been downloaded separately from Refinitiv. As the reopening data only provide amounts outstanding in order to obtain the issuance amount on each relevant date, the outstanding amount on the previous date is subtracted from the outstanding amount on that given date. These calculated issuance amounts are converted on the transaction date using USD foreign exchange data from Refinitiv. To ensure consistency and comparability, the same method is used for all bonds, including those which have not been subject to reopening.

Exchange offers and certain bonds in the dataset have been manually excluded when they did not have any identifier (ISIN, RIC or CUSIP) and when they have not been able to be manually confirmed by comparing with official government data.

The issuance amounts are presented in USD, converted on the transaction date.

Calculations excluded a series of bonds issued by countries that are part of the CFA franc zone. These bonds, issued in West African CFA, amount to a total of USD 6.29 billion and were issued between 2020 and 2021. Issuer countries were: Benin, Burkina Faso, Côte D'Ivoire, Guinea Bissau, Mali, Niger, Senegal, and Togo. Maturities ranged from 27 days to 15 years. None of these securities was classified as being green and, under use of proceeds, Refinitiv classified the proceeds from these securities as being used for "pandemic" purposes.

Survey respondents and groupings

The survey on "Approaches to incorporating ESG factors into public debt management, including the issuance of sovereign green bonds," was circulated to Delegates to the OECD Working Party on Debt Management in the third quarter of 2021. Thirty-four of the 38 OECD countries responded to the survey. Ireland, Korea, Norway and the Czech Republic did not take part.

The survey on "Approaches to incorporating ESG factors into public debt management including issuance of sovereign ESG-labelled bonds" was circulated to a sample of selected non-OECD countries, with a particular focus on emerging market economies in February 2022. Tthe following 17 countries responded to this survey: Argentina, Benin, Brazil, Bulgaria, Cambodia, Cameroon, Croatia, Ghana, Indonesia, Jamaica, Morocco, Philippines, Rwanda, Seychelles, Thailand, the United Arab Emirates and Uruguay.

Notes

[1] The Paris Agreement is developed under the United Nations Framework Convention on Climate Change (UNFCCC) to combat climate change. The agreement's main goal is to limit the global temperature increase in this century to below 2 degrees Celsius above pre industrial levels, and to work towards limiting the increase to 1.5 degrees. The Paris Agreement was drafted in December 2015, and went into effect as of November 2016. Currently, there are 189 countries that are party to the agreement, and 195 signatory countries. Many companies set their climate related targets to be in line with the goals of the Paris Agreement (Source: https://unfccc.int/process-and-meetings/the-paris-agreement/the-paris-agreement).

[2] The United Nations Sustainable Development Goals were adopted in September 2015, with the aim to protect the planet and improve quality of life globally. The UN SDGs refer to the 17 categories of targets to achieve a broad range of aspirational goals, including ending poverty and hunger, improving education, and protecting the environment (https://www.undp.org/sustainable-development-goals).

[3] More recently, the war in Ukraine has raised energy security concerns and therefore reinforced the need to accelerate the transition away from fossil fuels, especially in Europe. This could in turn provide additional impetus for countries' climate policies and sustainable finance (IEA, 2022[40]).

[4] Despite strong policy advices and commitments towards 'build back better', progress so far has been limited. For example, the 2021 *OECD Government at a Glance* report highlights that as of July 2021 only 17% of the pandemic-related recovery spending of OECD countries and key partner economies has been allocated to environmentally positive spending, while the remaining 83% will either have no environmental impact or, worse, a negative impact (OECD, 2021[41]).

[5] In the Glasgow Climate Pact, 190 countries agreed to phase down unabated coal power, 137 countries committed to halt and reverse forest loss and land degradation by 2030, and over 100 countries pledged to reduce methane emissions by 30% by 2030 (UN, 2021[3]).

[6] In a number of countries, governments have established various high level bodies to lead these efforts across government. They are often tasked with developing and implementing policies to tackle with the risks from climate change, from under-investment or poor treatment of the workforce, from poor executive behaviour. For example, in the United Kingdom National Economy and Recovery Taskforce was established on public sector recovery and the Better Regulation Committee was established to co-ordinate a regulatory reform agenda. At the same time, non-profit initiatives such as Green Building Councils have been launched to bring together business leaders from a cross-section of industries and sectors to advise governments on green and green growth policies such as infrastructure, innovation and investment.

[7] As of 2020, more than a third of OECD countries (14) practice some form of green budgeting, with an additional 5 countries (Chile, Greece, Latvia, Poland and Slovenia) indicating plans to introduce green budgeting in the future. Furthermore, initiatives such as the European Green Deal by the European Union and other political commitments across the OECD suggest that interest in green budgeting will continue to grow in the near future (OECD, 2020[4]).

[8] The International Capital Market Association (ICMA) is a self-regulatory organisation and a body for capital markets participant, whose mission is that of promoting resilient well-functioning international and globally coherent cross-border debt securities markets. Its market standards and conventions have affected global debt markets in recent decades. (Source: https://www.icmagroup.org/About-ICMA/mission/).

[9] The Principles also improve financial market players' knowledge of the relevance of environmental and social impact, with the goal of attracting more finance to support sustainable development. They also aim to raise awareness of the importance of environmental and social impact among market participants, with the aim of attracting more finance to support sustainable development (ICMA, 2022[13]).

[10] Beyond the direct impacts, there are a range of other ways that climate change and social issues will affect government finances such as the impact of uncertainties on business and social unrest.

[11] The impact of climate change on the economy is classified under "physical risks", which express the consequences of environmental impact, and "transition risks", which are the results of policies aimed at reducing climate change.

[12] In addition, some countries specified that if they do not have such a strategy yet, this is because they are at the beginning of the process that will allow them to include ESG factors in their debt management practices. Brazil and the United Arab Emirates reported being in the process of building the ESG framework.

[13] Relevant websites are as follows: Central government debt management - Sustainability and Finnish Government Bonds (treasuryfinland.fi) and les Objectifs du Développement Durable visés par le Bénin - République du Bénin (odd.gouv.bj).

[14] 'Greenwashing' refers to conveying a false impression or providing misleading information about an economic activity regarding its contributing to a climate or environmental objective.

[15] At the time of the surveys, 30 out of 51 countries issued or were in the process of issuing a form of ESG-labelled bond and were able to answer this question.

[16] All ratings in this section are from Fitch Ratings, updated as of December 2021.

[17] This committee is co-chaired by Finance Canada as well as Environment and Climate Change Canada. Several other departments (e.g. Natural Resources Canada, Transport Canada, and Infrastructure Canada) are also part of this committee given their important roles in delivering on the government's environmental priorities.

[18] German's Inter-Ministerial Working Group includes: the Federal Ministry of the Interior, Building and Community, the Federal Ministry for Economic Affairs and Energy, the Federal Ministry of Food and Agriculture, the Federal Ministry of Transport and Digital Infrastructure, the Federal Ministry for the Environment, Nature Conservation and Nuclear Safety, the Federal Ministry of Education and Research and the Federal Ministry for Economic Cooperation and Development.

3 Sovereign debt issuance trends in emerging-market economies

Emerging Market and Developing Economies (EMDEs) have faced various challenges since the outbreak of the pandemic in 2020. Many EMDE sovereigns experienced a considerable decline in their economic activity and tax revenues while having to increase fiscal stimulus and social spending to fight the negative impacts of the pandemic, which resulted in an unprecedented surge in debt issuance globally. Strong immediate policy support and accommodative financial conditions have helped to contain financial distress and allowed economies to recover to some extent. However, various risk factors such as inflationary pressures, monetary tightening in advanced economies and new COVID-19 variants may affect capital inflows to EMDEs and expose vulnerabilities in some countries.

This chapter presents an overview of sovereign debt issuance trends in EMDEs in 2021 and provides an update on the impact of the COVID-19 crisis on the issuance conditions of EMDE sovereigns.

3.1. Introduction

Chapter 3 of last year's *Outlook* explored the impact of the COVID-19 pandemic on debt issuance trends in emerging markets and developing economies (EMDEs) with a focus on currency and maturity structures. This year, the chapter on emerging market and developing economies (EMDEs) provides an overview of the most recent developments in borrowing conditions and sovereign debt issuance by different income levels and geographic regions, as well as an evaluation of debt quality and borrowing costs across regions during the pandemic.

The key source of information is a dataset comprising over 7 500 sovereign government securities issued by 95 EMDE sovereign issuers in 2021 (see Annex 3.A for details of the methodology used).

Key findings

- The impact of the COVID-19 pandemic spurred a rise in EMDE sovereign debt issuance. These country groups issued around a record of USD 3.5 trillion of debt in financial markets in 2021, roughly 40% higher than the pre-pandemic three year average. In 2021, the issuance amount remained stable at approximately the same level as in 2020, despite the increasing borrowing costs in most regions, especially towards the end of the year. In terms of net debt issuance, all income categories except low-income countries (LICs) decreased net issuance considerably in 2021 compared to 2020. Net debt issued by LICs reached record highs in 2021 despite having consistently decreased since 2015. In 2021, LICs issued USD 7.8 billion of net debt, more than double the USD 3.2 billion issued in 2020.

- In 2021, China remained the largest issuer, although its share declined slightly, while Emerging Asia and China combined constituted more than half of the EMDE sovereign debt issuance. Despite significant differences within regions, the share of Middle East and North Africa (MENA), Sub-Saharan Africa (SSA) and Latin America and Caribbean (LAC) picked up above 2020 levels, suggesting a restoration of market access and increased financial needs for these regions.

- Borrowing costs varied widely across regions with an overall increase in yields for all EMDEs in 2021. SSA and MENA faced the highest yields in foreign currency denominated securities, whereas Emerging Europe and Emerging Asia regions enjoyed relatively cheaper funding.

- The share of foreign currency denominated debt issuance in total issuance continued to decrease in 2021, falling below 2020 levels. The decline was most pronounced in MENA and LAC regions where costs were fairly high. Though the share of FX denominated debt of SSA picked up considerably, it was still below pre-pandemic levels as access to international money markets remained constrained for most sovereigns.

- In the face of high uncertainty and rising financing needs, sovereigns issued high amounts of short-term debt during the pandemic. This increased share of short-term debt has worsened the redemption profile of EMDE sovereigns, with high amounts of debt needing to be repaid within the next three years. LICs bear the highest rollover risk as 45% of their outstanding debt will need to be repaid or refinanced in the next three years.

- In 2021, the average maturity of new borrowing decreased in almost all regions except SSA and LAC regions. Particularly in SSA, the average maturity increased mainly due to a few large issuances in international capital markets.

- Debt quality in EMDEs has been deteriorating in some regions over the last two years, with a record of 59 downgrades issued in the wake of the pandemic and a further 15 downgrades issued in 2021, also reflected in increased risk premia and borrowing costs. The region bucking

> this trend is emerging Asia, where debt quality remained high and stable both before and after the pandemic.
>
> - As countries were slowly recovering from the COVID-19 pandemic, Russia's invasion of Ukraine is expected to put additional strain on inflation, economic growth and fiscal accounts in many EMDEs. This coincides with increased refinancing needs and deteriorated credit conditions in some low- and lower-middle income countries. It is important for these countries to receive financial and technical support from international financial institutions to manage both the risk of short-term refinancing risk and long-term debt sustainability, and to prevent these countries from resorting to opaque borrowing methods.

3.2. Borrowing from the markets by EMDE sovereigns continued to increase despite tightening financial conditions

At the initial outbreak of COVID-19, many EMDE governments faced considerably increased financing needs to deal with the turmoil caused by the pandemic and mitigate its economic consequences. This resulted in unprecedented levels of debt issuance in 2020, which reached USD 3.5 trillion, around 35% increase on the 3-year average before pandemic. Supported by major central banks' asset purchase programs and generous pandemic recovery packages, accommodative financial conditions in many advanced economies helped to support global liquidity, allowing EMDEs to access funds and rollover their existing debt at relatively low cost. In 2021, however, the strengthening global economic recovery and rising inflationary pressures have led many advanced economies to reduce pandemic related policy support and tighten monetary policy. Moreover, several EMDEs central banks' have also increased their policy rates in face of surging food and energy prices, which may pose new challenges for EMDEs, especially when refinancing their considerably high legacy debt from the pandemic.

3.2.1. Funding needs remained high in 2021 while EMDEs face new challenges which may affect future capital inflows

As was the case for almost all sovereigns, EMDE sovereign funding needs drastically surged with the outbreak of the pandemic in March 2020, in response to lower fiscal revenues and higher expenditure on health and support for vulnerable groups. Sovereign debt issuance gradually increased and reached a record high in July 2020, stabilising afterwards at levels significantly higher than prior to the pandemic. In 2021, EMDEs' financing needs remained elevated, in total, EMDE sovereigns issued more than USD 3.5 trillion, similar to the level issued in 2020. With this, they borrowed from financial markets at record level for two years in a row.

Monthly debt issuance was also volatile, as the relatively steady debt issuance in the first half soared significantly in the summer, reaching record highs in August, and stabilised again at levels slightly lower than 2020 in the last quarter of 2021 (Figure 3.1).[1] Most of the debt issuance surge in August came from Argentina's Sinking Fund/Amortisation Pay of USD 121.7 billion, which alone constituted 30% of the debt issuance in August. Excluding Argentina's high amortisation pay, the monthly debt issuance by EMDE sovereigns has been mostly steady.

Figure 3.1. Central government gross debt issuance by EMDEs

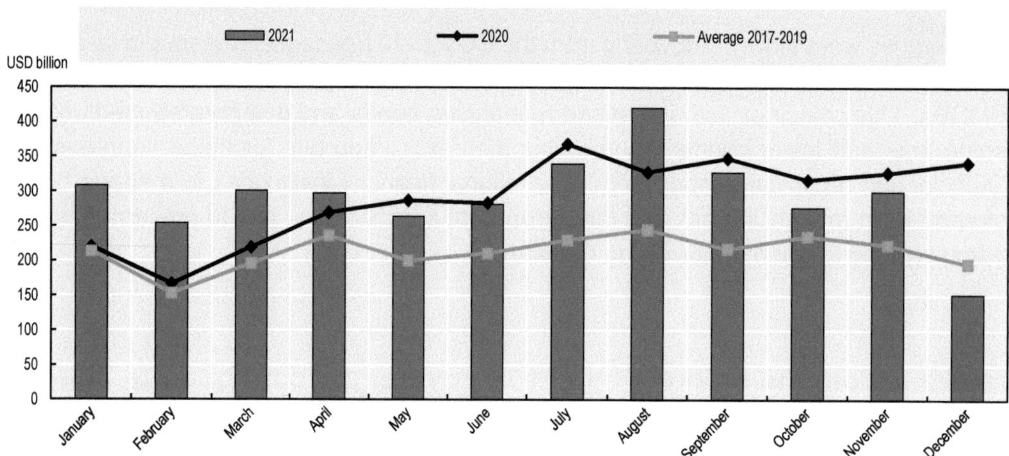

Notes: Data show sovereign bond issuances up to 15 December 2021.
Source: OECD calculations based on data from Refinitiv.

A number of factors played an important role in explaining the issuance trends during the pandemic; notably higher levels of gross issuance throughout the year; and the significant increase during the summer 2021. Despite recent increases in interest rates, financing conditions have been favourable in the period under review, as major central banks in advanced economies maintained a low interest rate policy, which supported global liquidity and mitigated financial distress in the markets, supporting capital inflows to EMDEs. In addition, substantial policy efforts were made to support recovery of low-income countries (LICs) from the pandemic such as the Debt Service Suspension Initiative (DSSI) and additional financing support programmes including new Special Drawing Rights (SDR) allocations by the IMF.[2] These programmes helped to enhance debt resilience and further facilitated sovereigns to issue new debt and rollover existing ones at very low costs, allowing the unprecedented increase in EMDE debt issuance during the pandemic.

The outlook suggested a normalisation from the period of acute financial distress with relatively steady monthly issuances in 2021, but EMDE financing needs remain significantly higher in 2021 than pre-pandemic averages. Moreover, various risk factors posed challenges for EMDE sovereigns, affecting capital inflows into EMDEs as well as the sustainability and the cost of debt. Notably, the policy support which had created ample liquidity and buttressed investor sentiment has been gradually reduced. Many advanced economies have initiated or planned to reduce their monetary and fiscal support in 2021. Global financial conditions have also started to tighten in the face of increased energy and food prices. Although still being accommodative, policy rates in some advanced economies have increased, since the second half of 2021. Given already elevated debt levels and the high financing needs of EMDE sovereigns, interest rate hikes may expose vulnerabilities in some countries, especially if they come faster than anticipated (IMF, 2021[1]).

Another major source of concern is the recent Russian invasion of Ukraine, which may have adverse implications for EMDEs. Having pushed energy prices even higher, the war may also spur agricultural commodity price increases as both Russia and Ukraine are major exporters of grain (OECD, 2022[2]). Increases in the price of energy and food, which typically form a larger share of household consumption of EMDE countries, may bring additional inflationary pressures and accelerate interest rate hikes (FitchRatings, 2022[3]). Higher borrowing costs, on the other hand, could raise debt sustainability concerns and trigger rating downgrades and even sovereign defaults, especially in countries which have high amounts of debt maturing in the near-term. Global liquidity conditions have also tightened, reflecting greater risk aversion and uncertainty, with higher risk premia and currency depreciations also occurring in many emerging-market economies and Central and Eastern European economies with relatively strong ties with Russia (OECD, 2022[2]). One exception is that capital flow into other regions, for example the LAC region, is picking up as some investors shift away from the countries in conflict to other emerging economies (OECD, Forthcoming[4]).

3.2.2. Monetary policy normalisation is now occurring amid increased inflationary pressures

Global inflationary pressures have shifted central bank policy rate expectations upwards for advanced economies, creating a major challenge for EMEs, as the increased borrowing costs would aggravate their debt problems and risks. The surge in commodity and energy prices added to the existing pressure on price levels coming from the recovery in demand and encouraging developments in vaccination rollouts. In particular, the price of crude oil picked up by more than 50% between the end of 2020 and 2021 and the global commodity price index excluding fuel prices increased by around 14% over the same period.[3] A rise in energy prices may allow some oil exporting EMEs to reduce their financing needs, but adds a negative drag on the economic activity of oil importing countries, which in turn affect their fiscal balances (IMF, 2015[4]).

Financial conditions have tightened globally, those countries who have borrowed in foreign currencies face higher exposure to currency risk and may have to refinance their debt under less accommodative terms. New COVID-19 variants and supply-chain disruptions have spurred price increases and accelerated interest rate hikes. In this regard, EMEs have faced a difficult trade-off between sustaining a stimulative financial environment to support the economic recovery or tightening monetary policy to maintain price stability as well as to preserve a real interest rate differential over US yields.

Figure 3.2. Change in the main policy interest rate of EME central banks and EME local currency bond spreads over ten-year US Government bond yields

Panel A: EME central bank policy rates
Panel B: EME local-currency bond yield spreads over ten-year US Government bonds

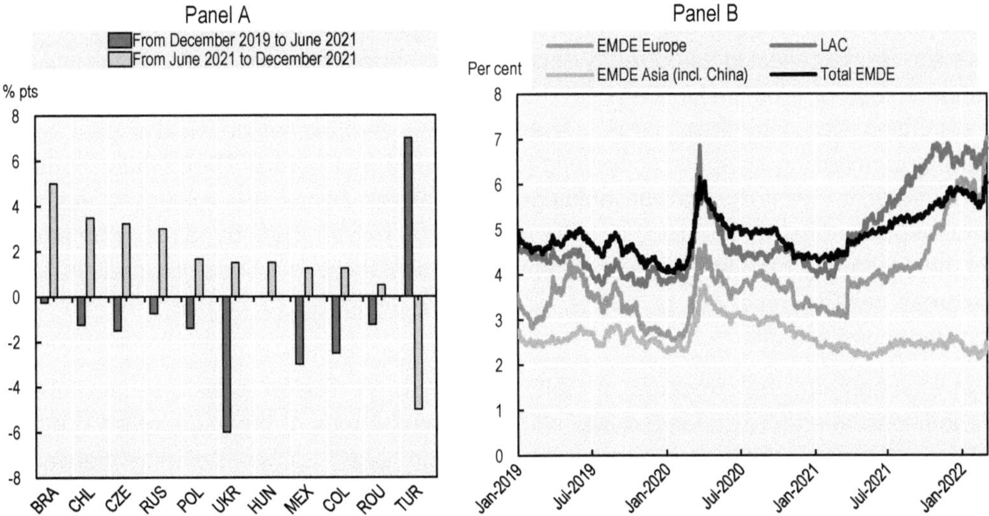

Source: OECD calculations based on Refinitiv data.

To this end, many EME central banks took an aggressive stance against rising inflation and increased their policy rates, especially during the second half of 2021, gradually widening the EME local-currency government bond yield spreads over ten-year US Government bond yields (Figure 3.2, Panel B). Along with others, the Central Bank of Brazil raised its benchmark rate seven times in 2021, from 2% to 9.25% and marked the steepest hike among EMEs. One exception to the trend was the Central Bank of Turkey, who cut its policy rate several times in 2021 despite soaring inflation. The policy rate set below inflation spurred further currency depreciation as well as a rise in inflation expectations and a surge in risk premia (OECD, 2021[5]).

The capacity to use fiscal policy varied widely among countries as the pandemic has weighed differently on various regions and income categories. In several LICs, recovery from the pandemic has lagged far behind the rest of the world due to their weak macroeconomic fundamentals, low vaccination rollouts and pre-existing vulnerabilities (IMF, 2021[6]). Lacking fiscal space, these countries may find it more challenging to balance the opposing needs of supporting the economy through the recovery and combatting inflation by monetary tightening.

3.2.3. Central bank bond purchases in EMEs have helped to restore financial stability in times of acute market distress

In response to financial market strains in the wake of the pandemic, central banks of EMEs deployed a number of measures, including liquidity support, and foreign currency interventions and swap lines. Some emerging-market economy central banks have also launched asset purchase programmes – for the first time since the adoption of inflation targeting frameworks in the late 1990s – in response to the massive government bond sell-off during the initial months of the COVID-19 crisis. For example, Brazil, India, Indonesia, South Africa, Thailand and Turkey have engaged in asset purchases with a particular focus on government bonds. These purchases, while often small compared to those of major advanced economies, were effective in restoring financial stability, guided price discovery and curbed further surges in local benchmark bond yields (Box 2.1).[4] Overall, bond purchases by EME central banks remained limited in 2021.

Box 3.1. Central bank bond purchases may mitigate the effects of a sovereign bond sell-off

This box sketches a model (Figure 3.3) to assess the efficacy of central bank (CB) asset purchases in EMEs (Sunel and Mimir, forthcoming[7]). The environment is a small open economy with a bank-based financial sector. Banks collect local-currency deposits from households and foreign-currency funds from foreign lenders. Banks then make loans to producers of intermediate goods by purchasing local-currency securities issued by these firms – financing their demand for physical capital – and to the government by purchasing local-currency, long-term government bonds. These latter bonds are also held by non-resident investors. Foreign holdings of sovereign bonds are subject to investor sell-off shocks and respond negatively to rising country risk premia. Government bonds may be purchased by the CB on the secondary market if there is exceptional financial stress.[1] These purchases, financed by issuing interest bearing reserves to banks, are mainly designed to compensate for the market dislocation from bond sell-offs.

In such an environment, the exposure of EME sovereigns to foreign investors can tighten overall financial conditions when foreign lenders sell off government bonds of these countries during a stress episode (Figure 3.4). If the CB does not undertake asset purchases, domestic commercial banks absorb the bonds sold off by foreigners, which pushes down their price and raises the excess yield on sovereign bonds over US interest rates. This crowds out bank credit to non-financial firms, bids down private firm bond prices and leads to a widening of intermediation margins.[3] Hence, the external bond sell-off shock has spill-over effects on domestic financial conditions. The foreign borrowing capacity of domestic banks is hindered by their weaker balance sheets due to depressed asset prices exacerbating the initial

---

net capital outflows from the sovereign bond sell-off. The ensuing depreciation of the currency raises import prices and passes through to aggregate prices, inducing conventional monetary policy to tighten to stabilise inflation.

Figure 3.3. A model of sovereign borrowing, financial intermediaries and asset purchases

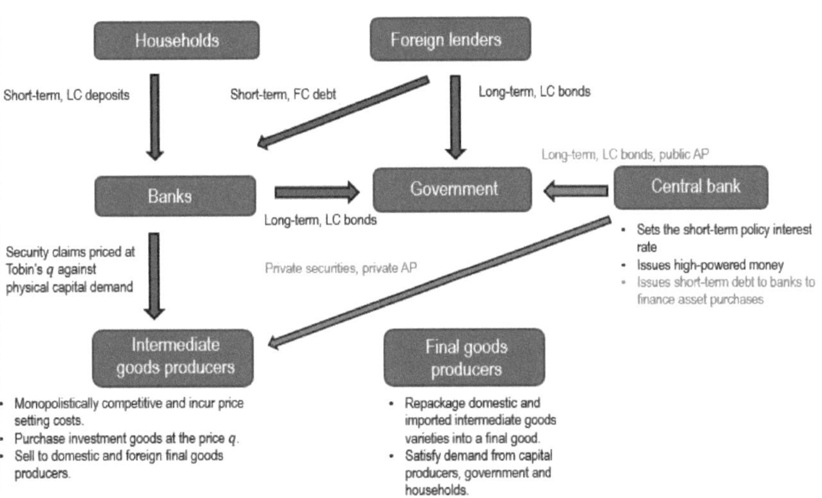

Note: LC and FC denote "local-currency" and "foreign-currency". AP denotes "asset purchases". Arrows indicate money flows.

Figure 3.4. Transmission of a sovereign bond sell-off by non-resident investors

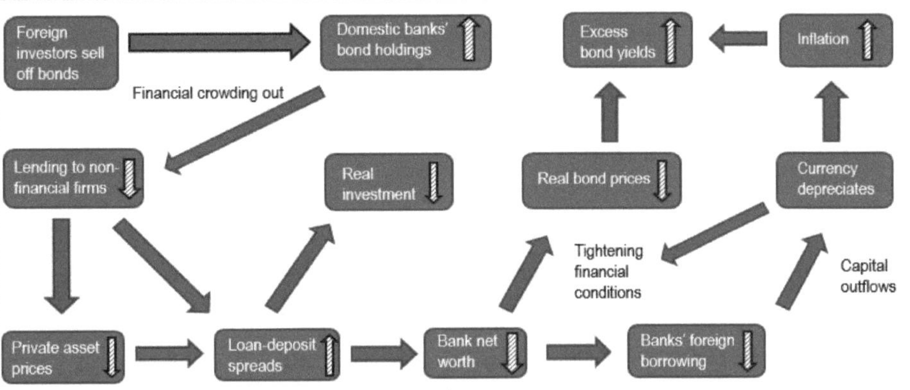

Note: "Bonds" denotes domestic-currency, long-term emerging-market economy sovereign bonds.

CB bond purchases could address the market dislocation so that commercial banks are no longer required to absorb the bond sell-off by foreign investors.[4] This would limit the crowding out of credit to firms and the collapse in sovereign bond and non-financial corporate bond prices. Stronger asset prices would in turn reduce the tightening of financial conditions as measured by excess bond yields and loan-deposit spreads. Stronger private domestic bank balance sheets would provide better foreign-borrowing prospects for banks, limit capital outflows, reduce currency depreciation and create room for manoeuvre for monetary policy.

1. Purchases on the secondary rather than the primary market (hence not monetising newly issued public debt) reflect the commonly observed modality of EME government bond purchases during the COVID-19 crisis (Fratto et al., 2021[8]).
3. Domestic banks absorbed around 90% of the increase in outstanding local-currency government bonds in emerging-market economies that implemented asset purchases between February and June 2020 (IMF, 2020[9]). CB holdings represented close to 30% of that increase, slightly exceeding the *decline* in non-resident investor holdings (about 25% of the change in total bonds).
4. For a quantitative analysis of the transmission of CB government bond purchases upon bond sell-offs, see (Sunel and Mimir, forthcoming[7]).

Although potentially useful in extreme stress episodes, central bank bond purchases in EMDEs are not always effective. Firstly, high-frequency estimates suggest that asset purchases during the pandemic resulted in only short-lived reductions in bond yields. This was because the level of bond purchases in EMDEs was not large enough to bring a sizeable and persistent easing of financial conditions (Sunel and Mimir, forthcoming[7]). Secondly, if bond purchases lead to a de-anchoring in inflation expectations, they bring a smaller reduction in real excess bond yields while leading to higher and more persistent inflation. Finally, a larger central bank balance sheet, especially if not scaled down once domestic financial conditions normalise, could elevate fiscal dominance risks and raise concerns that investors perceive future monetary policy tightening as less likely because of the potential for central bank losses on bond holdings.

3.2.4. An uneven recovery from the pandemic affected issuance amounts across regions and income levels

Similar to the total issue amount, shares of issuance by income categories in 2021 presented a similar picture as in 2020. In EMDEs in 2021, upper-middle income countries (UMIC) continued to be the largest group in terms of their gross issuance, representing 61% of the debt issued in 2021. It is worth noting that some major issuers, such as Brazil and China, significantly decreased their new debt issuance in 2021, as their new funding needs reduced compared to 2020. In contrast, several countries including Kazakhstan, Malaysia, Mexico, Peru and Thailand issued more sovereign bonds than their 2020 levels. High income countries (HIC) in EMDEs accounted for 10% of the gross debt issuance in 2021, slightly higher than their share in 2020. The rise in the share of HIC was mostly driven by Chile's increased issuance, followed by Bahrain, Oman, Panama and Uruguay. The share of lower-middle income countries (LMIC), on the other hand, slightly reduced from 30% in 2020 to 28% in 2021. Their issuance in the financial markets somewhat reduced in the fourth quarter of the year, when interest rates started to rise slowly (Figure 3.5, Panel B).

Figure 3.5. EMDE sovereign debt gross issuance by regional and income categories

Panel A: Issuance by selected income categories
Panel B: Regional composition of debt issuance

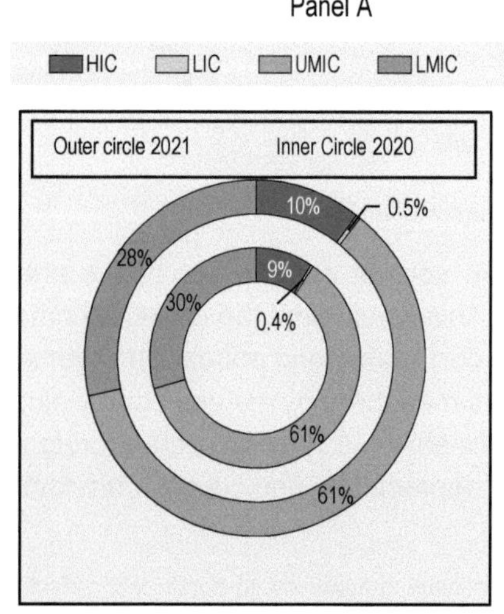

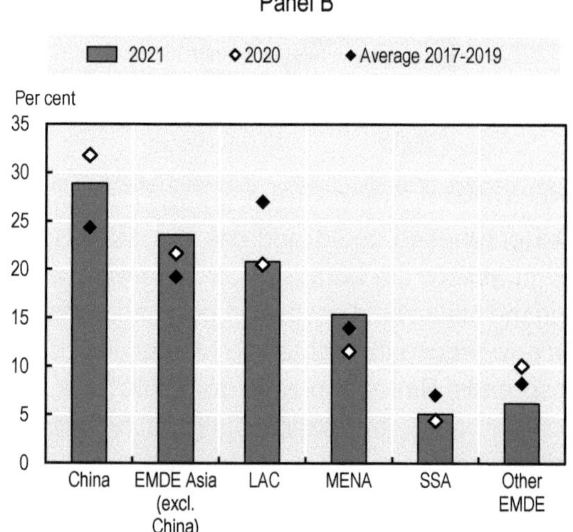

Source: OECD calculations based on Refinitiv data.

The regional composition of EMDE sovereigns' gross debt issuance has changed widely in 2021 (Figure 3.5 Panel A). Emerging Asia including China accounted for more than half of the EMDE debt issuance in 2021, while the relative share of China, which is the largest single issuer, fell from 32% to 29%, approaching its lower pre-pandemic levels. Excluding China, the share of the Emerging Asia region has continued to grow, accounting for almost one-quarter of the total EMDE issuance as of 2021.

After falling below its historic share in 2020, the share of Latin America and the Caribbean (LAC) of the gross debt issuance remained at the same level of 21% in 2021 as in 2020. Sub-Saharan Africa and MENA, which had also fallen short of their pre-pandemic averages in 2020, increased their issuance both in relative and nominal terms in 2021. Particularly, MENA's issuance share exceeded its 3-year pre-pandemic level, while Sub-Saharan Africa remained below their pre-pandemic average. Although it was important for MENA countries to increase fiscal spending to finance public health expenditures and support the most vulnerable households and businesses, the pandemic debt also came with a cost. Many MENA countries faced higher borrowing costs, despite the global low interest rate environment, as their default risk picked up sharply in 2020 due to their elevated debt levels, chronic low growth compared to peers and pre-existing vulnerabilities including governance and low transparency (Gatti et al., 2021[10]).

Figure 3.6.Net debt issuance by income categories, EMDE countries (USD billion)

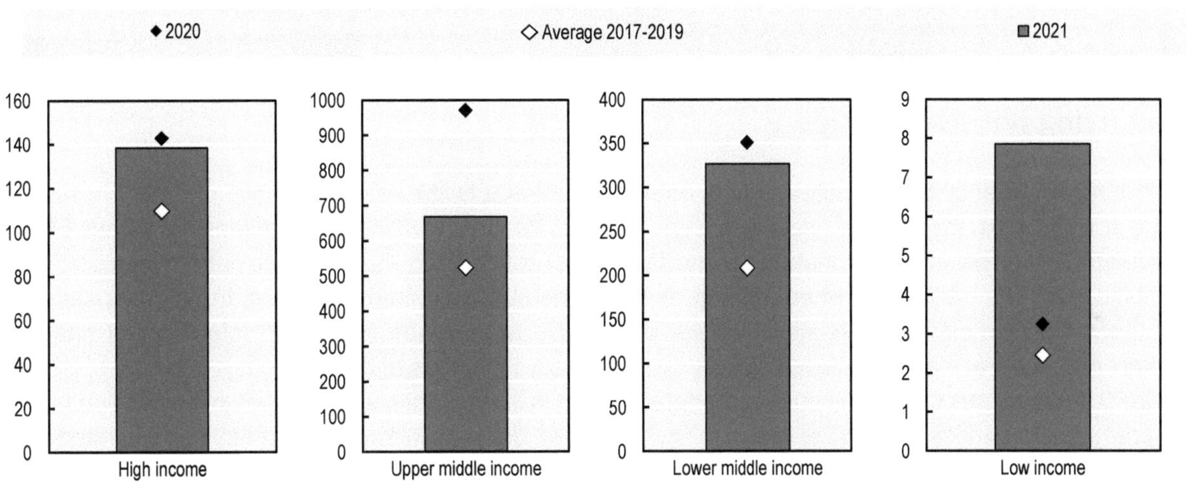

Note: Scales in each chart vary.
Source: OECD calculations based on Refinitiv data.

In 2020, net debt issuance by EMDE sovereigns soared drastically for all income categories compared to pre-pandemic levels and reached USD 1.5 trillion, as governments turned to bond markets to meet their increased financing needs in the face of restricted economic activity, lower tax revenues and additional health and social expenditures (Figure 3.6). Upper-middle-income countries (UMICs) with high financing needs and developed institutional frameworks had strong demand following the recovery of money markets from the initial shock. UMICs issued a record level of USD 970 billion which constituted 66% of the total net debt issuance in 2020. Similarly, lower-middle income countries (LMICs) also drastically increased their net debt issuance and issued 69% more than their pre-pandemic level. On the other hand, high income countries (HICs) and LICs increased their net debt issuance only by about 30% and issued substantially lower amounts of net debt. However, it should be noted that, even though the level of net debt issuance by HICs is considerably lower than the amount issued by UMICs, these categories are a subset of EMDEs. The USD 138 billion net debt issued by HICs in 2021 came from 18 sovereigns whereas USD 668 billion was issued by a higher number of 43 UMIC countries.

Sovereign net debt issuance in EMDEs declined in 2021 compared to 2020 but remain higher than pre-pandemic levels. As a result, indebtedness in EMDEs continues to grow and raises sustainability concerns in the future give the macroeconomic and macro financial context. In 2021, EMDE sovereigns issued USD 1.1 trillion net debt, 22% lower than the 2020 levels. While UMICs remained the largest group in terms of net debt issuance, their share of the total net issuance declined more than 8% but increased in all other income groups. In nominal terms on the other hand, LICs were the only group that increased their net issuance in 2021 compared to both 2020 and pre-pandemic levels.

Notwithstanding the consistent decline of net debt issuance by LICs since 2015, the pandemic resulted in record levels of LIC net debt issuance, marking the steepest increase among other income groups. In particular the amount of net debt issuance by LICs declined from USD 5.4 billion in 2015 to USD 1 billion in 2019. This number picked up to USD 3.2 billion in 2020 and reached more than USD 7.8 billion in 2021. In all other income categories, the volume of net debt issuance fell significantly below 2020 numbers, reflecting the uneven recovery for LICs who were more negatively affected by the pandemic. Due to their structural challenges and slower access to vaccines, LICs are still struggling to recover from the pandemic and face high financing needs. In this regard, international policy efforts were made to help ease the liquidity constraints in these economies such as the DSSI led by G20 countries and IMF financial assistance through various lending facilities, including the Rapid Credit Facility (RCF), the Rapid Financing Instrument (RFI) and the Catastrophe Containment and Relief Trust which have in total provided USD 250 billion to member countries since March 2020, a quarter of IMF's USD 1 trillion lending capacity.[5]

3.3. The share of debt issued in foreign currency continued to decrease in 2021 amid rising borrowing costs

While foreign currency denominated debt is often avoided due to the risk of potential currency mismatch on the sovereign balance sheets, issuing foreign-currency securities in international markets allows EMDE sovereigns to borrow in longer maturities and face lower refinancing risk, and alleviate the pressure on domestic investors particularly when funding needs surge suddenly. In this context, the global pandemic and the resulting heightened financial needs of EMDEs have made access to international financial markets more critical than ever. At the same time, especially in periods of financial crisis, the cost of issuing in hard currency soars drastically due to the deterioration in investor risk sentiment of investors and higher risk premium. In periods of financial stress there have been declines in foreign currency denominated debt issuance.

3.3.1. Foreign currency denominated debt issuance decreased across EMDE groups with the exception of Sub-Saharan Africa

Domestic currency securities have dominated EMDE issuance in the last decade, representing about 88.7% of all debt being issued in domestic currencies before the pandemic, suggesting a deepening of local currency bond markets and an improvement in currency risk exposures in EMDEs. The share of debt issued in domestic currencies increased further in 2020 and reached 91% as the foreign currency (FX) debt share shrunk drastically for some regions. Some countries with weak fundamentals could not regain market access following the initial shock of the pandemic. In 2020 for instance, Sub-Saharan Africa, despite its considerable foreign currency needs, could only issue 7.4% of its total debt in foreign currency, less than half of the 16.4% share before the pandemic, reflecting a loss of international market access in the wake of the COVID-19 crisis (OECD, 2022[11]).

In 2021, the overall share of foreign currency denominated debt in EMDEs fell further to 7.5%, lower than the pre-pandemic and 2020 levels (Figure 3.7). Emerging Asia and other emerging Europe countries who enjoyed relatively lower borrowing costs, both increased their share of foreign-currency denominated debt in 2021. Emerging Asia, which has deep and strong local-currency bond markets, issued about 4.2% of its total debt in foreign currencies, higher than its 2020 levels. On the other hand, Sub-Saharan Africa, which had experienced a significant loss of market access following the pandemic outbreak, issued around 16%

of its total debt in foreign currency, despite the considerably higher costs.[6] It should be noted that the majority of the large Eurobond issuance in 2021 came from Benin, Ghana and Nigeria, together constituting 65% of the total foreign-currency denominated debt issued in Sub-Saharan Africa. Overall, only 9 out of 30 sovereigns in the region issued FX-denominated securities, suggesting that the international market access for many Sub-Saharan Africa countries remained constrained in 2021, with the exception of a few, who managed to borrow large amounts of foreign denominated debt with fairly long maturities. In addition, sovereigns who issued ESG labelled securities, enjoyed strong investor demand and were able to borrow at longer maturities and at relatively low costs, allowing them to extend their debt maturity profiles and lower their exposure to future interest rate hikes and rollover risks. For instance, Benin raised USD 1.2 billion with its 14-year ESG labelled Eurobond, at a yield of 5.25%, one of the lowest yields achieved in the region. On the other hand, many Sub-Saharan Africa countries also relied on domestic markets and official creditors, as well as various debt relief programmes and restructuring.

MENA and Latin America and the Caribbean regions reduced their foreign-currency denominated debt issuance significantly in 2021. This took place amid increasing cost of FX-denominated debt issuance for most sovereign issuers in these regions, particularly in MENA.[7]

Figure 3.7. Foreign currency denominated debt issuance within emerging-market economy groups

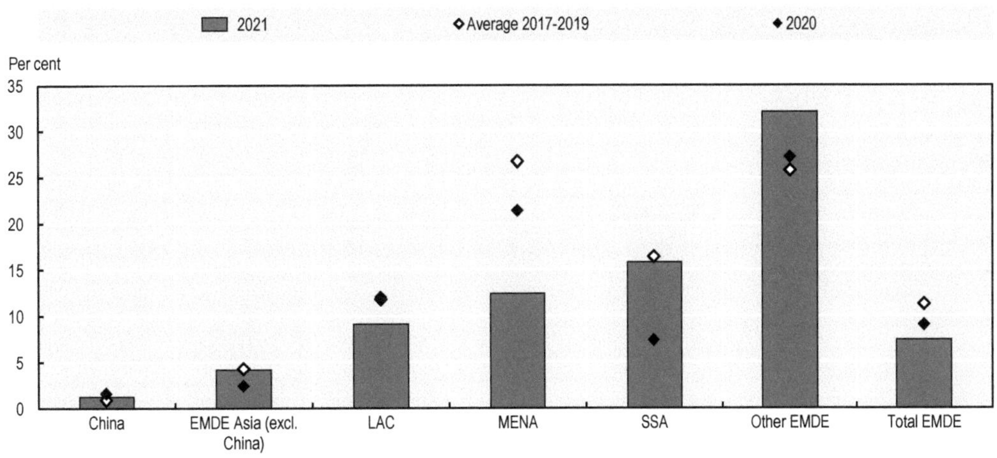

Notes: Other Emerging category covers mainly Emerging Europe issuers
Source: OECD calculations based on data from Refinitiv.

Although the foreign currency composition of total EMDE sovereign debt issuance in global markets has been limited in recent years, the results should be interpreted with caution with respect to currency risk assessments in EMDEs. First of all, the higher share of foreign-currency debt issuance in countries like Argentina,[8] Bulgaria, Romania and Turkey may make these economies more vulnerable to abrupt fluctuations in exchange rates. The rapid rise in foreign currency debt issuance by Benin and Nigeria is also worth noting. In addition, in some EMDEs, the rise in foreign-currency private sector liabilities has also been very substantial and needs to be considered when assessing overall currency risk exposure of countries.

3.3.2. Foreign currency borrowing costs for EMDEs increased, with wide variations between countries

In 2021, nearly one-fifth of the EMDE total fixed-rate USD-denominated government bonds were issued with a yield under 3%; 37% with a yield between 3% and 5% and 43% with a yield above 5% in the primary markets (Figure 3.8).[9] The share of FX-denominated bonds sold with a yield of 5% or more increased from 37% in 2020 to 44% in 2021.

Looking at regional groups, the cost of USD-denominated bonds was relatively favourable for Emerging Europe issuers with 42% of their issuance having a yield of less than 3%. Sub-Saharan Africa on the other hand, issued USD denominated debt with the highest cost, all of it with a yield above 5% and about one-third being with a yield of more than 8%, followed by MENA who issued more than two-thirds of its USD denominated debt with a yield above 5% yield. Out of ten EMDE issuers who borrowed with the highest yields on fixed-rate USD-denominated bonds, eight belong to either Sub Saharan Africa or MENA, with the exception of Turkey (5.5%) and Ukraine (6.7%).

Overall in EMDEs, the weighted yield-to-maturity (YTM) increased from 4.1% in 2020 to 4.6% in 2021 when all EMDE issuances are included. However, this finding should be interpreted with caution. Restricting the countries to those that issued fixed-rate USD denominated bonds in 2021 (35 EMDE sovereigns) and comparing their YTM between 2020 and 2021 shows that the change is much more moderate, from 4.5% to 4.6%. This difference suggests that the change in EMDEs' overall yield was mainly affected by the composition of countries who issued each year, the presence or absence of countries with high yields and their volume share of issuance, rather than a drastic change in yields for each given issuer. A number of countries who issued fixed-rate USD-denominated government bonds with high yields in 2020 did not issue in 2021. For instance, Bahamas and El Salvador who issued with 9.5% and 9.2% yields in 2020 did not issue in 2021, while there are countries where the opposite is also true. Countries with relatively higher yields such as Kenya (6.3%); Nigeria (7.3%); Pakistan (7.1%) and Rwanda (5.5%) who did not issue fixed-rate USD-denominated securities in 2020 issued in 2021, contributing to the overall yield increase. In LAC region, more than 90% of the fixed-rate USD-denominated government bonds were issued with yield less than 5%.

Figure 3.8. Volume share by yield group of fixed-rate USD denominated bond issuance by EMDEs in 2021

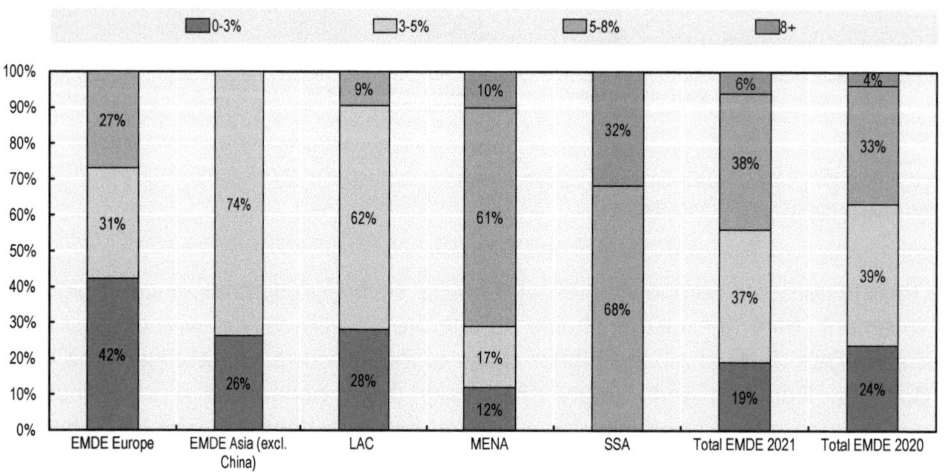

Notes: Yields are calculated using fixed-rate USD-denominated securities with maturity longer than 365 days. Comparison between EMDE yields between 2020 and 2021 is based on the same 35 EMDE sovereigns who issued fixed-rate USD denominated bonds in 2021 and their corresponding yields in 2020.
Source: OECD calculations based on data from Refinitiv.

3.4. Average maturity of debt issuance in most regions declined as T-Bill issuance prevailed among EMDEs

During the past two decades, EMDEs have weathered several financial crises, which commonly stemmed from currency and maturity mismatches. When sovereigns have large amounts of short-term debt and the economic outlook worsens, debt service becomes extremely costly and sometimes even impossible, leading to a sovereign default. Although issuing short-term debt is associated with higher risks and rollover vulnerabilities, options for EMDE sovereigns to shift towards longer maturities are often limited due to a number of factors. Most importantly, facing a higher risk premia and hence higher borrowing costs on long-term debt, it is more attractive for many EMDE issuers with shallow local bond markets to borrow at shorter maturities. Moreover, investor demand may be lower for fixed-rate long-term domestic-currency denominated securities from risky borrowers due to the moral hazard problem, that the governments are able to create inflation to lower the real value of their debt. This is not an issue with foreign currency denominated debt and less likely to occur for a shorter maturity debt (Broner, Lorenzoni and Schmukler, 2011[12]). Given that longer-term debt is often issued in foreign currency, issuing short-term debt also goes hand in hand with a higher share of domestic currency denominated securities. This is especially the case during crisis periods where the cost of longer-term debt soars drastically, and issuers depend more heavily on short-term domestic securities. Overall, EMDE sovereigns face a tough choice between issuing long-term debt, which mitigates the rollover risk, and short-term debt which reduces the cost of borrowing.

Figure 3.9. Average term to maturity (ATM) of gross issuance for EMDE regions, weighted by issue amounts

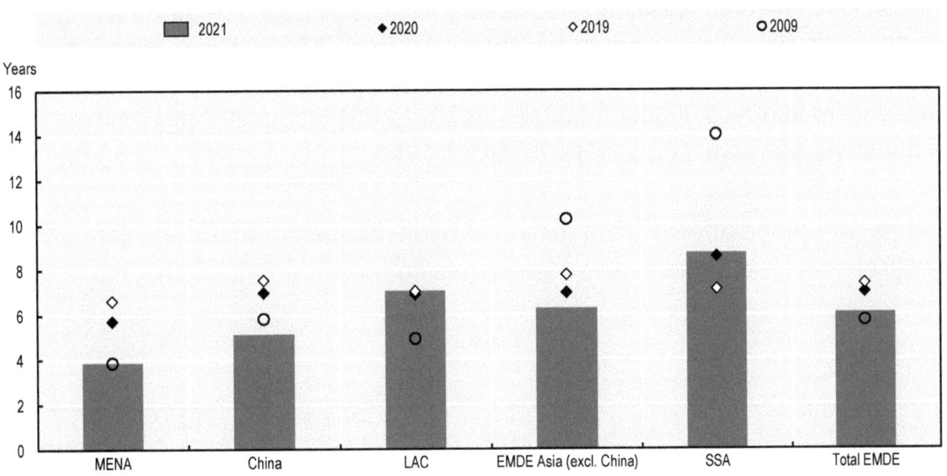

Notes: Data used on ATM calculation includes all gross issuances by EME sovereigns except short-term securities which had to be repaid in less than 31 days as these are mostly used for cash management purposes rather than debt management.
Source: OECD calculations based on data from Refinitiv.

Between 2009 and 2019, EMDEs have managed to lengthen the average maturity of their new debt issuance from 5.7 to 7.4 years, allowing EMDEs to improve their risk profile, which is particularly important as they are more prone to capital outflows and sudden stops during times of financial crises (Figure 3.9) (See Annex 3.A for details of the methodology used). Mitigating sovereigns' exposure to rollover risks with higher maturities came at the expense of higher currency risk, as the majority of the longer-term securities have been issued in foreign currencies over the past years, making EMDE sovereigns vulnerable to exchange rate shocks (Chen et al., 2018[13]). In times of financial distress, EMDEs long-term and foreign currency denominated debt issuance often decreases due to the lack of investor demand and higher hard currency borrowing costs. Meanwhile, sovereigns turn to their domestic markets where they can borrow for shorter maturities from domestic investors. Following both the burst of the 2001 dot-com bubble and the 2008 Global Financial Crisis (GFC), the weighted average maturity for EMDEs' new debt issuance decreased by about two years, and the numbers suggest that a similar pattern is occurring in the aftermath of COVID-19 pandemic. Looking at the maturity structure of EMDEs (Figure 3.9), overall maturities have decreased both in 2020 and 2021, falling from 7.4 years in 2019 to 6.1 years in 2021. Nevertheless, this decline is much less pronounced on the average maturities of outstanding debt, suggesting that the rollover risk associated with shortened maturity of new debt issuance during the pandemic remained relatively constrained. At the regional level, average maturity decreased considerably across all regions with the exception of Sub-Saharan Africa, which lengthened its maturity from 7.1 years in 2019 to 8.7 years in 2021, becoming the region with the longest average maturity among EMDEs. Average term-to-maturity of debt issuance by the Latin America and the Caribbean (LAC) has remained the same in the review period. Despite the general outlook of the region, 10 out of 12 LAC sovereigns who issued debt in 2021 managed on average to borrow with maturities higher than five years.

In the Sub-Saharan Africa, a country specific breakdown shows that the average maturity of new debt issuance varied widely between issuers, notably some large issuers like Benin and Nigeria had 14.6 and 9.4 years of ATM respectively (partially due to the recent Social bond issuance by Benin and long-term borrowings in Nigeria for infrastructure investments) while countries like Mauritius and Zambia had average maturity around three years, which raises concerns about debt sustainability and rollover risks in the short-term. However, it is worth noting that many Sub-Saharan African sovereigns also benefit from official creditors' lending (such as World Bank, IMF and Development Banks) which is not included the data used for this report. Often given in foreign currency with long maturities, a decade or longer, official creditors' funding helps buttress financial resilience and debt sustainability in the region. In addition, several Sub-Saharan Africa countries who had maturity less than three years in 2020 improved their maturity profile significantly, notably Cameroon, Rwanda and Senegal increased their average maturity from less than six months to 11 years; from three years to ten years and from 2.9 years to 12 years respectively. This suggests that some non-investment grade countries who were shut out of the markets at the wake of the pandemic were able to borrow at longer maturities in 2021 amid improved risk sentiment in 2021 largely due to global monetary and fiscal policy response to the crisis.

Figure 3.10. Maturity composition of debt issuance by investment and non-investment grade categories in 2021

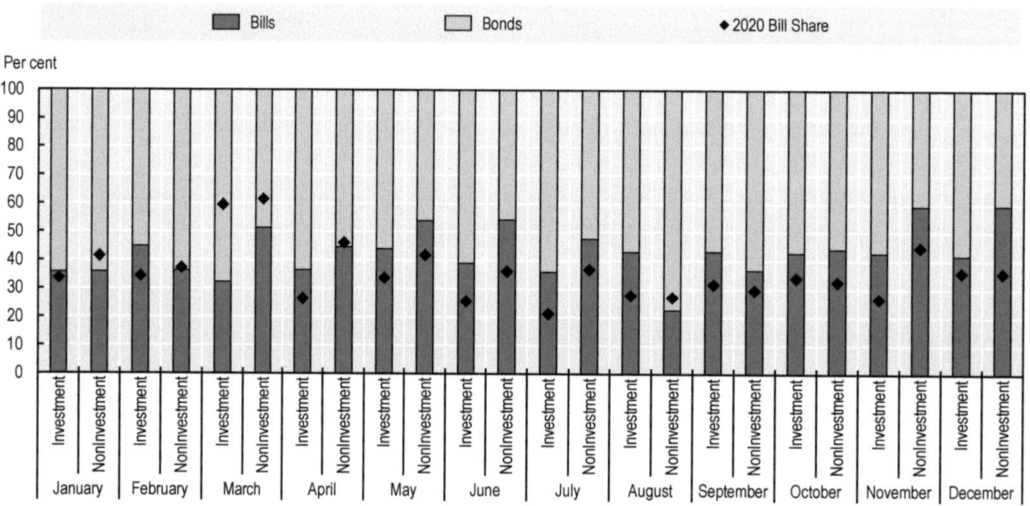

Source: OECD calculations based on data from Refinitiv.

In the wake of reduced investor risk sentiment and uncertainty about the future at the height of the pandemic, EMDE governments increased their T-Bill issuance as their long-term instruments faced less demand and became more costly.[10] In March 2020, at a time of acute market distress, the share of local-currency T-Bills surged dramatically (Figure 3.10), accounting for 61% of total issuance by non-investment grade and 59% for investment-grade categories. On average, T-Bills accounted for 33% and 39% for the investment and non-investment grade sovereigns in 2020 as the former were able to switch towards longer maturities in the months following the pandemic and benefit from favourable financial conditions, whereas non-investment grade issuers had to depend more heavily on shorter-term debt. In 2021, the share of T-Bill issuance constituted 40% of the total issuance of investment-grade issuers, lower than the 42% bill share issued by non-investment grade sovereigns (Figure 3.10). Monthly figures indicate that share of T-Bill issuance increased towards the end of 2021 for both investment- and non-investment grade issuers.

A total of 20 investment grade EMDE sovereigns issued more than USD 900 billion worth of T-Bills while 60 non-investment grade sovereigns issued USD 664 billion of bonds in 2021. It is important to note that the increase in the share of T-Bill issuance by investment-grade sovereigns has been mainly driven by China, which alone accounted for about 30% of the investment grade bill issuance in 2021, followed by India (20%) and Thailand (16%).

Given the reduced share of foreign investors in local bond markets, much of the pandemic-related debt was bought by local banks in EMDEs. For example, between 2019 and 2021, domestic bank holdings of government securities increased by more than 10% in Argentina, Chile, Egypt and Thailand (Arslanalp and Tsuda, 2014[14]). This highlights the importance of a resilient banking system in helping to absorb shocks, but at the same time raises concerns about the sovereign-bank nexus, particularly in jurisdictions where the government has a high level of debt. This suggests a need to develop deeper local markets to absorb medium to long-term local sovereign debt. This will help foster a broader domestic investor base that can mitigate the impact of outflows of foreign capital (Box 2.1).

3.5. Redemption profiles remain risky with high amounts of debt due in the next three years

The sharp increase in short-term borrowing associated with the COVID-19 pandemic has affected the redemption structure of debt, increasing the rollover risk for EMDEs. In 2020, higher financing needs and the decline in revenues resulted in increased borrowings by EMDEs with a considerable amount of new short-term debt being issued. Against this background, a considerable share of EMDE government debt will be repaid in the next three years. The amount of outstanding debt maturing by the end of 2024 constitutes 36% of debt held by EMDEs, 18% of which is due in the next year (Figure 3.11). The income category which has the lowest share of debt due in the next three years is Lower Middle-Income countries (LMIC). Nevertheless, the amount of debt to be rolled over by LMICs is still high, with nearly half of it being due in the next year. The LICs on the other hand, bear the highest rollover risk as 45% of the outstanding debt of these countries will need to be repaid or refinanced in the next three years. Given LICs' lower vaccination rollouts, weak macroeconomic fundamentals and already elevated debt levels, refinancing their short-term debt might be challenging for some countries, especially under less accommodative financial conditions. Despite their high rollover risk, there is also a slight improvement in the redemption profile of LICs in 2021, as both the share of outstanding debt maturing in the next year (19%) and the following two years (26%) have decreased in 2021, suggesting a slight improvement in the redemption profile and a reduction in the rollover risk relative to 2020.

Figure 3.11. Outstanding government debt due within the next three years

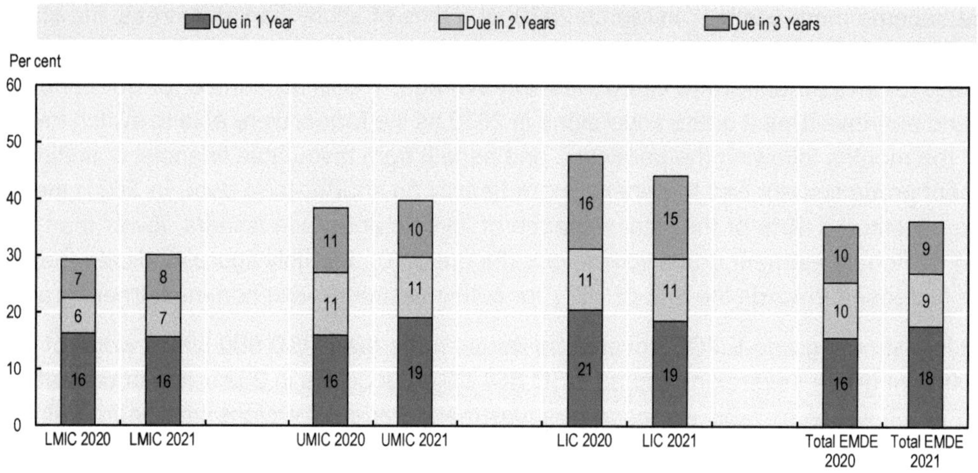

Source: OECD calculations based on data from Refinitiv.

3.6. The credit quality of EMDE sovereigns has continued to deteriorate in most regions after the record rating downgrades issued in the wake of the pandemic

Figure 3.12. Changes in EMDE sovereign credit ratings

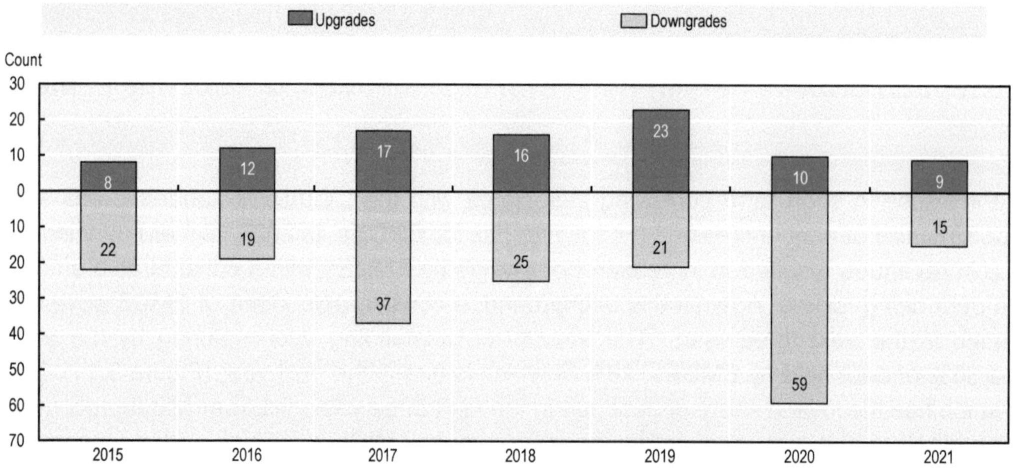

Source: OECD calculations based on data from Refinitiv.

Following the pandemic outbreak in March 2020, a record number of 59 downgrades were issued to EMDE sovereigns, reflecting a surge in the perceived risks associated with investing in EMDE debt (Figure 3.12). In 2020, a number of sovereigns including Lebanon, Oman, South Africa and Zambia were downgraded several times by different rating agencies as the macroeconomic outlook continued to worsen amid the pandemic. In particular, nine EMDE issuers (such as Bahamas, Cameroon and Gabon) who were classified as investment grade before the pandemic were downgraded to non-investment grade in 2020. This is particularly important for sovereigns that rely on foreign investors, as the inclusion of bonds in benchmark bond indices is mainly driven by credit ratings. It is worth noting that the majority of the downgrades in 2020, namely 44 out of 59, occurred in the non-investment category while only seven investment grade sovereigns (including Bulgaria, Chile, India and Mexico) were downgraded. In 2021, a considerably smaller number of EMDEs were downgraded. In total, 15 downgrades and nine upgrades were given to 9 and 8 countries respectively. In contrast with 2020, the majority (9 of 15) of downgrades were issued to investment grade category while only six out of 15 downgrades were issued to four non-investment grade countries. In addition, none of the countries were pushed towards non-investment grade rating in 2021. More than half of the downgrades in 2021 were given to Latin America and the Caribbean countries (8), followed by MENA (5); Sub-Saharan Africa (1) and Asia (1).

Figure 3.13. Evolution of credit quality for a selected group of EMDEs

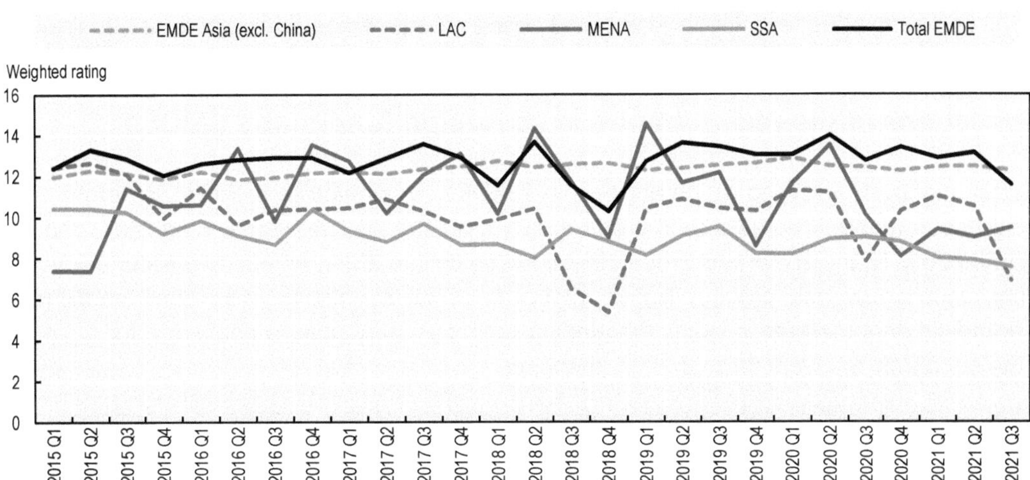

Note: Debt quality reflects the average rating of gross debt issuance at each quarter, it is not a measure for rating quality of outstanding debt. The value of 12 for the weighted rating constitutes a threshold for investment grade issuance (Annex 3.A.).
Source: OECD calculations based on data from Refinitiv.

Figure 3.13 shows the change of EMDE sovereign credit ratings weighted by their issue amounts between 2015 and 2021. Given the pandemic spurred a rating downgrade wave in EMDEs, a sharp decline in the weighted debt quality was observed in 2020, mainly driven by MENA and LAC regions. The decline was most pronounced in the second and third quarters as the majority of the downgrades occurred in March, April and May, which was reflected in the weighted debt quality in the following months, as downgraded sovereigns issued new debt. An exception to this trend was the Asia region, which received only seven out of 59 downgrades issued to EMDE sovereigns in 2020 and remained on average in the investment grade category during the pandemic.[11] In particular, 5 of these 7 downgrades were given to Sri Lanka, which explains the overall stable outlook of the region during the pandemic. All other regions, namely Latin America and the Caribbean, MENA and Sub-Saharan Africa, were below the investment grade rating throughout the pandemic. While MENA and Latin America and the Caribbean regions received 16 downgrades each (including Argentina, Chile, Lebanon, Mexico, and Oman), Sub-Saharan Africa countries were given 17 downgrades, the highest number issued to a region in 2020. In particular in Africa, the ten biggest issuers were rated below investment grade in 2021, with the exception of Mauritius. However, the weighted debt quality seems to have improved in Sub-Saharan Africa, increasing from 8.21 at the last quarter of 2019 to 9.02 (approximately from B+ to BB- or B1 to Ba3) in the third quarter of 2020. Given that no upgrades were given to Sub-Saharan Africa during this period, the reason for the increase observed in the debt quality of the region was mainly due to the change in the composition of issuers between quarters and their relative issue amounts. For instance, Gabon who had issued debt in the first quarter of 2020, did not issue any debt after being downgraded by Fitch on April 2020. Angola, who had been downgraded by all three rating agencies, also did not issue any debt throughout 2020, and therefore is not reflected in the debt quality of issuance in the region. Zambia, who received the highest number of downgrades given to a single country in Africa (six downgrades in total, three times each by Fitch and S&P), issued the least amount of debt in each quarter, which conceals the overall impact of the downgrades in the weighted debt quality of the region.

A similar story is also true for 2021, in the Latin America and the Caribbean region, where the improvement in debt quality is not mainly due to rating upgrades (only one upgrade was given to Ecuador in 2021) but rather due to large issuers' (such as Argentina and Mexico who were downgraded two and three times in 2020 respectively by three rating agencies) lower gross issuance in the first half of 2021 compared to previous two quarters. Overall, the rating quality of gross debt issuance has not recovered from the unprecedented number of downgrades given at the wake of the COVID-19 pandemic. Regions, which were hit hardest by downgrades in 2020, received only four upgrades in 2021, suggesting that negative implications of downgrades (e.g. higher borrowing costs) mostly remained in place for countries in 2021.

3.7. Implications of the recent trends in sovereign funding by EMDEs

This chapter highlights growing vulnerabilities in EMDEs, in particular in LICs, in terms of elevated refinancing needs and deteriorated debt credit quality over the last two years. Financial conditions have already tightened in financial markets around the world since late 2021, reflecting greater risk aversion and uncertainty, with higher risk premia. Tighter global financial conditions, weakened credit ratings and shallow domestic debt markets in many developing countries may pose a challenge for governments to support the economic recovery through debt financing.

Due to the surge in EMDE debt issuance since the onset of the pandemic, refinancing needs are significantly higher than pre-pandemic levels. While recovering from the pandemic gradually, fiscal policy space in many EMDEs is more limited after two years of COVID-19-related budgetary support. Yet, other factors may put pressure on sovereign borrowing needs in EMDEs. Given that the DSSI, which provided the most vulnerable countries some breathing space, has ended as of the end of 2021, the recipient countries of this programme may now turn to international capital markets for their funding needs. With increased refinancing needs and deteriorated credit ratings LICs are more vulnerable to risks stemming from changes in funding conditions. In particular, the depreciation of EM currencies may present challenges for the issuers that have substantial FX-denominated debt that needs to be repaid or refinanced in coming periods.

In addition to elevated refinancing needs, many EMDEs will require additional sovereign funding support due to the economic and financial fallout from the war in Ukraine. Already, the war has produced substantial downward revisions to global growth forecasts, and upward revisions to already rising inflation (OECD, 2022[2]).[12] Soaring energy prices can add significant inflationary pressures and worsen the current account balances of net energy importing EMDEs, including Chile, India, the Philippines and Turkey. In particular, the war will have substantial consequences for neighbouring countries that have close trade and payment-system links with Russia and Ukraine. In addition, governments may need to introduce fiscal measures such as raising well-targeted government subsidies to mitigate the economic impact of the crisis on consumers and businesses, which in turn would increase sovereign borrowing needs. On the other hand, higher commodity prices should bolster fiscal revenues in commodity-exporting countries, providing some leeway to cushion the shock of higher food and energy prices on household incomes.

Debt financing, through security and loan issuance, is especially critical for development in EMDEs. At the same time, unsustainable debt levels as well as poor debt management and transparency practices pose important challenges, in particular for LICs. For the less developed economies, sovereign lending is often characterised by widespread informational opacity that not only impedes access to funding and undermines investor confidence but also contributes to less-informed policy formulation and an increased risk of financial instability (The Bretton Woods Committee, 2022[15]). In this context, efforts were made to improve debt management capacity and transparency through international initiatives such as the World

Bank's strengthening of debt management capacity in low and middle income countries, and the OECD's Debt Transparency Initiative, which operationalises the Institute of International Finance's (IIF) Voluntary Principles on Debt Transparency are most welcome.

Looking forward, in view of global risk factors, the increasing financing needs of EMDEs may need to be met in less favourable conditions. The sovereign issuers that have access to market funding may benefit from lengthening debt maturities and build-up contingency buffers through pre-financing programmes. On the other hand, the sovereign issuers with weak macroeconomic fundamentals, heavy debt repayments and underdeveloped local currency bond markets can be significantly challenged by the trade-off between expected cost and risk involved short-term and long-term financing strategies. An increase in the interest rate of the borrowing would put additional interest burden on budgets, and the decrease in the borrowing maturity would worsen the sovereign refinancing risk. In this context, lending and other financial support such as grant facilities by the IFIs to these countries will be critical in terms of the sustainability of their debts and supporting their economies, as well as preventing them from turning to non-traditional sources of funding and use of opaque lending facilities.

References

Arslanalp, S. and T. Tsuda (2014), "Tracking Global Demand for Emerging Market Sovereign Debt", *IMF Working Paper*, Vol. No. 14/39, https://www.imf.org/en/Publications/WP/Issues/2016/12/31/Tracking-Global-Demand-for-Emerging-Market-Sovereign-Debt-41399. [15]

Arslan, Y., M. Drehmann and B. Hofmann (2020), *Central bank bond purchases in emerging market economies*, https://www.bis.org/publ/bisbull20.htm. [18]

Broner, F., G. Lorenzoni and S. Schmukler (2011), *Why Do Emerging Economies Borrow Short Term?*, https://crei.cat/wp-content/uploads/users/working-papers/why.pdf. [13]

Chen, S. et al. (2018), *Debt maturity and the use of short-term debt : evidence from sovereigns and firms*, International Monetary Fund, https://www.imf.org/en/Publications/Departmental-Papers-Policy-Papers/Issues/2019/02/04/Debt-Maturity-and-the-Use-of-Short-Term-Debt-Evidence-form-Sovereigns-and-Firms-46240. [14]

FitchRatings (2022), *Russia-Ukraine Conflict Raises Risks for Some Emerging Markets*, https://www.fitchratings.com/research/sovereigns/russia-ukraine-conflict-raises-risks-for-some-emerging-markets-07-03-2022. [3]

Fratto, C. et al. (2021), *Unconventional Monetary Policies in Emerging Markets and Frontier Countries*, IMF, https://www.elibrary.imf.org/view/journals/001/2021/014/001.2021.issue-014-en.xml. [9]

Gatti, R. et al. (2021), *Living with Debt: How Institutions Can Chart a Path to Recovery for the Middle East and North Africa*, https://openknowledge.worldbank.org/handle/10986/35275. [11]

IMF (2022), , https://www.imf.org/en/Topics/imf-and-covid19/COVID-Lending-Tracker. [17]

IMF (2021), *COVID-19, Crypto, and Climate: Navigating Challenging Transitions*, International Monetary Fund, https://www.imf.org/en/Publications/GFSR/Issues/2021/10/12/global-financial-stability-report-october-2021. [1]

IMF (2021), "Macroeconomic Developments and Prospects In Low-Income Countries", *IMF Policy Paper*, https://www.imf.org/en/Publications/Policy-Papers/Issues/2021/03/30/Macroeconomic-Developments-and-Prospects-In-Low-Income-Countries-2021-50312. [7]

IMF (2020), *Global Financial Stability Report: Bridge to Recovery*, International Monetary Fund, https://www.imf.org/en/Publications/GFSR/Issues/2020/10/13/global-financial-stability-report-october-2020. [10]

IMF (2015), "The Commodities Roller Coaster", *Fiscal Monitor*, https://www.imf.org/en/Publications/FM/Issues/2016/12/31/The-Commodities-Roller-Coaster#. [5]

Medas, P., V. Salins and J. Danforth (2016), "How to Adjust to a Large Fall in Commodity Prices", *IMF Fiscal Affairs Department Hot-to Notes*, https://www.imf.org/en/Publications/Fiscal-Affairs-Department-How-To-Notes/Issues/2016/12/31/How-to-Adjust-to-a-Large-Fall-in-Commodity-Prices-44231. [19]

OECD (2022), *OECD Economic Outlook, Interim Report March 2022: Economic and Social Impacts and Policy Implications of the War in Ukrain*, OECD publishing, https://doi.org/10.1787/4181d61b-en. [2]

OECD (2022), *OECD Sovereign Borrowing Outlook 2022*, OECD Publishing, Paris, https://doi.org/10.1787/b2d85ea7-en. [12]

OECD (2021), *OECD Economic Outlook, Volume 2021 Issue 2*, OECD Publishing, Paris, https://doi.org/10.1787/66c5ac2c-en. [6]

OECD (2020), *OECD Sovereign Borrowing Outlook 2020*, OECD Publishing, Paris, https://doi.org/10.1787/dc0b6ada-en. [20]

OECD (Forthcoming), "Latin American Economic Outlook 2022". [4]

OECD/AUC/ATAF (2021), "Revenue Statistics in Africa 2021", https://doi.org/10.1787/c511aa1e-en-fr. [22]

Sunel, E. and Y. Mimir (forthcoming), *Asset purchases as a remedy for the original sin redux*, OECD. [8]

The Bretton Woods Committee (2022), *Debt Transparency: The Essential Starting Point for Successful Reform*, https://www.brettonwoods.org/sites/default/files/documents/SDWG_Debt_Transparency_The_Essential_Starting_Point_for_Successful_Reform.pdf. [16]

World Bank (2021), *Global Economic Prospects*, The World Bank, https://doi.org/10.1596/978-1-4648-1612-3. [21]

Annex 3.A. Methods and sources

Primary sovereign bond market data and country groupings

The key source of information is a dataset comprising over 7 500 sovereign government securities issued by 95 EMDE sovereign issuers in 2021. Primary sovereign bond market data are based on original OECD calculations using data obtained from Refinitiv that provides international security-level data on new issues of sovereign bonds. The data set covers bonds issued by emerging market sovereigns in the period from 1 January 2015 to 15 December 2021 and includes both short-term and long-term debt. Short-term debt ("bills") is defined as any security with a maturity less than or equal to 365 days but no less than 30 days, as bill issuances with maturity less than 30 days are considered to be done for cash management purposes and excluded from calculations. The database provides a detailed set of information for each bond issue, including the proceeds, maturity date, interest rate and interest rate structure.

The definition of emerging markets used in this report is consistent with the IMF's classification of Emerging and Developing Economies used in its World Economic Outlook. The regional definitions are also those used by the IMF, while the income categories used (high income, low income, lower middle income, upper middle income) are defined by the World Bank according to GNI per capita levels.

A number of bonds have been subject to reopening. For these bonds the initial data only provide the total amount (original issuance plus reopening). To retrieve the issuance amount for such reopened bonds, specific data on the outstanding amount on each reopening date for the concerned bonds have been downloaded separately from Refinitiv. As the reopening data only provide amounts outstanding in order to obtain the issuance amount on each relevant date, the outstanding amount on the previous date is subtracted from the outstanding amount on that given date. These calculated issuance amounts are converted on the transaction date using USD foreign exchange data from Refinitiv. To ensure consistency and comparability, the same method is used for all bonds, including those which have not been subject to reopening.

Exchange offers and certain bonds in the dataset have been manually excluded when they did not have any identifier (ISIN, RIC or CUSIP) and when they have not been able to be manually confirmed by comparing with official government data.

The issuance amounts are presented in 2021 USD and adjusted by US CPI.

Credit ratings data

Refinitiv provides rating information from three leading rating agencies: S&P, Fitch and Moody's. For each country that has rating information in the dataset, a value of 1 to the lowest credit quality rating (C) and 21 to the highest credit quality rating (AAA for S&P and Fitch and Aaa for Moody's) is assigned. There are 11 non-investment grade categories: five from C (C to CCC+); and six from B (B- to BB+). The ratings data are observed on a monthly basis. If a country has received several ratings in one month, the lowest one is used, except when that is a default rating (SD or D for S&P; RD or DDD for Fitch and C or / for Moody's).

The rating in question is then assigned to each relevant bond issued by that country (as at issuance or transaction date). In the case that there are ratings available from several agencies, their average is used. When differentiating between investment and non-investment grade bonds, if the final rating is higher than or equal to 12 it is classified as investment grade. If the final rating is below 12 but higher than or equal to 11 and at least two agencies have given a rating higher than or equal to 12, it is also classified as investment grade. All other bonds are considered non-investment grade.

The weighted debt quality analysis uses the rating information from three rating agencies (S&P, Fitch and Moody's). Every gross debt issuance is then assigned a rating by each rating agency based on the date of transaction and the last rating the sovereign was given by that agency. Overall the average of these assigned ratings is used and weighted by their corresponding issuance amounts to calculate weighted monthly debt quality of each region.

ATM Calculation

Average term-to-maturity (ATM) figures presented in Figure 3.9 are calculated for each region by taking the maturity of each bond issuance within the region weighted by their issue amount.

YTM Calculation

Yield-to-Maturity calculations presented in Figure 3.8 are calculated using fixed-rate USD-denominated securities with maturity longer than 365 days. Comparison between EMDE yields between 2020 and 2021 is based on the same 35 EMDE sovereigns who issued fixed-rate USD denominated bonds in 2021 and their corresponding yields in 2020.

Notes

[1] The data used in Figure 3.1 includes debt security issuances in the financial markets by the EMDE sovereigns up to 15 December 2021.

[2] From May 2020 to December 2021, the DSSI initiative suspended USD 12.9 billion in debt-service payments owed by participating countries to their creditors, according to the Word Bank.

[3] IMF Commodity Price Index.

[4] Prior to the adoption of inflation targeting, emerging-market economy central banks occasionally monetised government debt (World Bank, 2021[20]). Several recent studies elaborate the latest objectives of central bank asset purchases in EMEs and discuss their announcement effects on government bond yields (Arslan, Drehmann and Hofmann, 2020[17]; IMF, 2020[9]; Fratto et al., 2021[8]).

[5] Up to date as of 9 March 2022 based on https://www.imf.org/en/Topics/imf-and-COVID-19/COVID-Lending-Tracker.

[6] OECD Revenue Statistics in Africa highlights that African governments have both increased their level of external government debt and seen an increase in borrowing costs. Between 2010 and 2019, among 26 Revenue Statistics in Africa countries, 19 registered an increase in their external government debt as a percentage of GDP as well as in the ratio of interest payments paid to debt stock. Over this period, the average ratio of debt interest payments to debt stock for these countries rose from 1.6% to 3.1% (OECD/AUC/ATAF, 2021[22]).

[7] For example, the share of fixed-rate USD denominated bond issuance with yield more than 5% picked up from 31% in 2020 to 69% in 2021.

[8] The Executive Board of the International Monetary Fund (IMF) approved on 25 March 2022, a 30-month extended arrangement for Argentina (equivalent to USD 44 billion) under the Extended Fund Facility (EFF).

[9] Fixed rate government bonds constituted nearly 90% of bonds issued in 2021.

[10] Securities that need to be repaid in 365 days or less but no less than 30 days are categorised as T-Bills.

[11] Investment grade category is considered having a grade higher than or equal to BBB- for Fitch and S&P, Baa3 for Moody's which is equivalent to 12 in Figure 3.13.

[12] OECD simulations suggests that the war in Ukraine will be a 1% negative shock to world in 2022 (OECD, 2022[2]).

Annex A. OECD 2021 Survey on Primary Markets Developments

This annex belongs to the OECD Sovereign Borrowing Outlook 2022.
Thirty-seven of the 38 OECD countries responded to this survey.
Countries which responded to the survey but did not provide comments to a question may not appear in the table of answers. The requested date for a response to the survey was 15 October 2021.
Source: 2021 Survey on Primary Markets Developments by the OECD Working Party on Debt Management.

Table of contents

Table A.1. Overview of issuing procedures 119
Table A.2. Q1 Overview of issuing procedures – country notes 119
Table A.3. Q1b Overview of recent changes in issuing procedures and techniques 121
Table A.4. Q2 Have you issued or plan to issue any new types of securities like inflation-linked bonds, variable rate notes, green bonds, and longer dated securities? 123
Table A.5. Q2 New type of instrument that was issued in the LAST 12 months 124
Table A.6. Q2 New type of instrument that will be issued in the NEXT 12 months 125
Table A.7. Q2 Other types of securities 126
Table A.8. Q3 Major challenges experienced over the last 12 months 127
Table A.9. Q3 Specified OTHER major challenges experienced over the last 12 months 128
Table A.10. Q3 Major challenges experienced over the last 12 months – Country notes 129
Table A.11. Q4 Major risk factors/events faced in the last 12 months 132
Table A.12. Major risk factors/events which might affect your operations in the next 12 months 134
Table A.13. Q4 Specified OTHER major risk factors/events that might affect the DMO operations in the next 12 months 136
Table A.14. Q4 major risk factors/events that your DMO faced last 12 months or might affect your operations in the next 12 months – Country notes 137
Table A.15. Q5 How do you manage these risks (e.g. contingency funding plans, continuity plan etc.)? 138
Table A.16. Q6 Do you consider potential risk factors when preparing your financing plan (e.g. auction calendar)? 141
Table A.17. Q7 How has the maturity structure of your 2021 issuances changed compared to 2020? 143
Table A.18. Q7 maturity structure of your 2021 issuances – country notes 144
Table A.19. Q8 Have you changed your funding strategies during 2021 compared to any original 2021 funding plan? 146
Table A.20. Q9 How have you adapted your funding strategies and operations in response to the pandemic in last 12 months? 147
Table A.21. Q9 How have you adapted your funding strategies and operations in response to the pandemic – Country notes 149
Table A.22. Q10 Have you observed any changes in investors behaviour in participating in auctions or/ Syndications (e.g. oversized orders)? 150
Table A.23. Q11 Do you have a liquidity buffer? 152
Table A.24. Q12 Please indicate areas of key lessons learned from the COVID-19 crisis. 154
Table A.25. Q13 Do you plan to review the long-term funding strategy as a consequence of increased debt levels following the COVID-19 pandemic? 155
Table A.26. Q14 Potential implications of the pandemic for future debt management 157
Table A.27. Q14 Specified OTHER implications of the pandemic for future debt management 159
Table A.28. Q14 Potential implications of the pandemic for future debt management – Country Notes 159
Table A.29. Q15 To what extent are you concerned about the adequacy of investor demand? 161
Table A.30. Q15 Please indicate situations or factors that give rise to concerns about future investor demand (e.g. changes in global liquidity conditions, regulations)? 162
Table A.31. Q16 Following the pandemic which operations do you now plan to carry out remotely (including at least partially) as standard that you did NOT do remotely prior to the pandemic? 163

Table A.1. Overview of issuing procedures

	Auctions		Auction type		Tap issues		Syndication
	Long-term	Short-term	Single-price	Multiple-price	Long-term	Short-term	
Australia	X	X		X	X		X
Austria	X	X	X	X	X	X	X
Belgium	X	X		X	X	X	X
Canada	X	X	X	X			X
Chile	X	X	X		X	X	X
Colombia	X	X	X		X		X
Costa Rica	X			X	X		
Czech Republic	X	X	X	X	X		
Denmark	X	X	X		X		X
Estonia		X		X			X
Finland	X	X	X		X	X	X
France	X	X		X	X	X	X
Germany	X	X		X	X	X	X
Greece		X	X		X		X
Hungary	X	X		X	X	X	X
Iceland	X	X	X				X
Ireland	X	X	X		X	X	X
Israel	X	X		X	X	X	
Italy	X	X	X	X	X	X	X
Japan	X	X	X	X			
Korea	X	X	X	X	X	X	
Latvia	X			X	X		X
Lithuania	X	X		X	X	X	
Luxembourg							X
Mexico (local market debt)	X	X	X	X	X	X	X
Mexico (external market debt)							X
Netherlands	X	X	X	X	X	X	
New Zealand	X	X		X	X		X
Norway	X	X	X				X
Poland	X	X	X	X	X	X	X
Portugal	X	X	X	X	X	X	X
Slovak Republic	X	X	X	X	X	X	X
Slovenia	X	X	X		X		X
Spain	X	X		X	X	X	X
Sweden	X	X		X		X	X
Switzerland	X	X	X		X		
Turkey	X	X		X			
United Kingdom	X	X	X	X	X	X	X
Total	**34**	**34**	**22**	**26**	**29**	**20**	**29**

Table A.2. Q1 Overview of issuing procedures – country notes

	Country notes
Australia	
Austria	In August 2021, Austria has started with regular auctions for Austrian Treasury Bills (ATBs). ATB auctions are single-price whereas Austrian government bond (RAGB) auctions are multiple-price. In general, syndications are used for new government bond issues only. Over the past years, Austria has successfully conducted parallel auctions (tap of two bonds at one auction) and dual-tranche syndications (syndicated issuance of two bonds at the same time).

	Country notes
Belgium	
Canada	Canada issues most of its domestic debt through multiple-price auction format. All nominal bonds and treasury bill auctions are multiple-price, whereas real return bonds (inflation-indexed bonds) and the ultra-long bonds are issued through a single-price auction format. In 2014, Canada initially issued its 50-year bond through a syndication format. As of August 2017, Canada now issues its ultra-long bond through a modified single-price auction format. Canada issues foreign currency global bonds through syndication, Medium Term Notes (MTNs) /Euro Medium Term Notes (EMTNs) on a reverse inquiry basis and operates a Commercial Paper program in USD.
Chile	
Colombia	Our local bonds are issued mainly through auctions and our external debt through a book building process with a syndication of banks. We also have loans with development banks and multilateral organizations as part of our funding sources. Our Global Bonds are issued by book building and are 10 years or longer.
Costa Rica	Ministry of Finance of Costa Rica conducts multiple-price auctions with allocation under the Dutch methodology. In 2018, the last and only syndication was carried out, known as "contratos de colocación".
Czech Republic	· Primary market (auction type) T-bonds: multi-price auction T-bills: single-price auction Secondary market operations (auction type) Tap-issues: single-price auction Exchange operations: single-price auction
Denmark	Syndication is used in relation to foreign issuance, i.e. EMTN issues.
Estonia	Estonia has no regular issuance calendar.
Finland	
France	Syndication mainly used for curve extension or new products
Germany	Traditionally, we issue and tap securities for long- and short-term borrowing via multi-price auctions. This year, two syndicates were carried out: adding a new 30-year maturity segment to the green segment (€ 6bn) refreshing the Bund curve with the a new 30-year benchmark (€ 5.5 bn)
Greece	
Hungary	After bond auctions there can be a non-competitive top-up tender, which is a single-price (average auction price) issuance. Some types of T-bills and bonds are sold via tap issuance or via subscriptions for retail investors. Syndication is used only for the issuance of foreign exchange bonds in the international markets.
Iceland	Single price format used for T-bills and T-bonds. Syndication is used for foreign debt borrowing
Ireland	
Israel	The majority of the issuing is by Tap.
Italy	The Italian Treasury makes use of two kinds of auction: - a competitive (multi-price) auction on a yield basis, for T-bills; - a marginal price (single-price) auction - where the auction price and the quantity issued are determined discretionally by the Treasury within a preannounced range of amounts in issuance - for all medium-long terms bonds (nominal fixed and floating rate bonds, and inflation indexed bonds). The Treasury normally makes use of syndication: - in case of issuance of new types of bonds (for instance, BTP€i in 2003 and CCTeu in 2010) or benchmarks in new segments of the nominal and European inflation curves (e.g.: 7-year BTP, 5-year BTP€i with a new coupon cycle); - in case of issuance of new nominal bonds with maturities above 10 years and new inflation linkers with maturities of 10 years or more. Starting from 2020 the Italian Treasury has started to make use of the syndicated placements even for the launch of new benchmark, both nominal and inflation-linked, with maturity equal or lower than 10 years. However, this may occur in exceptional circumstances, when the market conditions require since the beginning an efficient allocation among final investors and the achievement of a size that guarantees a good performance on the secondary market. As for the BTP Italia (linked to the Italian inflation) and starting from 2020 also for the BTP Futura (dedicated to retail investors), the Treasury makes use of a specific method of issuance, which allows for collecting purchase orders through the retail screen-based market for government bonds, the MOT platform of Borsa Italiana. A minimum coupon rate (for BTP Futura a set of annual minimum coupon rates) is announced the day before the starting of the issuance process, while the final coupon rate (for BTP Futura a set of annual coupon rates) is determined at the end of the placement period based on market conditions, whereas the issue price is fixed at par. For the BTP Italia the placement period is divided into a First Phase and a Second Phase. The First Phase is reserved to retail investors, while during the Second Phase all investors (including banks and other institutional investors) are allowed to participate. For the BTP Futura only retail investors are allowed to buy the bond during the placement period. Starting from April 2020 and consistently with what announced in the Update of the Guidelines for Public Debt Management for 2020, the Italian Treasury has introduced a new modality to issue one or more off-the-run securities through the electronic trading system ("TAP ISSUE"). These Tap reopening operations of off-the-run bonds are executed outside the auction calendar and are reserved to Specialists in Government Bonds. Moreover, the opportunity and type of bonds to be issued are evaluated according to specific demand requirements.
Japan	Price-competitive & multiple-price auction methods are used in Japan, except for the auctions for: 40-year bonds (yield-competitive & single-price auction), Inflation-indexed bonds (price-competitive & single-price auctions) and Liquidity Enhancement Auctions (yield-spread-competitive & multiple-price auctions). Also, reopening is conducted for JGBs except for T-Bills and 2-year bonds.
Korea	We introduced single-price auction type from March (originally planned to operate till September)
Latvia	The Answer is based on the actual funding program of 2021, when Latvia did not issue any short term securities. However if the question is about procedures available, then in terms of the short term debt - the same type of procedures would apply to it as to the long term debt.

	Country notes
Lithuania	The Government borrows by issuing both short– and long–term securities in the auctions and later tapping them. However, since 2015, due to market conditions (low interest rates) short-term securities were issued just once in April 2020.
Luxembourg	
Mexico (local market debt)	Local Market Debt The quarterly issuing calendar remains as one of the most important tools for the announcement of the future issuing plan as it details the issuing scheme for zero coupon bonds, nominal bonds, inflation-linked bonds and floaters. Regarding the bonds auction pricing, the floaters are currently the only type of bonds that use both auction types of pricing, single and multiple. Syndicated auctions, are only used when there is a new instrument to be issued and used in the quarterly calendars. Given the weekly frequency of auctions Tap Issues occur quite regularly.
Mexico (external market debt)	External Market Debt The process of Mexico's debt issuances in international financial markets is made through a syndication. The characteristics of any debt issuance will depend on market conditions and the specific objectives the Federal Government has at the time, that been said its very important to mention that Mexico has a large access to the USD dollar, the euro and the yen market which means that practically all the tenors are available for Mexico in those markets. Also, tap issues it's a very common tool the Federal Government uses in both the US dollar and the euro market.
Netherlands	
New Zealand	New bond lines are issued via syndication, whilst existing bond lines are generally issued by weekly tenders. Treasury Bills are issued via weekly tenders.
Norway	New bonds are introduced by syndication, while new Treasury bills are issued through uniform price auctions. Both bills and bonds are regularly reopened by auctions. Auctions are conducted via the Bloomberg Auction System. Only primary dealers are authorised to participate in the auctions. They are obliged to participate in every auction of bills and bonds. The issue amount and tenor are published two days prior to the auction.
Poland	Single price auction is used in T-bill and T-bond regular sale auctions as well as T-bond switching auctions. Multiple price model is used in buy-back auctions. There is a possibility of placing non-competitive bids on T-bond and T-bill sale and T-bond switching auctions. Primary Dealers, that purchased Treasury securities at the sale auction, have the right to purchase on the auction day additional Treasury securities at the minimum (stop) price set at the sale auction (additional sell). Syndication has been mainly used for Treasury securities issues on foreign markets.
Portugal	Syndications: T-Bonds only. Auction type: T-Bonds: Single Price T-Bills: Multiple Price *Tap issues correspond to reopening the series via auctions for both T-Bonds and T-Bills. T-Bonds can also be tapped via syndication or other formats, such as exchange offers.
Slovak Republic	Single price only for T-Bills, currently all other auctions with multiple price
Slovenia	Auctions apply for Treasury Bills only – Slovenia is not performing bond auctions. Syndication remains the exclusive issuance method for the government bonds. However, the auctions system and auction rules for the government bond auctions are in place.
Spain	The Spanish Treasury usually does the first issuance of longer-term bonds through syndications. Afterwards, these benchmark bonds are tapped through auctions, until they are "filled", with a size of approximately €20 bn. After a benchmark is filled, or it is no longer representative of its point on the curve, a new benchmark is issued. For shorter-term bonds and bills, only auctions are used, both for initial issuance and taps.
Sweden	Sweden issued a 50-year government bond in June 2021, via syndication procedure.
Switzerland	Almost all of our debt (bills as well as bonds, both new issues and reopenings) is issued under an auction system with a Dutch tender (the one exception are our "own tranches", see below). The reopening of already issued bonds (implemented by auction) is comparable with the auctioning of new bonds. To support market liquidity, we aim to have only one outstanding bond per year with a volume of around 4 billion CHF at maturity. Because of our limited financial needs and limited market demand, we do not auction the entire volume at once but reopen individual bonds several times over their entire lifetime until they reach our target volume. Between auction dates, the Federal Treasury sells so called "own tranches" from time to time to support market liquidity and cover extraordinary market demand. Own tranches are Government Bonds owned by the Confederation and can be sold on demand at market prices (own tranches are not yet placed/settled, the whole issuance process is completed except the sale to the investor à primary market transaction). Every time we auction a bond, we reserve own tranches of up to 300 million CHF of the issued bond (in addition to auctioned volume) if required. We consider the selling of own tranches as tap issues. Year to date we have sold own tranches of around 0.6 billion CHF (roughly 10 percent of total bond issuance) to bolster market liquidity. In the years before the pandemic we did not sell any own tranches due to limited financial needs.
Turkey	Domestic debt securities are issued mainly through auction (multiple-price auction system). On the other hand, sukuk (lease certificate) issuances in the domestic market are held by direct sale method.
United Kingdom	We hold single-price auctions for inflation-linked gilts and multiple-price auctions for nominal gilts.

Table A.3. Q1b Overview of recent changes in issuing procedures and techniques

Australia	The AOFM increased usage of syndications to achieve the required funding rate in 2020/2021
Austria	Austria introduced a new program for EUR Austrian Treasury Bills (ATBs) under Austrian law in July 2021. Under the new ATB programme there will be regular auctions - the first one was successfully held on the 24th of August 2021. The existing ATB programme, under English law, was renamed to ACP programme (Austrian Commercial Paper) in August 2021 for

	differentiation purposes and in order to be able to address future demand of short-term foreign currency issuances. The decision to create a second short-term funding programme was also made in order to increase Austria's financial flexibility and expand Austria´s investor base.
Belgium	No changes compared to 2020. What was new in 2020 and 2021 has been the use of loans under the EU SURE program as an additional source of funding.
Canada	Canada's current debt distribution framework has been in place since the late 1990s. There have been no notable changes to the issuing procedures. The MTN program was re-introduced in 2012. The EMTN program was re-introduced in 2013. In 2014, Canada initially issued its 50-year bond through a syndication format. As of August 2017, Canada now issues its ultra-long bond through a modified single-price auction format.
Chile	During a long time, the normal process to issue were the Dutch auction. In order to reach international investors and promote their participation, the book building process was implemented in 2017. Recently, due to the situation derived from COVID, the MoF decided to issue in shorter maturities, and thus T-bills have been recently issued.
Colombia	In 2021, the Government of Colombia issued the first Green Bond through auctions in the local bond market following the structure of twin bonds in the 10 year tenor.
Costa Rica	The Ministry of Finance of Costa Rica approved in April 2021 the standardized internal debt issuance plan of the Central Government, which defines the general guidelines for the issuance of internal debt. Likewise, since January 2019 the Ministry of Finance publishes a calendar of auctions to the market with information on the dates of the events, the deadlines, the currency, the trading platform, and auctions are held every 15 days, and also operations of management of liabilities such as debt swaps. For the month of February 2021, the Ministry of Finance approved and published the debt strategy of the Central Government.
Czech Republic	No recent changes.
Denmark	
Estonia	
Finland	
France	Slight adjustment in our auction calendar following the pandemic (additional auction in August)
Germany	
Greece	
Hungary	There has been no change.
Iceland	No changes since the last survey.
Ireland	In general our issuance techniques have not changed. However in 2021 we conducted more three-line auctions, and have also tapped more off-the-run bonds in response to PD requests for liquidity
Israel	The issuing procedures hasn't change recently.
Italy	There are no changes in issuing procedures and techniques occurred in the last 12 months.
Japan	Cap of the amount of a bid of the Non-Price Competitive Auction II (*1) was lowered from 15% to 10% of each participant's total successful bids in the competitive auction and Non-Price Competitive auction I (*2) from an auction in January 2020. Non-Price Competitive Auction II for the Inflation-Indexed Bonds has been canceled since April 2020. (*1) Non-Price Competitive Auction II is an auction carried out after the competitive auction is finished. The price offered is equal to the weighted average accepted price in the price-competitive auction or issuance price in Dutch-style competitive auction. Only the JGB Market Special Participants are eligible to bid in this auction. Each participant is allowed to bid up to the amount set based on the result of its bids during the preceding two quarters. (*2) Non-Price Competitive Auction I is an auction in which biddings are offered at the same time as for the price- competitive auction. The maximum issuance amount is set at 20% of the total planned issuance amount and the price offered is equal to the weighted average accepted price of the price- competitive auction. Only the JGB Market Special Participants are eligible to bid in this auction. Each participant is allowed to bid up to the amount set based on the result of its successful bids during the preceding two quarters.
Korea	
Latvia	No changes have taken place in the procedure or technics of issuing government securities. The only change that happened for local market was introduced in October 2020 introducing Eurobond TAPs (auctions of reopening outstanding XS Eurobonds under English law)
Lithuania	Issuing procedures and techniques haven't changed recently. With a slight exception that since September 2021, syndicated issues are also being re-opened in the auctions.
Luxembourg	None
Mexico (local market debt)	Local Market Debt Recently, the Mexico's Federal Government has made use the communicating vessels scheme for floaters, allowing us to identify and locate the investors demand and appetite; therefore, focusing our issuing plans on those particular nodes.
Mexico (external market debt)	External Market Debt No changes have taken place in the process of issuing debt in international financial markets.
Netherlands	No significant changes
New Zealand	In response to COVID-19, 2019/20 and 2020/21 issuance included tap syndications of existing bond lines to help to quickly issue increased volumes. Given the size of our forecast borrowing programmes, we do not intend to issue via tap syndication in the 2021/22 fiscal year.

Norway	The auction terms were changed in June 2021. Norges Bank will normally auction off the announced sales volume, but is not obliged to do so. In special situations where the total volume of accepted tenders is lower than the announced sales volume, Norges Bank may cancel the auction or issue a lower volume. Norges Bank has the right to reject tenders that are not submitted on market terms.
Poland	No changes in the current year.
Portugal	There were no relevant changes in the issuing procedures and techniques in the last 12 months. During this year, issuing procedures and techniques were standard: both via syndications and auctions.
Slovak Republic	No changes compared to 2020.
Slovenia	No changes recently.
Spain	We have carried out larger auctions due to the temporary increase in funding needs and carried out a few more syndications, but the overall strategy described in the previous paragraph has not changed. One small change made for our auctions was to carry out the second-round (greenshoe) at the marginal price of the auction, instead of the average weighted price. This was done to increase the attractiveness of our primary market issuance.
Sweden	
Switzerland	No recent changes
Turkey	No change.
United Kingdom	Auctions remain the primary issuance method along the maturity curve. In the 2021-22 financial year (which starts on 1 April 2021), the UK DMO has raised approximately £139bn (as at 5 October 2021); 79% of proceeds (approximately £110bn) have been raised via the auction programme and the post-auction option facility (PAOF), whilst the remaining 21% (£29bn) of proceeds have been raised via the syndication programme. In financial year 2020-21, (starting on 6 April 2020), in light of the expanded issuance programme necessitated by the UK government's response to the COVID-19 pandemic, the DMO adapted its auction schedule to include some days where two auctions are held on the same day. We have continued to allow for this approach in financial year 2021-22, although days on which two auctions are held have become less frequent due to the relatively smaller size of the financing programme this year. Two bidding windows were established for the two different auctions: from 9.00am to 10.00am for the first auction and from 10.30am to 11.30am for the second. The DMO also maintained the availability of the post auction option facility (PAOF) but the length of the window has been condensed. In the period prior to these changes, when only one auction was held on any day, auctions closed at 10:30am and the PAOF window was open from midday to 2pm on the same day as the auction. In order to ensure that we are able to offer the PAOF at both auctions where two are scheduled on the same day, the respective PAOF windows are open for a shorter period. In cases where there is a single auction on one day, the PAOF window operates from 12.30pm to 1.00pm. In cases where there are two auctions on one day, the PAOF windows operate from 12.30pm to 1.00pm for the first auction and from 2.00pm to 2.30pm for the second auction. On 21 September 2021, the UK launched via syndication its inaugural green gilt (0⅞% Green Gilt 2033). The transaction raised approximately £10bn (cash) and was the largest sovereign green bond issue to date. On 1 October 2021, the DMO announced its intention to launch a new green gilt maturing in 2053 via syndication, in the week commencing 18 October 2021, subject to demand and market conditions. Green gilt issuance is a key priority for the UK government to help finance projects that will tackle climate change and to finance infrastructure investment.

Table A.4. Q2 Have you issued or plan to issue any new types of securities like inflation-linked bonds, variable rate notes, green bonds, and longer dated securities?

	YES, new types of securities were/will be issued		NO new types of securities were/will be issued	
	Last 12 months	Next 12 months	Last 12 months	Next 12 months
Australia			X	X
Austria	X	X		
Belgium			X	X
Canada		X	X	
Chile	X			
Colombia	X			
Costa Rica		X	X	
Czech Republic			X	X
Denmark		X		
Estonia			X	X
Finland			X	X
France			X	X
Germany			X	
Greece		X	X	
Hungary	X	X		

	YES, new types of securities were/will be issued		NO new types of securities were/will be issued	
	Last 12 months	Next 12 months	Last 12 months	Next 12 months
Iceland			X	X
Ireland			X	
Israel			X	
Italy	X			X
Japan			X	X
Korea	X			
Latvia		X		
Lithuania			X	X
Luxembourg	X			X
Mexico (local market debt)		X	X	
Mexico (external market debt)	X	X		
Netherlands	X	X		
New Zealand	X			X
Norway			X	X
Poland			X	X
Portugal			X	X
Slovak Republic			X	X
Slovenia	X			X
Spain	X			X
Sweden	X			
Switzerland			X	X
Turkey			X	X
United Kingdom	X	X		
Total	**14**	**11**	**22**	**20**

Table A.5. Q2 New type of instrument that was issued in the LAST 12 months

	Inflation-linked bonds	Longer dated securities	Variable rate notes (such as floating rate notes)	Green bonds	Social Bonds	Sustainable bonds	Infrastructure bonds	Sukuk	Others
Australia									
Austria									X
Belgium		X		X					
Canada									
Chile						X			
Colombia				X					
Costa Rica									
Czech Republic	X		X						
Denmark									
Estonia									
Finland									
France									
Germany									
Greece		X							
Hungary		X		X					
Iceland									
Ireland									
Israel									

	Inflation-linked bonds	Longer dated securities	Variable rate notes (such as floating rate notes)	Green bonds	Social Bonds	Sustainable bonds	Infrastructure bonds	Sukuk	Others
Italy				X					
Japan									
Korea									X
Latvia									
Lithuania									
Luxembourg						X			
Mexico (local market debt)									
Mexico (external market debt)									X
Netherlands				X					
New Zealand		X							
Norway									
Poland									
Portugal									
Slovak Republic									
Slovenia		X				X			
Spain				X					
Sweden		X							
Switzerland									
Turkey									
United Kingdom				X					
Total	**1**	**6**	**1**	**7**	**0**	**3**	**0**	**0**	**3**

Note: Infrastructure bonds and Sukuk were also available as options to select but no country ticked either of these boxes.

Table A.6. Q2 New type of instrument that will be issued in the NEXT 12 months

	Inflation-linked bonds	Longer dated securities	Variable rate notes (such as floating rate notes)	Green bonds	Social Bonds	Sustainable bonds	Infrastructure bonds	Sukuk	Others
Australia									
Austria				X					
Belgium				X					
Canada				X					
Chile									
Colombia				X					
Costa Rica	X			X	X	X			
Czech Republic	X								
Denmark				X					
Estonia									
Finland									
France									
Germany									

	Inflation-linked bonds	Longer dated securities	Variable rate notes (such as floating rate notes)	Green bonds	Social Bonds	Sustainable bonds	Infrastructure bonds	Sukuk	Others
Greece		X		X	X				
Hungary									
Iceland									
Ireland									
Israel									
Italy									
Japan									
Korea									
Latvia						X			
Lithuania									
Luxembourg									
Mexico (local market debt)		X	X						X
Mexico (external market debt)									X
Netherlands				X					
New Zealand									
Norway									
Poland									
Portugal									
Slovak Republic									
Slovenia									
Spain									
Sweden									
Switzerland									
Turkey				X					
United Kingdom				X					
Ttal	2	2	1	10	2	2	0	0	2

Note: Infrastructure bonds was also available as an option to select but no country selected this.

Table A.7. Q2 Other types of securities

	Others issued in the LAST 12 months	Others issued in the NEXT 12 months
Australia		
Austria	Specify (i): Austrian Treasury Bills auction programme	
Belgium		
Canada		
Chile		
Colombia		
Costa Rica		
Czech Republic		
Denmark		
Estonia		
Finland		

	Others issued in the LAST 12 months	Others issued in the NEXT 12 months
France		
Germany		
Greece		
Hungary		
Iceland		
Ireland		
Israel		
Italy		
Japan		
Korea	Specify (i): shorter dated securities (2y)	
Latvia		
Lithuania		
Luxembourg		
Mexico (local market debt)		Specify (i): SDG aligned bonds
Mexico (external market debt)	Specify (i): SDG aligned bonds	Specify (i): SDG aligned bonds
Netherlands		
New Zealand		
Norway		
Poland		
Portugal		
Slovak Republic		
Slovenia		
Spain		
Sweden		
Switzerland		
Turkey		
United Kingdom		

Table A.8. Q3 Major challenges experienced over the last 12 months

	Changes in government's funding needs	Cash flow forecasting	Market volatility	Understanding investor behaviour	Operational challenges	Lack of investor demand	Communication with fiscal & monetary authorities	Communication with market participants	Others
Australia	X	X	X		X				
Austria	X	X							
Belgium		X							
Canada	X	X	X		X				
Chile	X	X	X			X			
Colombia		X	X						
Costa Rica				X					X
Czech Republic	X	X	X		X				
Denmark	X	X				X			
Estonia	X	X							
Finland	X	X							
France		X			X				
Germany	X								
Greece	X	X	X	X					

	Changes in government's funding needs	Cash flow forecasting	Market volatility	Understanding investor behaviour	Operational challenges	Lack of investor demand	Communication with fiscal & monetary authorities	Communication with market participants	Others
Hungary	X		X	X					
Iceland	X	X	X				X		
Ireland	X	X	X						
Israel	X	X	X	X	X				
Italy	X	X	X	X					
Japan									
Korea	X		X					X	
Latvia	X	X	X						X
Lithuania	X			X		X			
Luxembourg	X				X				
Mexico (local market debt)			X	X		X			4
Mexico (external market debt)	X		X						
Netherlands	X	X			X				
New Zealand	X	X	X						
Norway						X			
Poland	X	X	X		X		X		
Portugal	X	X	X						
Slovak Republic	X	X	X	X					X
Slovenia	X		X						
Spain	X				X				
Sweden	X	X							
Switzerland	X	X		X	X		X	X	
Turkey	X	X	X		X	X			X
United Kingdom	X	X	X		X				
Total	**31**	**26**	**22**	**9**	**12**	**6**	**3**	**2**	**8**

Table A.9. Q3 Specified OTHER major challenges experienced over the last 12 months

Australia	
Austria	
Belgium	
Canada	
Chile	
Colombia	
Costa Rica	(i) please specify: Lack of demand for issues in foreign currency: US dollars and variable rate.
Czech Republic	
Denmark	
Estonia	
Finland	
France	
Germany	
Greece	
Hungary	
Iceland	
Ireland	
Israel	
Italy	
Japan	

Korea	
Latvia	(i) please specify: Monetary policy changes, announcements, decisions
Lithuania	
Luxembourg	
Mexico (local market debt)	(i) inflation dynamics, (ii) monetary policy adjustments, (iii) capital outflows, and (iv) short-term refinancing needs
Mexico (external market debt)	
Netherlands	
New Zealand	
Norway	
Poland	
Portugal	
Slovak Republic	(i) please specify: Act on Fiscal Responsibility (Debt Brake)
Slovenia	
Spain	
Sweden	
Switzerland	
Turkey	(i) please specify: Pandemic
United Kingdom	

Table A.10. Q3 Major challenges experienced over the last 12 months – Country notes

Australia	
Austria	The major challenge remains cash flow forecasting and to manage the changes with regards to Austria's funding needs as budgetary developments around COVID-19 remain volatile.
Belgium	The overall funding needs are turning out to be very close to initial estimates. Detailed cashflow forecasting has remained challenging in a year where the economy and fiscal revenue improved drastically, but costs linked to the pandemic remained very high.
Canada	The Government of Canada has decreased its planned gross issuance by $81 billion compared to last fiscal year, from $593 billion (FY2020-21) to $512 billion (FY2021-22). Similar bond auction sizes in the long end of the curve and decreased bond auction sizes in the medium to short-term bonds have amounted to $286 billion for the gross bond issuance, down by $88 billion compared to $374 billion (FY2020-21). A significant proportion of extraordinary borrowings to date in 2021-22 has consisted of short-term instruments, mainly treasury bills as the "shock absorbers", given the ability to issue these instruments in volume quickly to raise needed funding. By the end of the fiscal year, the treasury bill stock is expected to be $226 billion, about $7 billion higher than the level at the end of 2020-21. The Bank of Canada has also launched several measures and facilities to support well-functioning markets, including increasing the amount of Government of Canada securities it purchases at treasury bill auctions and bonds in secondary markets. These facilities have been very important in maintaining well-functioning markets in Canada. Canada is taking a prudent approach to financing the deficit by adding a third objective to its debt management strategy to significantly increase long-term bonds to lock in funding at historically low interest rates. This will ensure Canada's debt remains affordable and sustainable for future generations and less vulnerable to increases in interest rates.
Chile	
Colombia	
Costa Rica	
Czech Republic	Czech Republic faces monetary policy interest rate hikes by central bank (Czech National Bank). Czech National Bank increased 2W repo rate from 0.25% to current 1.50% in three steps in 2021 and additional hikes are expected. This environment strongly influences government bond yields, which are increasing since the beginning of 2021, with negative impact to state debt service. Short end of the yield curve is more sensitive to monetary policy interest rate hikes, while yields on the long end of the yield curve are increasing with the lower pace resulting in flat yield curve of government bonds in this time. Czech Republic is taking steps to inclusion of the Czech government bonds denominated in EUR and issued on domestic market under Czech law among the eligible assets under Eurosystem credit operations (ECB eligibility). Relatively time consuming process due to ECB additional assessment procedure of the CSD Prague to the CSDR regulation.
Denmark	Uncertainty related to the government's funding needs has been higher than usual.
Estonia	
Finland	
France	

Germany	We did not perceive any major risk factors/events affecting our primary market operations. In year 2 of the COVID-19 pandemic the adjusted funding strategy and new communication formats are already in place and are working properly / are well received in the market
Greece	
Hungary	
Iceland	
Ireland	Markets continued to face volatility as the Covid-19 pandemic evolved and financing forecasts needed to change throughout the year as needs changed.
Israel	
Italy	Please refer to the answer to the point 4.
Japan	
Korea	
Latvia	
Lithuania	
Luxembourg	
Mexico (local market debt)	Local Market Debt The greater challenges for the local debt market in the last 12 months have been the foreign capital outflows for 200 billion pesos (~10 bn USD), the local and global inflation growing adjustment, and the uncertainty of the central bank monetary policy decisions, which increases the complexity of issuing. Particularly, the central bank monetary policy decisions have been crucial in the development of local debt market curves. Due to their inflation evolution perspectives and the Central Bank's monetary policy decisions in the current year (some of them surprising participants), participants are more cautious, therefore making careful movements in their positions.
Mexico (external market debt)	External Market Debt Most of this volatility was related to the hike seen in the US references rates through the first quarter 2021 (the 10-year rate increased 83 basis points from January 1st to March 31st while the 30-year rate increased 81 basis points from January 1st to March 18th). However it's very important to mention that despite of all this volatility Mexico's market risk perception (measured by the spread between the US 10-year rate and Mexico's 10-year US dollar denominated bond) has maintained stable; currently this measure it's at a level of 143 basis points, which means an increase of only 3 basis points on a YTD basis. Given that the local market faced several disruptions given the circumstances derived from the pandemic, the Federal Government intended to satisfy its needs with external market financing.
Netherlands	
New Zealand	
Norway	Lack of investor demand led to a very poor auction result in early June 2021. Consequently, we changed to auction terms allowing us in special situations to allot a lower volume than the pre-announced sales volume.
Poland	
Portugal	
Slovak Republic	Issuance plans of Slovakia must be in line with prudent Act on Fiscal Responsibility (Debt Brake).
Slovenia	Due to the COVID-19 crisis the government's funding needs increased significantly. Besides, the pandemic development is difficult to predict which requires higher attentiveness in debt management.
Spain	Operational challenges: It's worth highlighting that we were subject to an extreme weather event (Filomena storm), which made it impossible to reach the location where auctions are usually carried out. The pandemic also posed operational issues, having to work from home for many operations that were normally done in-person. All this has tested our procedures and proven that we can indeed carry out our issuance with great success (both through auctions and syndications) both remotely and in-person, even in the most difficult of circumstances. Changes in government's funding needs: This was especially relevant in 2020, where the government's needs varied drastically from initial projections. In 2021 a conservative estimate was put forth, due to the uncertainty brought about by the pandemic, which was later revised downward.
Sweden	
Switzerland	The funding needs of the Swiss government changed throughout the year due to the unpredictable nature of the pandemic. The pandemic and its impact on the funding needs were – and still are – linked to great uncertainty (e.g. what and when the government will decide; how the economy will respond; whether the government can meet its higher financing needs without negative effects on its financing conditions; how increased government funding needs will affect the financing conditions of other market participants). This led to challenges in cash flow forecasting and in the communication with fiscal and monetary authorities on the one hand and in the communication with the markets on the other. The communication with market participants was especially challenging as the funding needs of the government changed throughout the year. In order to achieve the Federal Treasury's goal of maintaining a constant and reliable market presence, a trade-off had to be found between transparency and maintaining the necessary flexibility to adjust the funding plan. At the end of the first quarter, the expected government expenditures for the year 2021 increased sharply due to the second wave of the pandemic and the corresponding countermeasures to soften the economic impact. For this reason, the Treasury significantly increased its issuance target. After the summer, it became clear that the financing needs of the government would be smaller than previously thought (lower expenditures, higher tax

	revenues). Therefore, the Treasury had to lower its issuance target.
Turkey	
United Kingdom	There have been some unusually large revisions to the DMO's financing requirement, including large increases in financing in the period due to the government's response to the COVID-19 pandemic, as well as an unusually large reduction in April 2021 as the government's cash needs decline from the peak level seen in 2020. In the context of challenging conditions in the sterling money markets, the DMO has also worked closely with HM Treasury and the Bank of England to identify ways in which the DMO's cash management responsibilities can be further supported.

Table A.11. Q4 Major risk factors/events faced in the last 12 months

	COVID-19 pandemic's risks on a global basis	COVID-19 pandemic's risk on a national basis	Global financial risks	Local financial risks	Political risks	Changes in the government's borrowing needs	Materialization of contingent liabilities including state guarantees	Liquidity risk	Revisions to the financial regulations	Operational risks	Cyber risk
Australia	X	X				X		X		X	
Austria	X	X				X					
Belgium	X	X								X	X
Canada		X	X			X				X	
Chile	X	X				X					
Colombia	X	X	X					X		X	
Costa Rica	X	X									
Czech Republic	X	X			X	X				X	
Denmark	X	X				X					
Estonia		X				X					
Finland	X	X				X					
France	X	X									
Germany		X				X					
Greece	X	X	X	X		X					
Hungary	X	X	X			X		X			
Iceland	X	X				X		X			
Ireland	X	X				X					
Israel	X	X	X	X	X	X		X			
Italy	X	X	X		X	X					
Japan		X				X				X	
Korea	X	X	X			X					
Latvia	X	X	X			X					
Lithuania	X	X			X	X				X	
Luxembourg		X				X	X	X		X	
Mexico (local market debt)	X	X	X	X	X	X		X			

	COVID-19 pandemic's risks on a global basis	COVID-19 pandemic's risk on a national basis	Global financial risks	Local financial risks	Political risks	Changes in the government's borrowing needs	Materialization of contingent liabilities including state guarantees	Liquidity risk	Revisions to the financial regulations	Operational risks	Cyber risk
Mexico (external market debt)	X	X	X	X	X	X		X			
Netherlands	X	X				X				X	
New Zealand	X	X			X	X					
Norway	X		X			X					
Poland	X	X	X			X				X	
Portugal	X	X	X			X					
Slovak Republic	X	X	X		X	X			X		
Slovenia	X	X				X					
Spain	X	X				X				X	
Sweden	X	X	X			X					
Switzerland	X	X				X	X	X		X	
Turkey	X	X						X		X	
United Kingdom	X	X	X			X				X	
Total	**33**	**37**	**16**	**4**	**8**	**33**	**2**	**10**	**1**	**14**	**1**

Table A.12. Major risk factors/events which might affect your operations in the next 12 months

	COVID-19 pandemic's risks on a global basis	COVID-19 pandemic's risk on a national basis	Global financial risks	Local financial risks	Political risks	Changes in the government's borrowing needs	Materialization of contingent liabilities including state guarantees	Liquidity risk	Revisions to the financial regulations	Operational risks	Cyber risk
Australia	X	X				X				X	X
Austria		X	X			X					
Belgium	X	X	X							X	X
Canada		X	X			X				X	
Chile											
Colombia			X		X					X	
Costa Rica			X		X	X					
Czech Republic	X	X	X			X				X	
Denmark											
Estonia		X				X					
Finland			X			X					
France	X	X	X		X						
Germany			X			X					
Greece	X	X	X	X		X	X	X			
Hungary	X	X	X		X	X		X			
Iceland	X	X				X		X			
Ireland	X	X	X		X						
Israel	X	X	X	X	X	X					
Italy	X	X	X		X	X					
Japan		X				X				X	
Korea	X	X	X		X	X			X		
Latvia	X	X	X		X	X					
Lithuania	X	X			X	X				X	
Luxembourg											
Mexico (local market debt)	X	X	X	X		X		X			

	COVID-19 pandemic's risks on a global basis	COVID-19 pandemic's risk on a national basis	Global financial risks	Local financial risks	Political risks	Changes in the government's borrowing needs	Materialization of contingent liabilities including state guarantees	Liquidity risk	Revisions to the financial regulations	Operational risks	Cyber risk
Mexico (external market debt)	X	X	X	X		X		X			
Netherlands	X	X	X			X				X	X
New Zealand	X	X				X					X
Norway			X								
Poland	X	X	X			X				X	
Portugal	X	X	X			X					
Slovak Republic	X	X	X		X	X			X		
Slovenia	X	X	X		X						
Spain	X										
Sweden	X	X	X		X	X	X				X
Switzerland	X	X	X			X	X	X		X	
Turkey	X	X				X		X		X	
United Kingdom	X	X	X			X				X	

Table A.13. Q4 Specified OTHER major risk factors/events that might affect the DMO operations in the next 12 months

Australia	
Austria	
Belgium	
Canada	
Chile	Specify (i):
Colombia	
Costa Rica	
Czech Republic	
Denmark	
Estonia	
Finland	
France	
Germany	
Greece	
Hungary	
Iceland	
Ireland	
Israel	
Italy	
Japan	
Korea	
Latvia	
Lithuania	
Luxembourg	
Mexico (local market debt)	Specify (i): inflation convergence, (ii) monetary normalization
Mexico (external market debt)	Specify (i): inflation convergence, (ii) monetary normalization
Netherlands	
New Zealand	
Norway	
Poland	
Portugal	
Slovak Republic	
Slovenia	
Spain	
Sweden	
Switzerland	
Turkey	
United Kingdom	

Table A.14. Q4 major risk factors/events that your DMO faced last 12 months or might affect your operations in the next 12 months – Country notes

Australia	
Austria	
Belgium	The main uncertainties remain linked to the further evolution of the pandemic. If the current economic expansion continues and the pandemic remains under control, monetary policies and inflation expectations may indeed change which could lead to higher borrowing costs. Throughout the pandemic, the change in the work situation has been a very important new element but the setup with still a lot of work from home continues to function well. Staffing can become more challenging in a rapidly improving economic context. Cyber risks remain a point of attention.
Canada	COVID-19 has caused a significant disruption in the Canadian economy. Real GDP fell by a record 13 per cent over the first half of 2020. Activity in Canada declined about three times as much as in the 2008-09 recession, in a much shorter time. The average of private sector economic forecasts released as part of the Budget 2021 expect the real GDP to rebound from a contraction of 5.4 per cent in 2020 to growth of 5.8 per cent in 2021 and 4 per cent in 2022, a faster recovery than the growth rates of, respectively, 4.8 per cent and 3.2 per cent projected in the November 2020 Fall Economic Statement. Based on the Fiscal Projections in the Budget 2021, a budgetary deficit of $121.2 billion is expected for 2021-22 (6.4 per cent of GDP versus 16.1 per cent of GDP in 2020-21). While this year's deficit estimate is still high compared to historical levels, it is in line with the fiscal response to the COVID-19 pandemic deployed by Canada's peer countries and was necessary to avoid a more significant economic impact and prolonged economic and fiscal challenges. A fourth or fifth wave of COVID-19 could cause further changes to the Government of Canada's borrowing needs if additional response is needed to support the Canadian economy and individuals as was the case with the previous waves of COVID-19.
Chile	Uncertainty derived from the pension system, and the consequences that it could have on the investor demand
Colombia	
Costa Rica	
Czech Republic	
Denmark	
Estonia	
Finland	
France	In the next 12 months, the main risk we foresee would be a more rapid than anticipated normalization of ECB monetary policy (even if unlikely). Resurgence of the pandemic whether at national or international level remains a risk.
Germany	
Greece	
Hungary	
Iceland	
Ireland	Impact of the Covid-19 pandemic
Israel	
Italy	Despite 2021 has been marked by a strong recovery of economic activity, the evolution of the COVID-19 pandemic has continued to represent a risk factor. Moreover, the uncertainties regarding the trend of inflation and the attitude of central banks in the coming months, have led to an increase in volatility on all securities markets, including of course the government segment, especially in the second half of the year. On the other hand, the maintenance of the Central Banks' purchase programmes (APP and PEPP) contributed to the consolidation of a constructive climate in financial markets. At a national level, the completion of the SURE programme and the launch of the Next Generation EU programme together with the stability of the national political framework, the strong growth of Gross Domestic Product for the current year and the good prospects for next year – which, among other things, have made it possible to anticipate the decline in the debt/GDP ratio -, have contributed decisively to maintaining low levels of volatility and to limit the increase of yield curve for Italian government securities.
Japan	
Korea	
Latvia	
Lithuania	
Luxembourg	
Mexico (local market debt)	The response to this question is not split into local and external debt.
Mexico (external market debt)	The response to this question is not split into local and external debt.
Netherlands	
New Zealand	
Norway	Norwegian interest rates are highly correlated with foreign interest rates. Sudden international events related to monetary

	policy as well as asset purchasing programs can therefore affect the demand for Norwegian government bonds significantly.
Poland	
Portugal	
Slovak Republic	
Slovenia	
Spain	Given the high vaccination rate in Spain, we do not expect significant Covid-19 risks on a national level for Spain in the next 12 months. However, if other countries suffer problems in the next 12 months, this could affect Spain's economy, and therefore our role as a DMO.
Sweden	
Switzerland	The risks over the next 12 months will mainly be the same as the risks that arose during the pandemic and were relevant in 2020 and 2021. In addition to the challenges described in question 3 (e.g. higher funding needs, operational challenges, uncertainty), there is still a risk that a prolonged pandemic could lead to mass defaults in the corporate sector which in turn could trigger a financial crisis. This could lead to the materialization of contingent liabilities and further fiscal policy measures and therefore lead to an even higher need for government borrowing. Ultimately, this could lead to a liquidity risk, if the cash buffer of the Treasury were to be depleted. Because Switzerland is a small and open economy, developments abroad also play a major role. At present, there are no indicators that predict this chain of events and the risk gets less likely as the pandemic gets under control. Nevertheless, it is important to monitor signs of these risks and to react quickly if they should materialize (e.g. by keeping a sufficient liquidity buffer).
Turkey	
United Kingdom	The DMO is mindful of the impact that the COVID-19 pandemic may still have both in terms of how the size of the financing requirement may evolve over the next year and how this will affect the design and implementation of the financing programme. The DMO's Exchequer cash management responsibilities may also be impacted given uncertainties over the borrowing profile in the next year in a context where there are known challenges in the period ahead (e.g. large gilt redemptions).

Table A.15. Q5 How do you manage these risks (e.g. contingency funding plans, continuity plan etc.)?

Australia	The AOFM's usage of short-term financing continues to significantly be higher than pre-2020 levels.
Austria	The Republic of Austria mitigates funding risks with its diversity of funding sources and instruments as well as financial flexibility due to its scarcity. We also try to spread issuances over the year in order to minimize concentration risk and diversify interest rate risk.
Belgium	We have business continuity plans that are regularly reviewed and updated. In terms of funding there is a close follow-up of fiscal revenue and spending in order to gauge the outcome of overall funding needs. Throughout 2021, because of large funding transactions early in the year (including SURE loans), we have held larger cash positions than usual.
Canada	· The Government of Canada employs an open and collaborative approach for its debt management function. Actions such as publishing market notices, which act as information communiques containing operational details, and/or new program announcements, have been effective. Senior government officials have also effectively communicated changes in funding needs and information on programs and operations during public appearances/speeches. This approach has helped to ensure the well-functioning of the Government of Canada markets and favorable conditions for market liquidity in both the primary and secondary Government of Canada securities markets. In addition, new programs and changes to existing programs that have been announced by the Government to support key financial markets to ensure that they continue to function properly have been well received by market participants and primary dealers (PDs). Given the government's unprecedented borrowing requirements due to COVID-19, Government officials have also communicated directly to PDs in order to reinforce PDs significant role in Government of Canada Debt Distribution Framework (DDF) in helping to manage the huge increase in Government issuance and providing secondary market liquidity to the GoC market. Being open and transparent in the communication strategy with PDs has also been an effective approach to motivating dealers to provide liquidity to the market and to support primary market issuance. The following are three examples of Canada's transparency in communication with financial market participants: Publication of the quarterly bond schedule prior to the start of each quarter in advance of auctions Publishing details for each operation in a call for tender a week prior to the auction Regular consultations with market participants: The Government of Canada and the Bank of Canada seek the views of government securities distributors, institutional investors, and other interested parties on issues related to how the Government of Canada securities market is performing and views for the design and operations of the domestic debt program.
Chile	There is still a strong space in the external market, as well as a capacity of the local market to absorb short-term instruments. When the local appetite reduced, the DMO increased the issuances in the external markets and reduced the tenor of LC issuances (up to 10 years). When the appetite for long maturities reduced, the DMO decided to issue more T- Bills.
Colombia	Though manuals and procedures when applicable.
Costa Rica	The indicated risks are managed by defining an annual financing plan or strategy, with access to external financing (loans and Eurobonds issuance), in addition by prefunding the Government's cash flow and by adopting spending containment measures. and fiscal rule.

Czech Republic	Risks arising from domestic or global financial markets are managed operatively by flexible debt issuance strategy, which is published for following year and updated in the mid-term (quarterly in extraordinary cases). Additionally, the decisions related to gross issuance are discussed and approved by the Ministry of Finance management every quarter. Ministry of Finance also keeps sufficient liquidity buffer within single treasury accounts and forecasts future state debt service expenditure on high percentile.
Denmark	Increased government funding demand and increased uncertainty concerning government finances was mitigated by expanding the funding base to foreign issuance, both CPs and EMTN
Estonia	In order to mitigate the risk of changes in government's borrowing needs, a minimum liquidity requirement was introduced and committed credit facilities with the main local partner banks were established already in 2011. The minimum required level of the liquidity position equals the State's six-month negative net cash flow comprising: transactional requirements, meaning the excess of budgeted monthly outgoings over budgeted revenue (also taking into account entities such as the Health Insurance Fund and the Unemployment Insurance Fund whose cash management is consolidated with central government), including debt and interest payments during the next one-month period, and precautionary requirements, representing an estimate of the deterioration in budgeted tax revenues over the following six months in the event of an economic downturn of the severity experienced in 2009 and a provision for liabilities from guarantees given by the State that are expected to crystallise in the following six months. The actual liquidity position is calculated as (a) the Liquidity Reserve (deposits with maximum three months maturity, current accounts and bonds, liquid and high-grade) plus (b) undrawn amounts from facilities committed for at least the following three months (by banks). These facilities also serve to mitigate operational risks and to ensure that unexpected large outgoing payments can be made without having to liquidate investments. Borrowing strategy document was introduced in 2020 and is updated regularly.
Finland	For operational risk process guidelines and checkpoints. There are also contingency and continuity plans.
France	Cash buffer and flexibility on the short term funding programme.
Germany	Our issuance planning and market entrance allows for adjustments during the year. Short-term changes can, amongst others, be addressed by our bill instruments.
Greece	
Hungary	Flexible issuance plan, contingency plans, communication with market participants, prefinancing.
Iceland	Our auction program will have to be adapted to higher funding needs of the government due to consequences of the pandemic. The issuance plan has to be more flexible, more series will be issued and the maximum size of each series has been increased.
Ireland	Large cash balance in place, plan issuance schedule around known events
Israel	Our funding plans include several scenarios, and for each scenario we carefully built a detailed plan of action and several contingency plans.
Italy	The Italian Treasury funding plan is inspired by the principles of transparency and predictability. In order to handle possible risks deriving from a national and international geopolitical scenario, the funding strategy is oriented toward managing interest-rate and refinancing risks, so as to continue to keep exposure to such risks under control. Moreover, the Italian treasury has focused its debt management policy in increasing the average life of the debt to mitigate the risk of refinancing by diluting over time the volumes to place on the market and to decrease the issuer's exposure to sudden increases in interest rates. However, the above-mentioned factors are characterized by a level of uncertainty which makes difficult to predict their evolution over time. Therefore, the Treasury funding strategy keeps a sufficient degree of flexibility in order to quickly response and adapt its funding plan to the evolution of the market context, as occurred during the Covid-19 crisis.
Japan	In the case of rapid changes in fiscal demands, we will adjust the amount of front-loading Refunding Bonds in order to mitigate additional impacts on the JGB market. Also, we will deal with a decline in market liquidity through Liquidity Enhancement Auction, an additional issuance of off-the-run bonds.
Korea	Contingency plan
Latvia	We use pre-funding approach, maintaining liquidity buffer, to keep flexibility in context of issuance timing, terms and conditions, etc. We regularly review and update the total funding requirement and adjust the borrowing activities if necessary
Lithuania	When redeeming major (equivalent to EUR 1 billion and above) Eurobond issues, the risks are mitigated by allocating the required funds in advance. Also we can use the reserve (stabilization) fund for the debt redemptions. The taken amount must be returned to the fund within few years. Thus, we have high cash buffers or liquidity cushions, actively seek to reduce operational risk.
Luxembourg	contingency funding plans
Mexico (local market debt)	The response to this question is not split into local and external debt. Given that the pandemic remains a latent risk, the Federal Government has a contingency plan and can continue its payment and non-market related operations remotely without the need of daily on-site work.
Mexico (external market debt)	The response to this question is not split into local and external debt. Given that the pandemic remains a latent risk, the Federal Government has a contingency plan and can continue its payment and non-market related operations remotely without the need of daily on-site work.
Netherlands	Funding plans are drafted with sufficient flexibility to deal with unexpected changes, whilst at the same time maintaining sufficient predictability for investors. Interest rate risk is kept at acceptable levels through targets for the average time to refixing and the 12-month refixing rate of the portfolio. Operational risks are managed through business continuity plans among others. Liquidity risk is mitigated through maintaining a sizeable money market and having the option to store cash at the central bank.
New Zealand	Liquidity risk – As a result of our experience during the COVID-19 pandemic we have undertaken work to quantify the size of

	a larger, enduring liquidity buffer. We maintain a buffer of high quality liquid assets and also have a limited overdraft facility with the Central Bank if there are unforeseen funding needs in the short-term. We also have the option to increase Treasury Bill and ECP issuance in the short-term. COVID-19 pandemic risk – we take a long-term structured approach to our funding strategy, rather than trying to tactically respond to short-term market dynamics. Our intention is to provide as much certainty as possible and thereby reduce the uncertainty or illiquidity premiums that are applied to our bonds. Over the long-term we believe this will place us in the best possible position in the backdrop of global financial risks that are beyond our control. Political risks – we avoid syndications around the timing of elections. We emphasise to investors the continuity of fiscal prudence between parties, and that the strengths of the NZ sovereign rating are independent of a particular political party. Change in Government borrowing needs – we review the borrowing programme forecasts at two scheduled points during the year. Last year we were also able to seek out-of-cycle approval from the Minister of Finance to change the borrowing programme.
Norway	
Poland	Holding a cash buffer, flexibility in terms of issuance: instruments, markets, issuance techniques. Maintaining the relations with investors and developing the investor base. Emergency procedures are updated on a regular basis taking into account new types of security issues. Technical infrastructure allowing for running debt management processes from outside of the Ministry of Finance building is assured.
Portugal	When preparing the financing plan for the year, potential risk factors are taken into account, therefore we anticipate as much as we can the financial schedule aiming to comfortably raise the funds to cover not only the year needs but also prefunding at least 30% of the following year gross funding needs and/or execute liability management exercises with the cost of debt reduction and smooth of redemption profile objectives. We also have contingency funding plans – e.g. we can launch new financial instruments directed to local retail market at short notice if need be.
Slovak Republic	Sufficient liquidity buffer (currently higher than long-term average).
Slovenia	These risks are managed by DMO maintaining the flexibility under the scope of annual funding plan, which in turn enables a swift response when needed. Bonds with short term residual maturity were offered for buy-back in 3Q 2021 in order to decrease refinancing risk in the following two years.
Spain	When preparing our yearly funding strategy we take all these risks into account. Therefore, the net funding goal takes possible risk factors into account, providing us with a conservative estimate, given the information available at the time. Moving on to the actual execution of our funding plan, one of the ways we can manage possible risks (especially the high degree of uncertainty associated to the pandemic), is by front-loading our issuance. This was something done by many DMOs, including ourselves. The idea is that by front-loading our issuance, we avoid saturating the market later in the year, if it becomes necessary to increase our funding needs.
Sweden	The Debt Office´s strategy to meet a rapidly changing borrowing need is to initially handle with short term funding (adjusting T-bill issuance, CP and bonds in foreign currency) and then gradually adjusting the borrowing in long term funding. It is also important to have different borrowing methods (auction, syndications, private placements) and maintain short-term funding market (T-Bills, repos).
Switzerland	The Treasury develops its auction calendar and issuance program in close cooperation with the budgetary units of the Ministry of Finance. In addition, the issuance program is revised on a quarterly basis and, if necessary, adapted according to the funding needs of the government. These updates are also approved by the Asset & Liability committee of the Treasury, on which – among others – the budgetary units and the Swiss National Bank are represented. With this rolling planning, potential risk factors can be taken into account for the issuance program and at each quarterly adaption. Thanks to this process and the relatively large liquidity buffer (see Q11), there is enough time and flexibility to adapt the funding strategy in a timely manner should risks materialize.
Turkey	Debt and Risk Management Committee closely monitors and evaluates recent changes in global, local markets and budget realizations and government borrowing needs. With respect to these developments, if needed, the Committee determines new strategies for debt management. Regarding operational risks, we manage our operations according to our Operational Risk and Business Continuity Management frameworks. On the other hand, to manage pandemic related risks while ensuring business continuity; flexible and remote working arrangements had been continued until June 2021. As a result of the high vaccination rate and the decline in the spread of coronavirus, working arrangements in public sector got back to normal as of July 2021. Besides, Turkish Treasury has an emergency and business continuity plan to deal with the operational risks since 2011. The BCP is updated annually and whenever deemed necessary. In that regard, at the beginning of the pandemic, we updated the BCP in 2020 to cover the case of a pandemic, revised the critical roles, the skills needed to fulfil these positions, and replacements/substitutes for key individuals.
United Kingdom	In order to try and manage some of these risks (as set out in the table in question 4), the UK DMO has a longstanding predictable approach to debt issuance, providing as much transparency to the market about our supply plans as possible. We aim to provide timely updates on the quarterly issuance calendar following market consultation, and with respect to the timing of syndicated offerings, in particular. This approach has served the DMO and the market well, supporting gilt market functioning and smooth price adjustment. In addition, we regularly consult with the market about current demand conditions before confirming our detailed plans for the period ahead; this gives scope to reflect market feedback (e.g. about shifts in demand conditions) into our issuance programme on a regular basis. With respect to 'contingency funding' (for example, the rapid increase in financing required as a result of the COVID-19 pandemic), we scaled up the size of our syndications and increased the frequency and average size of our auctions. We adapted to the changing market conditions by increasing issuance across the curve, including shorter-dated gilts (e.g. 3-year maturity); doing so was an essential component of the programme necessitated as a means to help deliver a rapidly increasing borrowing requirement. With effect from 7 April 2020, we also

			increased the post auction option facility rate from 15% to 25% with the intention to provide to auction participants a greater incentive to participate in operations. Within cash management, we increased Treasury Bill issuance at certain points in the pandemic. We regularly review our business continuity plan to ensure that it remains fit for purpose, in particular, to mitigate against the risk that we might be unable to hold an operation due to some unforeseen circumstance.

Table A.16. Q6 Do you consider potential risk factors when preparing your financing plan (e.g. auction calendar)?

	Yes	No	Comment
Australia	X		
Austria		X	In general, potential risk factors (e.g. forthcoming elections, geo-political events, central bank meetings etc.) and competing supply are considered when preparing the financing plan. The RAGB and ATB auction calendar dates are announced in December for the forthcoming year in order to maintain the highest possible degree of predictability. We tend to stick to these calendar dates regardless of potential risk factors. However, we have flexibility with regards to the amount and bond(s)/bill(s) issued at each auction (which for bonds is announced on Thursdays in the week before the auction) depending on demand and market conditions. At bond syndications we have more room to adjust in function of known upcoming events. In 2022 we plan introduce a quarterly funding outlook to increase transparency and predictability.
Belgium	X		In terms of the auction programs we maintain the highest possible degree of predictability. For syndications we do of course have more liberty to adjust in function of known upcoming events.
Canada		X	Flexibility is built in our financing plan to adjust to lower or higher financial requirements (e.g., contingency planning). The quarterly bond schedule (auction calendar) is designed to ensure that there are no auctions taking place on the same days as the interest rate announcement dates in Canada and in the US. The potential impact of public speaking engagements of members of the Governing Council of the Bank of Canada is also considered and utmost care is utilized to avoid inadvertent impact on Government of Canada primary market auctions. Call for tenders for primary market auctions are released in the morning (instead of the afternoon) in the week before an auction week when the markets are closed for a long weekend (i.e. a national/provincial holiday). The auction calendar also provides information on the specific sector of the to-be auctioned security and total amounts maturing on the auction day (across other securities). Market participants are closely consulted as part of the process of developing the debt management strategy. To support a liquid and well-functioning Government of Canada securities market, the Government strives to promote transparency and regularity.
Chile	X		
Colombia	X		
Costa Rica	X		
Czech Republic		X	Financing plan is prepared in accordance with financing needs, state budget deficit development, state treasury development, internal forecast and last but not least with situation on domestic and foreign bond markets and primary dealers' demand. In the internal forecast Ministry of Finance takes into account relevant financial risks arising from the situations on global and local financial markets (i. e. estimate of expenditure on state debt service in particular years), political risk related to state debt management and expenditure on state debt service (state debt level, expenditure level) etc.
Denmark	X		Issuance is spread out over the year to reduce event risk.
Estonia	X		For a small country like Estonia it is essential to be prepared for different funding alternatives (multilateral loans, revolving lines, t-bills, bonds)
Finland		X	Annual funding plan is based on a baseline scenario
France	X		We take into account the most likely annual trajectory of our financing programme and try to smooth it by running a buybacks programme and sizing the t-bill programme.
Germany	X		We tried and try to consider (avoid) days of foreseeable high volatility / uncertainty while preparing our annual auction calendar.
Greece	X		
Hungary		X	We do that by making the financing plan rather flexible. The auction calendar used to be fixed until 2019 for the given calendar year, but since it then it can be changed within a year as well. The Debt Management Office (DMO) has flexibility in determining the offered amounts and the accepted amounts at the auctions, and it has other tools such as the non-competitive top-up phase after the auctions; all these help to adjust the financing by wholesale instruments. Short-term liquidity management instruments (mainly repos) are available for handling temporary situations and a sizeable cash buffer is also held on the Treasury Single Account and in Foreign Exchange (FX) deposits. The annual amount of FX bond issuance is also flexible in the financing plan, depending on the government's financing needs and the demand for local government securities. All these measures have been in effect for many years, and were revised and enhanced in the past two years due to the Covid pandemic.
Iceland	X		The goal is to maintain a high degree of predictability in the auction program. An auction calendar is published in December each year for the following year and a quarterly auction plan is published before the start of each

	Yes	No	Comment
			quarter. A degree of flexibility is attained in the financing plan by the amount issued in each auction.
Ireland	X		Auctions are announced quarterly. Consideration is given to known market events which may influence auction outcomes.
Israel	X		
Italy	X		
Japan		X	We put our focus on predictability of issuance in formulating annual JGB Issuance Plans. One of the tools for this end is front-loading issuance of Refunding Bonds, which allows us to avoid concentration of bond redemption in a specific year and easing volatility in the amount of JGB market issuance across fiscal years. For instance, when it is predictable that bond redemption will be concentrated in a certain fiscal year, which could lead to a sharp rise in the issuance of Refunding Bonds, the amount of JGB issuance across fiscal years can be levelled by issuing front-loading Refunding Bonds in a year before the concentration. Thus, front-loading issuance of Refunding Bonds can serve to address market impacts volatile fiscal needs may have.
Korea	X		
Latvia		X	During the COVID-19 and uncertainties caused by the pandemic, acknowledgment and monitoring the risks is very important (for example: budget execution and fiscal impact of the pandemic, general trends in markets, investor interests, general market expectation of rate development etc.)
Lithuania		X	Potential risk factors are considered to some extent, however, we publish our auction calendar for three months in advance and auction details 5 working days in advance, so we have little flexibility to react if markets open in a bad shape on the day of the auction. We tend to manage risk by adjusting the borrowing amounts if needed.
Luxembourg	X		
Mexico			The response to this question is not split into local and external debt. The Annual Borrowing Plan and Quarterly Securities Auction Calendars are designed taking into account potential risk factors. The auction calendars are flexible in order to respond to changes in demand from local and foreign investors, as well as cash flow needs in the treasury account.
Netherlands	X		
New Zealand		X	We take a strategic approach to our bond tender issuance, pre-announcing the full details of the auction calendar a month in advance. We avoid scheduling auctions: • On the day of meetings of the Reserve Bank of New Zealand (RBNZ), • On the day of significant fiscal announcements such as the Budget or release of Crown accounts, • During the New Zealand summer holiday period, where there is the risk of low participation. By contrast, the precise timing of syndications are based on a tactical assessment of when will provide optimal investor participation. Potential risk factors are considered in detail when choosing a date. We also maintain flexibility for the volume of Treasury Bill tender issuance by announcing the volumes and maturities the day prior to the tender.
Norway		X	Issuances in both bills and bonds are spread over the year. An auction calendar for the whole year is published in December the preceding year. The normal auction amount in reopenings is NOK 2-3 billion. Should we experience any challenges in covering the auctions, we might consider increasing the number of auctions and reduce the volume in each auction. Auctions may also be cancelled.
Poland		X	In the annual auction calendar, the dates of the auctions are planned on days when there are no decisions of central banks (ECB, Fed, NBP) nor rating agencies' decisions regarding Poland. In monthly plans, the offer of domestic T-bonds at auctions is adjusted on an ongoing basis to the current and forecast market and budget situation.
Portugal		X	IGCP does not have a defined auction calendar for T-Bonds (PGB). Instead, there are two issuance windows per month (2nd and 4th Wednesday of each month) and on the Friday of the week preceding the auction date we confirm (or not) the tender and announce the lines to be opened and the target size for the auction.
Slovak Republic		X	Potential risk factors are very important in Syndicate deals with large expected volumes to be sold. In regular auctions the risks are less important. We prepare the auction calendar (dates of the auctions) for the whole year and try to avoid any changes or cancelations. We announce particular type of the offered bonds in the auctions only few weeks before the auction, following the actual demand/feedback from the PD and investors
Slovenia	X		
Spain		X	We do not vary our auction calendar dates, because we consider having a regular issuance calendar to be crucial. However, given the large amount of auction dates, our auction calendar provides us with ample flexibility to adapt to these potential risk factors. When preparing our funding strategy, we do take these risks into account, as mentioned in the previous response.
Sweden		X	There continues to be great uncertainty about how the budget balance will develop in the future, but the Debt Office is well prepared for both increased and decreased borrowing. If the borrowing requirement in the short term is smaller than forecast, the Debt Office can allow funding within liquidity management to decrease or further reduce the T-bill borrowing. If the borrowing requirement becomes larger and it is not considered appropriate to further increase borrowing local currency (Swedish Krona), the Debt Office can borrow in foreign currency, both in bonds and commercial paper.
Switzerland	X		See Q5.
Turkey	X		We share the main framework of the yearly borrowing plan through the Treasury Financing Program

	Yes	No	Comment
			announcement. Throughout the year, in the end of each month further details on the auction calendar are shared in the 3-month borrowing strategy. During the preparations of each announcement, Debt Office receives monthly and yearly risk assessments from the Risk Department. These assessments include simulation based analyses that are carried out in order to assess the cost - risk profile of the debt stock and to design the main debt management policy of the Turkish Treasury. In addition to those quantitative assessments, other qualitative potential risk factors, like geo-political or operational, are also considered during the final evaluation stage.
United Kingdom		X	The key high level risks taken into account from the debt management perspective when preparing the annual financing remit are: interest rate risk, refinancing risk, inflation risk, liquidity risk and execution risk. An assessment of these risks (alongside an assessment of cost and the pattern of demand) will impact the skew of issuance both between nominal and inflation-linked gilts and, within conventional gilt issuance, the split between maturities. The assessment can also impact the number, type, size and scheduling of gilt operations. With respect to some of the larger risks cited in the table above (e.g. local/global financial risks and changes to monetary conditions), we simply aim to adapt to any changes in market conditions as appropriate, after consultation with a wide range of market counterparties.
Total	**35**	**1**	

Table A.17. Q7 How has the maturity structure of your 2021 issuances changed compared to 2020?

	LONGER on average	SHORTER on average	Around the same
Australia		X	
Austria	X		
Belgium	X		
Canada	X		
Chile		X	
Colombia	X		
Costa Rica		X	
Czech Republic	X		
Denmark	X		
Estonia		X	
Finland			X
France	X		
Germany		X	
Greece	X		
Hungary	X		
Iceland			X
Ireland	X		
Israel		X	
Italy	X		
Japan		X	
Korea	X		
Latvia	X		
Lithuania	X		
Luxembourg			X
Mexico (local market debt)		X	
Mexico (external market debt)	X		
Netherlands			X
New Zealand	X		
Norway			X

	LONGER on average	SHORTER on average	Around the same
Poland	X		
Portugal	X		
Slovak Republic	X		
Slovenia			X
Spain	X		
Sweden			X
Switzerland			X
Turkey	X		
United Kingdom	X		
Total	**22**	**8**	**8**

Table A.18. Q7 maturity structure of your 2021 issuances – country notes

	Country notes
Australia	
Austria	
Belgium	After stabilizing the average maturity of the debt portfolio over the past years, we decided to further extend the average maturity of the debt portfolio again in 2021.
Canada	The Government of Canada manages its funding plan according to the annual Debt Management Strategy (DMS) which is legislated to be tabled within 30 sittings days of the beginning of the fiscal year. The Government of Canada's fiscal year-end is March 31. The funding plan for fiscal year 2021-22 was released in April 2021 and can be found here: https://www.budget.gc.ca/2021/report-rapport/anx2-en.html As Canada moves towards economic recovery, the shift towards long-term debt issuance, which began in 2020-21, will continue. Funding more COVID-19-related debt through long-term issuance will help provide security and stability to the government balance sheet by lowering debt rollover while remaining fiscally prudent. Issuances with a maturity of 10 years or greater will be higher in 2021-22 than 2020-21 in both relative and absolute terms. As part of this move towards longer-term issuance, the government will re-open issuance of the ultra-long 50-year bond for 2021-22. Before the pandemic, 15 per cent of the bonds issued by the government were issued at maturities of 10 years or greater. Over the course of 2020, federal government allocations of long bonds rose to about 29 per cent. The government is now proposing to increase that proportion to 42 per cent. Over the next three years, the average term to maturity for Government debt is expected to increase to nearly 8 years, a level that is significantly higher than the historical average of 5.9 years seen in the period from 1981-82 to 2019-20.
Chile	The participation in the external market also increased (from 20% of the total stock to 30%, approx.). The effect on maturity was partially compensated by the decision to issue in longer maturities in the external markets.
Colombia	The average life of our debt increased from 8.69 years in August 2020 to 9.62 years in August 2021. In January 2021 we issued our first 40 year bond in the international markets.
Costa Rica	
Czech Republic	Czech Republic aims to issue instruments with longer maturities due to flat yield curve of CZK-denominated government bonds. Average time to maturity of newly issued government bonds in 2021 is 8,6 years, average time to maturity of the state debt is 6,6, which represents increase by 0,4 year compared to the end of 2020. On the other hand, Ministry of Finance has started to use stabilization repo operations on money market in higher extent aiming to short-term funding and strengthening of liquidity reserves.
Denmark	In 2021 the outstanding amount in the short-term papers, in particular the commercial paper programmes, have been reduced gradually.
Estonia	Risk for higher borrowing need did not materialize and pre-funding in 2020 allowed the DMO to issue T-bills instead of bonds to cover the uncertainty of 2021 cash-flow.
Finland	
France	Issuances on bonds have raised by 1 year on average in 2021 (from 11,6 to 12,6 years year to date)
Germany	Issuance volumes* 2020: € 237 bn capital market (excl. April issuances into own holdings), € 181 bn money market vs. 2021 (plan): € 256.4 bn capital market (excl. ILB volume to be auctioned on 2 November 2021), € 238 bn money market *incl. syndicates and issuance volumes of conventional twins into own holdings
Greece	
Hungary	
Iceland	ATM of the portfolio decreased in 2020 by approximately 1 year, but has remained more or less the same during 2021.
Ireland	

	Country notes
Israel	
Italy	Market conditions and management decisions made it possible to continue increasing the average life of debt which, at the end of 2021, relative to the stock of government bonds, was equal to 7.11 years (7.29 years including loans under the SURE and NGEU programs), a figure higher than that at the end of 2020 equal to 6.95 years. This was attributable to various issues on the long end of the yield curve, carried out both through auctions and with the launch - through a placement syndicate - of several new nominal benchmark securities (10-year, 15-year, 20-year and 50-year BTPs plus the BTP Green maturing in 2045).
Japan	Compared with the JGB Issuance Plan for FY2020 (Initial), the JGB Issuance Plan for FY2021 (Initial) increased offering for almost every maturities of bonds by biggest-ever amount, but it increased mostly offering for short-term bonds. This is because in FY2020 the Issuance Plan increased its amount significantly, especially of short-term bonds, which resulted in increasing issuance amount of Refunding Bonds in the Issuance Plan for FY2021 (Initial). Overall, the average maturity of JGBs (flow-basis) was shortened from 9 years 3 months (FY2020 (Initial)) to 6 years 10 months (FY2021 (Initial)). In addition, compared with the average maturity of JGBs (flow-basis) in FY2020 (3rd Supplementary Budget), the average maturity of JGBs (flow-basis) was lengthened from 6 years 8 months (FY2020 (3rd Supplementary Budget)) to 6 years 10 months (FY2021 (Initial)).
Korea	
Latvia	
Lithuania	Average maturity in auctions increased from 12.6 years in 2020 to 13.1 years in 2021 YTD.
Luxembourg	
Mexico (local market debt)	Average time to maturity (ATM) for local debt has reduced (and ATM for foreign debt has increased). In the average, the ATM of all market debt remains around the same.
Mexico (external market debt)	(Average time to maturity (ATM) for local debt has reduced and) ATM for foreign debt has increased. In the average, the ATM of all market debt remains around the same.
Netherlands	In 2020 we started to gradually shift money market funding to capital market funding (since money market funding was quite high following the covid crisis). This process has continued in 2021. The term structure of capital market funding has however stayed relatively stable in 2020 and 2021, with a focus on long maturities (between 10 and 30 years) while at the same time maintaining sufficient liquidity across the entire curve.
New Zealand	We extended the length of the nominal bond curve from 20-years to 30-years in September 2021. There is a lower funding requirement in 2021 relative to 2020. This has meant less emphasis on issuing volume into short-dated bonds where domestic demand is assured and allowed us to issue more mid to longer-dated bonds.
Norway	
Poland	The average maturity increased from slightly less than 6 years to more than 7 years.
Portugal	IGCP launched a new 30 year benchmark in February 2021 that significantly increased the average maturity of MLT debt issuance in 2021 compared to 2020.
Slovak Republic	
Slovenia	In 2021 Slovenia issued two 10-year lines in the total amount of €2.75bn. Nevertheless, it also issued a 60-year bond (€0.5 bn), which is the longest maturity issued ever. All in all, we would still opt for the answer "Around the same".
Spain	This lengthening of our maturity structure is in line with the trend the Spanish Treasury has followed in recent years, seeking to lengthen the maturity of our issuance, without causing a significant increase in the cost of issuance. The low interest rate environment of the past years has been helpful in this regard.
Sweden	
Switzerland	The bonds issued in 2021 (new issuance, reopenings, own tranches sold) had a time to maturity of 13.8 years; this is around the same as in the previous year (14.3 years). The amount of outstanding bills did also not change compared to 2020.
Turkey	We have comparatively more relied on 5 and 10 year fixed-rate bond issuances in 2021 and switched shorter-term bonds with longer-term bonds. At the end of 2020, 12-month moving average maturity of domestic borrowing was 37.2 months (switch auctions included), as of August 2021, this ratio has dramatically increased up to 56.5 months (switch auctions included).
United Kingdom	The skew of issuance, which shows the amount of issuance of short (1-7 years), medium (7-15 years) and long nominal gilts (15+ years) as well as that of inflation-linked gilts is decided on a financial year basis. The maturity structure of issuance in 2020-21 involved a larger proportion of short debt than issuance in 2021-22 to-date. This reflects the unprecedented size of the financing programme last year, which necessitated very large increases in short issuance in order to raise the required amount of cash in the period (i.e. short-dated auctions require a lower level of risk to be absorbed by the market relative to longer-dated issuance and, therefore, auction sizes can be larger, other things equal). In 2020-21 the weighted average maturity of issuance was 14.3 years, whereas in 2021-22, as at end-September 2021, the weighted average maturity of issuance stands at 16.1 years.

Table A.19. Q8 Have you changed your funding strategies during 2021 compared to any original 2021 funding plan?

	Yes	No
Australia		X
Austria	X	
Belgium		X
Canada		X
Chile	X	
Colombia		X
Costa Rica		X
Czech Republic	X	
Denmark	X	
Estonia	X	
Finland		X
France		X
Germany		X
Greece		X
Hungary	X	
Iceland		X
Ireland		X
Israel	X	
Italy	X	
Japan		X
Korea	X	
Latvia	X	
Lithuania	X	
Luxembourg		X
Mexico (local market debt)	X	
Mexico (external market debt)	X	
Netherlands		X
New Zealand	X	
Norway		X
Poland		X
Portugal	X	
Slovak Republic	X	
Slovenia		X
Spain	X	
Sweden	X	
Switzerland	X	
Turkey	X	
United Kingdom		X
Total	**20**	**18**

Table A.20. Q9 How have you adapted your funding strategies and operations in response to the pandemic in last 12 months?

	Number or volume of issuance of securities across the yield curve	Issuance of money market instruments	Introducing new maturity lines	Issuing new types of securities	Auction calendar	Frequency of auctions	Post-auction option facility	Use of syndications	Use of private placements	Others
Australia	Higher	Higher	Yes	No	No	Higher	Not applicable	Higher	Not applicable	Not applicable
Austria	Higher	Higher	No	Yes	No	No change	No change	No change	Higher	Please select
Belgium	Lower	No change	Yes	No	No	Lower	No change	Lower	No change	No change
Canada	No change	Higher	No	No	Yes	No change	Not applicable	No change	No change	Not applicable
Chile	Lower	Higher	Yes	Yes	Yes	Lower	No change	Higher	Not applicable	Not applicable
Colombia	No change	No change	Yes	Yes	Yes	No change	No change	Lower	No change	Not applicable
Costa Rica	No change	No change	No	No	No	No change	Not applicable	Not applicable	Not applicable	Not applicable
Czech Republic	Higher	Higher	Yes	No	Yes	Higher	No change	No change	No change	Higher
Denmark	Higher	Higher	Please select	No	No	No change	Not applicable	Not applicable	Not applicable	Higher
Estonia	Lower	Higher	Not applicable	Not applicable	Not applicable	Lower	Not applicable	Lower	Not applicable	No change
Finland	No change	No change	No	Not applicable	Yes	No change	Not applicable	No change	Lower	Not applicable
France	No change	Higher	No	No	No	Higher	No change	Higher	Not applicable	Please select
Germany	Higher	Higher	No	No	Yes	Higher	Not applicable	Lower	Not applicable	Higher
Greece	Higher	Lower	Yes	No	Yes	No change	No change	Higher	No change	No change
Hungary	Higher	Lower	Yes	Yes	Yes	Lower	No change	Higher	Not applicable	Higher
Iceland	No change	No change	Yes	No	No	No change	No change	No change	Not applicable	Higher
Ireland	Please select	Please select	Yes	Please select	Please select	Higher	Please select	Higher	Higher	No change
Israel	Lower	Lower	No	No	Yes	No change	Not applicable	Not applicable	Not applicable	Not applicable
Italy	Higher	Higher	Yes	Yes	No	No change	Higher	Higher	No change	Higher
Japan	Higher	Lower	No	No	Not applicable	Not applicable	Not applicable	Not applicable	Not applicable	Not applicable
Korea	Higher	Not applicable	Yes	No	Yes	No change	Higher	No change	No change	Higher
Latvia	Higher	No change	Yes	Yes	Yes	Higher	Not applicable	No change	Not applicable	Not applicable
Lithuania	Higher	No change	No	No	Yes	No change	No change	No change	No change	No change
Luxembourg	Higher	Not applicable	Yes	Yes	Not applicable	Not applicable	Not applicable	Higher	Not applicable	Not applicable
Mexico (local market debt)	Lower	Higher	Yes	No	Yes	No change	No change	No change	Not applicable	No change

	Number or volume of issuance of securities across the yield curve	Issuance of money market instruments	Introducing new maturity lines	Issuing new types of securities	Auction calendar	Frequency of auctions	Post-auction option facility	Use of syndications	Use of private placements	Others
Mexico (external market debt)	Higher	Not applicable	Yes	Yes	Not applicable	Not applicable	Not applicable	No change	Not applicable	Not applicable
Netherlands	Higher	Lower	Yes	No	No	Higher	No change	Not applicable	Not applicable	Not applicable
New Zealand	Lower	Lower	Yes	No	No	No change	Not applicable	Lower	Not applicable	No change
Norway	No change	No change	No	No	No	No change	Not applicable	No change	Not applicable	Not applicable
Poland	No change	Lower	No	No	No	No change	No change	No change	Lower	No change
Portugal	Lower	Lower	Yes	No	No	Lower	No change	Higher	No change	Not applicable
Slovak Republic	Higher	No change	Yes	No	Yes	Higher	No change	No change	No change	Please select
Slovenia	Higher	Lower	Yes	Yes	Yes	Lower	Not applicable	No change	No change	Not applicable
Spain	No change	No change	Not applicable	No	No change	No change	No change	Higher	No change	No change
Sweden	Higher	Higher	Yes	No	No	No change	Not applicable	Higher	Not applicable	Not applicable
Switzerland	Higher	No change	Yes	No	No	No change	Not applicable	Not applicable	Not applicable	No change
Turkey	Higher	No change	No	No	No	Higher	No change	No change	Please select	Please select
United Kingdom	Higher	Lower	Yes	Yes	Yes	Higher	Not applicable	Higher	Not applicable	Higher
Total: Higher	21	12				10	2	12	2	8
Total: Lower	7	10				6	0	5	2	0
Total: No change	9	12				19	17	15	12	10
Total: Yes			23	10	16					
Total: No			12	25	16					

Table A.21. Q9 How have you adapted your funding strategies and operations in response to the pandemic – Country notes

Australia	
Austria	
Belgium	This compares 2021 to 2020. The funding needs are significantly lower than in 2020 due to a combination of lower primary (fiscal) cash needs (although this will mostly be visible in the last months of the year) and lower debt redemptions.
Canada	N/A
Chile	
Colombia	In June 2021, we introduced a new bond due 2031 (10 year), to our local auctions. In September 2021, we issued our fist green bond through auctions in the local bond market following the structure of twin bonds with the recently launched 10 year tenor.
Costa Rica	
Czech Republic	Financing needs increased due to the crisis state budget deficit, which was increased from CZK 320 billion to CZK 500 billion in February as part of amendments to the Act on the State Budget in response to the ongoing SARS-CoV-2 coronavirus pandemic and also taking into account the effects of the amendment to the Income Tax Act effective from 1 January 2021.
Denmark	
Estonia	On contrary to the forecast in 2020 there has been no need to issue bonds. Due to better liquidity, only T-bills have been used.
Finland	
France	One more auction in August
Germany	The changes for 2021 in response of the pandemic were already included in the auction calendar for 2021, published in December 2020. On balance at year-end 2021, there will be only a very small adaption (€ 0.5 bn) of total issuance volume, compared to this planning. This adaptation as well as the introduction of new green maturities (5Y and 30Y) was not linked to the pandemic.
Greece	
Hungary	Frequency of auctions was increased at first in 2020, then lowered back to the original frequency in 2021.
Iceland	Use of non-marketable funding increased.
Ireland	
Israel	
Italy	Since the outbreak of the Covid-19 epidemiological crisis, in order to manage the increase of the funding needs, the Italian Treasury has made recourse to some element of flexibility in issuing procedures: Increase of both the amount offered at auctions and the shares of the supplementary placements reserved to the Specialists; Use of syndicated placement also for the launch of new benchmark securities with maturity ≤10 years; Introduction of a new modality to issue one or more off-the-run securities through the electronic trading system ("TAP ISSUE"). Issuance of retail instruments (BTP Italia and BTP Futura) specifically dedicated to finance the provisions adopted by the Government related to Covid-19 crisis. Even if not directly related to the response to the Covid-19 crisis, other two important changes in finding strategy occurred in 2021 has been: the introduction of the repurchase agreement (Repo) activity, which generated positive effects both in terms of efficiency in the collection of liquidity and in the management of distortions in the market. For the purposes of executing Repos with the aim of collecting liquidity, the Treasury has set up its own portfolio, composed of tranches of Government securities already in circulation in the nominal BTP segment. This portfolio will be periodically updated to adjust its composition and quantities in line with cash management needs and take into account the full implementation of Repo operations. Given the levels of market rates, for the first months of activity, the Treasury operated on the Repo market only in funding. However, as of 2022, the Treasury could have recourse to the Repo market also for liquidity use. The launch of the first Green BTP, the Italian government security dedicated to financing expenditure incurred by the State with a positive environmental impact, as provided for by the Italian Budget Law for 2020. Following the publication of the Green Bond Framework and the related Second Party Opinion, the syndicated issue of the first tranche of the BTP Green with maturity 30 April 2045 took place on 3 March, for an amount of 8.5 billion, of which more than half was subscribed by ESG (Environmental, Social and Governance) investors.
Japan	Comments on "Issuance of money market instruments (i.e. T-Bills and repos) compared to issuance of long-term bonds"; The shares of short-term bonds in the market issuance amount for FY2020 (2nd Supplementary Budget) was lower than those for FY2021 (Initial).
Korea	
Latvia	Pandemic in general globally together with uncertainties and inflation expectation impacted investors demand for certain tenors at particular time of the offering. Taking into account the flexibility of the borrowing strategy, Latvia used the strategy to raise funding with such bond tenors that created as low as possible burden on debt servicing costs to the budget.
Lithuania	
Luxembourg	

Mexico (local market debt)	
Mexico (external market debt)	
Netherlands	
New Zealand	Over the past 12 months, funding requirements have been lower and reduced relative to expectations in early 2020. As a result, tender volumes have been lower (although over the same number of bond lines) and we have undertaken fewer syndications. That said, these are both well above pre-COVID times, with multiple new bond lines now being introduced per annum (compared to 0-1 previously).
Norway	
Poland	
Portugal	In 2021 the execution of the funding program was according with the initial plan until July. In August and September, two T-Bill auctions were canceled and an expected T-Bond auction window in September was not used, mostly due to a better budget execution and instalments received under the NGEU program.
Slovak Republic	
Slovenia	Please note that changes in "Auctions" apply to treasury bill auction.
Spain	We have used more syndications to be able to decide on how our bond issuance is allocated among investors. This allows us to find investors who are more likely to contribute to stable secondary market prices. This is especially useful given the uncertainties brought about by the Covid-19 global crisis. Regarding our green bond issuance, we have just issued our first green bond, but this issuance is not related to the pandemic. It's more related to Spain's general green goals and the Spanish Treasury's aim to diversify its issuance instruments and investor base. Regarding our post-auction options, as mentioned in one of the initial paragraphs, we made a change to the price at which our green-shoe option is allocated. However, this change was done more than 12 months ago.
Sweden	In the beginning of the pandemic during the spring of 2020, The Debt Office increased the funding lines of T-bills. We also introduced a 50-year bond via syndication in June 2021.
Switzerland	There was no reason to fundamentally adjust our approach to funding. Thanks to our reliable issuance strategy and the frequent auctions in the money and capital markets, we can react quickly to increasing funding needs without introducing new instruments. Therefore, we did not introduce any new instruments or techniques and there are no plans to do so in the next 12 months. We changed the targeted issue volume several times due to high uncertainty (increases and decreases) There was an increased use of existing instruments (own tranches) and especially in the beginning of the pandemic a higher than usual share of T-Bills compared to T-Bonds.
Turkey	The effects of the pandemic on the government's financing needs in 2020, led us to increase the level and adjust the composition of the borrowing. In this context the share of short-term, CPI-indexed, TLREF-indexed and foreign currency bonds in the overall domestic borrowing composition was increased. On the other hand, in 2021, also thanks to the gradual alleviation of the effects of the pandemic on government budget and financing dynamics, we have been able to increase substantially the average maturity of domestic borrowing and the share of 5 and 10 year fixed-rate bonds in the overall borrowing composition. Moreover, according to our up-to-date financing program, we plan to borrow much less than the amount envisaged in the original annual financing program.
United Kingdom	Our funding strategy has remained consistent despite the unprecedented financing requirements – in historical terms – last year and in 2021-22. As set out previously, auctions remain the primary issuance method for us, with syndications remaining an important issuance method alongside to deliver a minority of the financing programme. The UK's decision to issue green gilts was not driven by the pandemic, rather by the UK Government's commitment to a green transition. However, financing raised via green gilt issuance will contribute to the meeting the overall financing requirement.

Table A.22. Q10 Have you observed any changes in investors behaviour in participating in auctions or/ Syndications (e.g. oversized orders)?

Australia	Behaviour in syndications and tenders over the past 12 months was broadly similar to the 12 months previous to that. Breakdowns of investor participation in syndications and tender statistics are available here https://www.aofm.gov.au/data-hub
Austria	In 2020 the average bid/cover ratio at government bond auctions was 2.81x and reached its highest value since 2005. In 2021YTD the bid/cover ratio normalized with an average value of 2.26x (until October), close to its long-term average of 2.3 (2009-2021YTD). At syndicated bond issuances oversubscription was 8.1 in 2020 (=second highest value ever recorded) and 8.2 in 2021YTD (=highest value ever recorded).
Belgium	We haven't observed any changes in auctions. In the syndications, we continue to witness the phenomenon of increasing order books that we have seen since -especially- 2018.
Canada	The increase in volatility seen at the beginning of the pandemic seems to have dissipated. Government of Canada Bond auctions across sectors as well as Treasury Bill auctions are performing well, with auction performance metrics returning to historical long-term average levels. Being open and transparent in the communication strategy with primary dealers has been an effective

	approach to motivating dealers to provide liquidity to the Government of Canada securities market and to support primary market issuance. Investors' continue to participate in Government of Canada securities auctions across the curve. Canada's reputation as a high-quality issuer of Government securities has remained strong in the investor community through the crisis period. Overall, no significant changes in investor behavior have been observed.
Chile	No
Colombia	From April to August Colombia has had positive net inflows from foreign investors.
Costa Rica	No greater has been observed in the patterns of investors, in general, it has been possible to reduce the interest rate in all the terms.
Czech Republic	In the first half of this year Ministry of Finance decided to utilize unusually high demand for government bonds and pre-financed all state debt redemptions this year, even before expected interest rate hikes by Czech National Bank.
Denmark	Demand from investors were lower in certain periods with market turmoil during the covid-19 pandemic.
Estonia	Improvement of competition in T-bills auction.
Finland	Fast money orders in syndications continue to be somewhat inflated
France	We have noticed an increased participation and order size for hedge funds and fast money investors. No specific change in auctions
Germany	In general, there is currently a high demand for green securities.
Greece	Yes, there was a tremendous increase in investors demand and appetite for sovereign bonds.
Hungary	No changes in this regard
Iceland	No significant change observed.
Ireland	No significant change
Israel	No specific change
Italy	During the past syndicated transactions, in some circumstances we have noted an inflated amount of orders coming from fast money accounts that could misrepresent the underlying value of the book.
Japan	Auction participant's behavior such as "successful Bids Share for JGBs by Investor type", "ratio of bid" at the time of auctions has not changed in particular.
Korea	
Latvia	Yes, at certain periods of the year the demand for longer tenor was limited due to the market expectations for rates increase
Lithuania	No significant changes
Luxembourg	Even more oversubscription than we usually have
Mexico (local market debt)	Local Market Debt Foreign investors are currently focusing on instruments on the long-end side of the curve, revealing preferences for 10 and 30 years bonds on the run. Retirement fund managers are currently increasing the demand for inflation-linked bonds in the short-side of the curve. Participants have shown higher demand for floating rates instruments. Additionally, some local participants have shown a preference for liquidity, demanding instruments on the short-side of the curve. The overall volume and liquidity have been decreasing.
Mexico (external market debt)	External Market Debt No changes have been observed in investors' behavior regarding debt issuances in international financial markets. Opposite to the local market, there has been a steady demand all across the curve, compressing differentials against US treasure curve in line with CDS performance.
Netherlands	No, we have not observed any changes in investor behaviour
New Zealand	No.
Norway	With the exception of one auction, investor demand has been unchanged from previous years. As regards syndications, there is a tendency by some market segments to place oversized orders.
Poland	No, average bid/cover ratio did not change significantly.
Portugal	IGCP has witnessed significant large orders in syndications, mostly from hedge funds accounts. This behavior leads a certain difficulty in assessing the quality of the demand and consequently to set the final price for new issuance.
Slovak Republic	We observed higher presence of hedge funds or fast money investors in Syndicate books.
Slovenia	The order books/bids are significantly oversubscribed.
Spain	Similarly to other sovereign issuers, we have noticed larger orders from certain investors in our syndications.
Sweden	No change
Switzerland	- For our T-Bills, the investor demand depends mainly on the prices of the last few auctions and the cross currency basis. This has not changed during the pandemic. The demand for our bonds depends on a number of factors (amount of other issuers, absolute yield, relative valuation compared to peers, current interest rate development, etc.). Because of this, it is sometimes difficult for us (and for other market participants) to predict the level of demand for certain maturities in the days before an auction. However, this is also not limited to the period of the pandemic. For both the bills and the bonds, the bidders/counterparties at the auctions have mostly been the same as before the pandemic.
Turkey	
United Kingdom	It has been reported to us anecdotally and we have observed oversized orders placed at syndicated offerings (i.e. where bidders submit bids that are larger than the amount they want/expect to be allocated in the transaction). We understand though that this

is not unique to the UK. We have communicated to our primary dealers that we do not find this approach to submitted orders to be helpful, in that it may make allocations more difficult for the dealers themselves, whose responsibility it is to decide the allocations based on the DMO's high level steer.		

Table A.23. Q11 Do you have a liquidity buffer?

	Yes	No	Have there been any changes in the last 12 months in terms of your liquidity buffer practice? Also has there been any problems in managing or communicating the use of the liquidity buffer?
Australia	X		The AOFM sets a minimum target asset balance, this amount has reduced slightly over the last 12 months in response to somewhat reduced government outlays. The AOFM also generally holds a minimum of around 4 weeks of net government outlays and debt refinancing requirements across the year.
Austria	X		In the past Austria did not have a liquidity buffer. This changed in mid-March 2020 due to the uncertainties around the exact cash flows surrounding the Austrian government corona package.
Belgium		X	We typically do not hold a formal liquidity buffer. However, in 2021 the liquidity we held was higher than usual (cf 5)
Canada	X		There have been no changes to the liquidity buffer practice since the announcement of the Prudential Liquidity Management plan in the March 2011 Federal Budget. Please refer to: https://www.budget.gc.ca/2011/plan/anx2-eng.html The liquidity plan is composed of government deposits held with financial institutions and the Bank of Canada, as well as the liquid foreign exchange reserves and are managed to provide one month's worth of coverage. Government cash balances in both 2020 and 2021 are running significantly higher than in comparison to 2019, largely because of anticipation of large funding requirements for COVID-19 programs that were announced by the Government of Canada in the first half of 2020. The Government temporarily increased the frequency and size of treasury bill auctions in H1 2020 and ramped up bond issuances. This has resulted in larger cash balances than were previously carried in 2019.
Chile	X		The liquidity buffer is nor formally established, although in practice, there are Treasury assets, maintained to cover short term expenses. The amount of these assets has reduced due to the pandemic.
Colombia	X		
Costa Rica		X	
Czech Republic	X		Since March the Ministry is active on the money market, with the aim of preventively strengthening the liquidity reserves of the CZK state treasury, when it successfully tested a new financing channel in the form of stabilization repo operations with maturities from 2W up to 3M (mainly 2W) with collateral mainly in the form of T-Bills. Czech Republic obtains CZK funds for 2W period at key monetary policy rate (2W CNB repo rate).
Denmark	X		The Danish DMO holds a minimum cash buffer. The targeted cash buffer has not changed.
Estonia	X		There have been no changes in our liquidity buffer practice. The liquidity buffer is the financial buffer used for the State's daily cash flow management to deal with normal mismatches of cash inflows and outflows within a month. Liquidity was increased by the DMO due to the uncertainty of cash-flow connected to COVID-19 crisis in H1 2020.
Finland	X		A lower buffer than in 2020 but still higher than before that
France	X		We increased our cash buffer following the crisis and decreased it in 2021.
Germany	X		
Greece	X		
Hungary	X		The targeted optimal liquidity buffer level was raised and the achieved TSA balance is even higher. The Hungarian Debt Management Office restarted cash placements in the market via repos in 2021 (these were suspended in April 2020), but with relatively low amounts.
Iceland	X		The pandemic has caused higher funding need of the government. The funding strategy has changed consequently with more emphasis on issuing short term bonds and T-bills. These measures have resulted in a more "stable" liquidity buffer.
Ireland	X		No
Israel	X		No changes in our liquidity buffer practices. We didn't use it during Covid-19.
Italy	X		Any change in our liquidity buffer practice has not been introduced in the last 12 months.
Japan	X		The fund balance on the Government Debt Consolidation Fund (GDCF) has decreased by reducing the amount of front-loading Refunding Bonds according to the 3rd revision of the issuance plan for FY2020.
Korea	X		
Latvia	X		Increased liquidity buffer is maintained due to additional funding needs to manage risks and mitigate fiscal impact of Covid-19 pandemic. No problems in managing or communicating the use of the liquidity buffer was observed.
Lithuania	X		No changes

	Yes	No	Have there been any changes in the last 12 months in terms of your liquidity buffer practice? Also has there been any problems in managing or communicating the use of the liquidity buffer?
Luxembourg	X		no
Mexico (local market debt)		X	The response to this question is not split into local and external debt. It has remained the same, there has not been any changes in our liquidity buffer. The Treasury has a minimum liquidity threshold that helps as a contingency buffer. Also, Mexico has access to the IMF' Flexible Credit Line and other International Financial Institutions resources. Regarding the short-term zero coupon bonds, there is always a buffer in order to capture more resources; furthermore, zero coupon bonds are on a range and they are communicated to participants on a weekly basis.
Mexico (external market debt)		X	The response to this question is not split into local and external debt. It has remained the same, there has not been any changes in our liquidity buffer. The Treasury has a minimum liquidity threshold that helps as a contingency buffer. Also, Mexico has access to the IMF' Flexible Credit Line and other International Financial Institutions resources. Regarding the short-term zero coupon bonds, there is always a buffer in order to capture more resources; furthermore, zero coupon bonds are on a range and they are communicated to participants on a weekly basis.
Netherlands	X		Temporarily the restraints on storing cash at the central bank have been relaxed.
New Zealand		X	Our liquidity buffer is materially larger than prior to the COVID-19 pandemic, to help manage funding and liquidity risk. The compliance requirements for the liquidity buffer has not yet been revised but we are currently quantifying the enduring level of the liquidity buffer. We plan to provide further guidance on this at future Economic and Fiscal Updates.
Norway	X		No changes
Poland	X		Due to extraordinary budget and market uncertainty the level of cash buffer was increased.
Portugal		X	The increase in volatility of government revenues and expenditures since March 2020 has put additional pressure on cash forecasting activities. Although IGCP was anticipating the increase in cash deposits at the end of 2020 to help in managing 2021 uncertainty, the cash excess surpassed the target significantly. As result, the execution of 2021 funding program needed to be adjusted (meaning reduce net issuance).
Slovak Republic		X	The liquidity buffer due to COVID19 increased. We have an ongoing internal debate about the sufficient size of liquidity buffer. There is a political challenge to correctly communicate higher gross debt increase vs. smaller increase of net debt. Potentially higher liquidity buffer than optimal due to overshooting cash deficit forecasts by the Ministry of Finance.
Slovenia	X		Slovenia has a significant liquidity buffer. The issue with managing liquidity buffer is negative interest rates. Communicating the use/size of the liquidity buffer is usually not a problem.
Spain		X	Given the large amounts of Government Spending and Tax Revenues that Spain carries out, and the possibility of cashflow/time mismatches, the Spanish Treasury always maintains a liquidity buffer to avoid cashflow tensions. In the last 12 months there have been two factors that have increased the need for this liquidity buffer: The higher uncertainty brought about by pandemic-related changes in Tax Revenues or Government spending. The implementation of the NGEU program. On the one hand, Spain must pay for NGEU related projects. On the other hand, Spain receives disbursements from the grant component of NGEU. It's possible that cashflow mismatches may arise, which would require a liquidity buffer.
Sweden		X	
Switzerland		X	Since the introduction of negative interest rates by the Swiss National Bank in 2015, the liquidity buffer has grown steadily and reached a year-end volume of around CHF 20 to 25 billion (between a quarter and a third of the yearly budget of the federal administration). Thanks to this high liquidity buffer, the Treasury had sufficient time to adapt the issuance strategy and increase the issuance activity slowly and without causing additional market stress. As a result of the pandemic, the liquidity buffer has decreased and we forecast it to reach around CHF 10 billion at the end of the year. This would be in line with our liquidity target. One key lesson of the pandemic was, that we can add liquidity quickly thanks to our well-established T-Bills program and that there is no need for an oversized liquidity buffer (opportunity costs).
Turkey	X		Keeping a strong level of cash reserve in order to reduce the liquidity risk associated with cash and debt management is one the main pillars of our borrowing strategy.
United Kingdom		X	N/A

Table A.24. Q12 Please indicate areas of key lessons learned from the COVID-19 crisis.

	The need to hold excess cash balances as a buffer	Need to maintain short-term funding market	Having different borrowing methods	Established communication with investors	Yield curve extension	Others
Australia	X	X	X	X	X	
Austria		X	X	X		
Belgium			X			
Canada	X	X			X	
Chile	X	X	X	X	X	
Colombia		X	X	X	X	
Costa Rica	X	X	X	X		
Czech Republic		X		X	X	
Denmark						The benefit of having a broad and diversified market access, including in foreign currency.
Estonia		X	X	X	X	
Finland	X	X	X	X		
France	X	X	X	X		Being able to work on remote
Germany		X	X			
Greece	X	X	X	X	X	
Hungary	X		X	X	X	
Iceland	X	X				
Ireland	X	X	X			
Israel	X	X	X	X		
Italy			X	X	X	
Japan				X		
Korea		X		X		
Latvia	X			X		Keep available also other funding options, like international financial institutions and utilize when necessary and if financially favourable borrowing conditions are offered
Lithuania			X	X		
Luxembourg	X	X				
Mexico (local market debt)		X	X	X	X	Use of liquidity buffers (trust funds)
Mexico (external market debt)		X	X	X	X	Use of liquidity buffers (trust funds)
Netherlands		X	X	X		
New Zealand	X	X	X	X		
Norway		X	X	X		
Poland	X	X	X	X		
Portugal	X	X			X	Existence of a

	The need to hold excess cash balances as a buffer	Need to maintain short-term funding market	Having different borrowing methods	Established communication with investors	Yield curve extension	Others
						business continuity/recovery plan to fall back toin case of need
Slovak Republic	X	X	X	X		
Slovenia	X	X	X	X	X	
Spain	X	X	X	X		
Sweden		X	X	X		
Switzerland	X	X		X		
Turkey	X	X		X		
United Kingdom		X	X	X		
Total	**21**	**31**	**28**	**29**	**13**	**6**

Table A.25. Q13 Do you plan to review the long-term funding strategy as a consequence of increased debt levels following the COVID-19 pandemic?

	Yes	No
Australia	X	
Austria		X
Belgium		X
Canada	X	
Chile	X	
Colombia		
Costa Rica		X
Czech Republic		X
Denmark	X	
Estonia		X
Finland		X
France		X
Germany		
Greece	X	
Hungary	X	
Iceland	X	
Ireland	X	
Israel		X
Italy		X
Japan		X
Korea		X
Latvia		X
Lithuania	X	
Luxembourg		X
Mexico (local market debt)		X
Mexico (external market debt)		X
Netherlands	X	
New Zealand	X	
Norway		X
Poland		X
Portugal		X

	Yes	No
Slovak Republic		X
Slovenia	X	
Spain		X
Sweden		X
Switzerland		X
Turkey	X	
United Kingdom		X
Total		

Table A.26. Q14 Potential implications of the pandemic for future debt management

	Boosting or establishing a cash buffer	Review of primary dealership systems	Issuance of new securities	Review of communication with Central Banks as major investors	Adaption of a business continuity/recovery plan	More emphasis on investor relations	Lengthening average maturity	Reassessment of issuance techniques	Others
Australia	X					X		X	
Austria					X			X	
Belgium	X						X		
Canada	X						X		3
Chile	X	X				X	X		
Colombia	X		X		X		X		
Costa Rica	X		X			X			
Czech Republic	X		X			X	X		
Denmark						X			
Estonia		X	X			X	X		
Finland				X	X				
France				X	X				
Germany									
Greece	X	X	X	X	X	X	X		
Hungary	X				X	X	X		
Iceland			X		X		X		
Ireland				X	X				
Israel					X	X		X	
Italy			X			X			
Japan					X		X		
Korea		X	X						
Latvia		X	X						
Lithuania		X			X		X	X	
Luxembourg	X				X				
Mexico (local market debt)	X	X		X		X		X	X

	Boosting or establishing a cash buffer	Review of primary dealership systems	Issuance of new securities	Review of communication with Central Banks as major investors	Adaption of a business continuity/recovery plan	More emphasis on investor relations	Lengthening average maturity	Reassessment of issuance techniques	Others
Mexico (external market debt)	X	X		X		X		X	X
Netherlands			X		X				
New Zealand	X		X	X	X		X		
Norway									
Poland	X	X	X		X	X			
Portugal					X		X	X	
Slovak Republic	X		X	X		X			
Slovenia	X				X	X			
Spain					X	X			
Sweden			X	X		X		X	
Switzerland						X			
Turkey						X			
United Kingdom									X
Total	**16**	**9**	**14**	**9**	**18**	**19**	**13**	**8**	**6**

Table A.27. Q14 Specified OTHER implications of the pandemic for future debt management

Australia	
Austria	
Belgium	
Canada	(i) Manage maturity structure of debt issuance and growing share of money market instruments (treasury bills). (ii) Assess whether the debt issuance mix used to raise funding during the pandemic should be modified or rebalanced.(iii) With the last two Debt Management Strategy plans, the government intends to issue a historic level of long-term bonds to manage the significant increase in debt resulting from the response to COVID-19. In light of the unique situation posed by the COVID-19 crisis, the government will continue to review the Debt Management Strategy for opportunities to borrow at longer maturities and lock in historically low interest rates, as well as enhance the predictability of debt servicing costs.
Chile	
Colombia	
Costa Rica	
Czech Republic	
Denmark	
Estonia	
Finland	
France	
Germany	
Greece	
Hungary	
Iceland	
Ireland	
Israel	
Italy	
Japan	
Korea	
Latvia	
Lithuania	
Luxembourg	
Mexico (local market debt)	more flexible mechanisms in order to issue more if the market demand conditions allow it
Mexico (external market debt)	more flexible mechanisms in order to issue more if the market demand conditions allow it
Netherlands	
New Zealand	
Norway	
Poland	
Portugal	
Slovak Republic	
Slovenia	
Spain	
Sweden	
Switzerland	
Turkey	
United Kingdom	N/A

Table A.28. Q14 Potential implications of the pandemic for future debt management – Country Notes

Australia	*Operational lessons learned from the pandemic will be incorporated into BC planning *The wisdom of having extended the yield curve and lengthened the average term of the portfolio in the years prior to the pandemic has been demonstrated over the past 18 months (i.e. lower debt refinancing task, more diversity in investor base and more points on the yield curve to fund)

	*Maintaining investor relation activities remains integral to AOFM operations
Austria	
Belgium	As answered in question 11, there is no formal liquidity buffer but we tend to finance our needs earlier in the year in order to be able to cope with a deteriorating situation/unexpected needs. The strategy of debt lengthening was underway before the pandemic but could potentially be slightly accentuated.
Canada	As Canada moves towards economic recovery, the shift towards long-term debt issuance, which began in 2020-21, will continue. Funding more COVID-19-related debt through long-term issuance will help provide security and stability to the government balance sheet by lowering debt rollover while remaining fiscally prudent.
Chile	
Colombia	
Costa Rica	
Czech Republic	
Denmark	
Estonia	
Finland	
France	
Germany	
Greece	
Hungary	
Iceland	
Ireland	
Israel	
Italy	The Italian Treasury funding strategy has always been based on the principles of transparency and predictability. In order to handle possible risks deriving from a national and international geopolitical scenario, the funding strategy has always oriented toward managing interest-rate and refinancing risks, so as to continue to keep exposure to such risks under control. However, the outbreak of Covid-19 crisis has shown how the above-mentioned factors are characterized by a high level of uncertainty which makes difficult to predict their evolution over time. Therefore, more emphasis will be placed on the maintenance of a high degree of flexibility (in the choice of issuance methodologies and instruments) in order to quickly response and adapt the funding plan to the evolution of the market context.
Japan	Comments on "Adaption of a business continuity/recovery plan"; We reaffirm the importance of developing the business environment where operations can be conducted remotely, based on the experience of the pandemic. Comments on "Lengthening average maturity"; Since the JGB market issuance amount, especially in the short–term zone, has rapidly increased in response to the COVID-19 pandemic, the flow-basis average maturity has shortened from 9 years to 6 years 10 months. We think that average maturity adjustment will be essential in the future.
Korea	
Latvia	The new Primary Dealer joining the system in 2021 positively impacted auction results with additional demand. Review/enlargement of Primary Dealer system might be a topic in further years. The recently established Latvia`s Sustainability Bond framework enables us to issue Green, Social and/or Sustainability Bonds in future.
Lithuania	Some of the implications were not a direct consequence of a pandemic, e.g. we reassessed our issuance techniques because of increased Government debt and the need to manage it more effectively, which in turn was caused by the pandemic (to an extent).
Luxembourg	
Mexico (local market debt)	The response to this question is not split into local and external debt.
Mexico (external market debt)	The response to this question is not split into local and external debt.
Netherlands	
New Zealand	
Norway	
Poland	
Portugal	Portugal has been running cash reserves in excess of 40% of its gross funding needs for some years and during the pandemic crisis this instrument allowed the DMO to better time the market and to delay new funding until better knowledge of the true size of the additional funding needs.
Slovak Republic	
Slovenia	
Spain	The Spanish Treasury's overall DMO strategy was effective in the face of the pandemic. However, the sharp and sudden increase in net funding needs was, of course, a challenge. In 2020 the Spanish Treasury had to revise its net funding needs upwards from €32.5 bn to €130 bn, and later down to €110 bn. This experience was shared by many DMOs across the globe,

	given that no one expected the pandemic back in 2019, when the 2020 Funding Strategies were devised. Despite this drastic increase, we were able to handle the increase in funding needs quite smoothly thanks to: (1)the diversity of instruments available, (2)the deep investor pool that the Spanish Treasury enjoys, (3)the coordination with other Euro-area DMOs, and (4) stable issuance strategy followed by the Spanish Treasury, as wellas many other aspects, we were able to handle the increase in funding needs quite smoothly. However, it's always possible to keep reinforcing our strategy and policies. To highlight two factors: Investor relations are key, to better understand what investors look for and keep these needs in mind with our issuance. Keeping a flexible strategy and having contingency plans is key for a DMO, given the importance of our role. In this respect, having faced extreme weather events and the pandemic itself, the Spanish Treasury understands that this type of planning is crucial.
Sweden	
Switzerland	The issuance procedures and techniques in place have proven to be adequate and flexible enough and the existing liquidity buffer was sufficient (if not too high). Therefore, there is no need to add new instruments or fundamentally change the issuance process or the liquidity management. One point that we may review is the regularity of communication with market participants in times of high uncertainty and the resulting trade-off between flexibility and planning certainty.
Turkey	
United Kingdom	The UK DMO regularly reviews its funding strategy, issuance techniques, and the primary dealer system to ensure that its practices are in line with the government's debt management objective to minimise, over the long-term, the costs of meeting the government's financing needs while taking into account risk. While COVID-19 has certainly required us to adapt our existing issuance practices, it has not fundamentally changed the primary market issuance model and we do not anticipate any change to the long-term strategic approach.

Table A.29. Q15 To what extent are you concerned about the adequacy of investor demand?

	Very Concerned				Not concerned
Australia					X
Austria				X	
Belgium				X	
Canada					X
Chile		X			
Colombia				X	
Costa Rica					X
Czech Republic					X
Denmark				X	
Estonia					X
Finland				X	
France				X	
Germany					X
Greece	X				
Hungary	X				
Iceland		X			
Ireland			X		
Israel					X
Italy			X		
Japan					X
Korea			X		
Latvia		X			
Lithuania			X		
Luxembourg					X
Mexico (local market debt)		X			
Mexico (external market debt)					X
Netherlands				X	
New Zealand					X

	Very Concerned				Not concerned
Norway				X	
Poland				X	
Portugal			X		
Slovak Republic		X			
Slovenia					X
Spain					X
Sweden					X
Switzerland				X	
Turkey	X				
United Kingdom				X	
Total	**3**	**5**	**5**	**11**	**14**

Table A.30. Q15 Please indicate situations or factors that give rise to concerns about future investor demand (e.g. changes in global liquidity conditions, regulations)?

Australia	
Austria	
Belgium	Lower debt purchases by central banks will impact the funding cost for borrowers going forward. However, we believe underlying demand for fixed income instruments will remain strong.
Canada	As part of business continuity planning, many risk scenarios are reviewed, and these scenarios can evolve and change over time. As part of a recent playbook manual that was prepared for a table-top exercise for debt management preparedness, one of the broad stress scenarios where the Government's access to funding could be jeopardized was confidence crises: a persistent structural funding pressure due to insufficient demand for Government of Canada securities as a result of deterioration in market confidence and/or as a result of a potential credit downgrade. Various contingency plans have been developed to respond to different scenarios involving investor demand.
Chile	The main risk is a significant change in the pension fund system, which affect the demand from pension managers.
Colombia	Changes in global liquidity conditions.
Costa Rica	
Czech Republic	Investor demand for CZK- or EUR-denominated government bonds maintains relatively high levels. Share of domestic investors is increasing (mainly domestic banks), while share of non-resident holders decreased from 40% in 2019 to 30 % at the end of September.
Denmark	
Estonia	Estonia has minor funding needs.
Finland	A poorly communicated or executed exit from QE by the Central Banks
France	Regulation changes for long-term investors (e.g. pension funds, insurers), change in central banks monetary policies
Germany	
Greece	
Hungary	Monetary policy changes (QE tapering); households' demand; inflation
Iceland	
Ireland	Change in investor dynamics as the ECB QE buying reduces
Israel	
Italy	The slowing path of ECB Purchase Programme would probably affect the investor's demand in the near future in a relevant way.
Japan	
Korea	
Latvia	Climate related matters and respective demand driven by ESG investors. Global growth and inflation expectations and investors demand for duration.
Lithuania	The issues we face are not related to the lack of investor demand but rather to the current market conditions were there is no significant difference in cost of borrowing for issuers of different rating categories
Luxembourg	
Mexico (local market debt)	Local Market Debt The foreign capital outflows. Retirement fund managers have reduced their appetite for investment in local currency against a potential dollar strengthening. Increasing government financial needs. Increasing maturities for the debt portfolio. Monetary policy normalization. China has been incorporated into Global Debt Indexes; consequently, they have

	captured an important amount of capital flows addressed to emerging markets.
Mexico (external market debt)	
Netherlands	Increased competition in European bond markets (more issuance by all European Debt Management Offices (DMO's) in response to corona, but also an increased presence of the European Commission), regulation impacting investor demand.
New Zealand	
Norway	
Poland	Changes in monetary policy of national and key foreign central banks.
Portugal	The end of PEPP program by the ECB could lead to a decrease of investor demand in general for the EGB market. In addition, the rise in inflation could significantly increase the rates and affect the investor demand for PGB market.
Slovak Republic	Concerned of ECB tapering and replacement of ECB position by new investors outside of domestic market.
Slovenia	
Spain	Given how varied our investor base is, thanks to the efforts carried out in past years directly by the Spanish Treasury and through our Primary Dealer Network, we do not see a specific risk in this regard. We expect investor demand to remain strong throughout possible regulation or liquidity changes. However, of course, if there were a market-shaping event, such as the Global Financial Crisis, investor behavior could be seriously affected. This means that maintaining open communications with our investor base is crucial, and something we put special emphasis in.
Sweden	Sweden is a AAA country with a sound fiscal policy and a debt to GDP ratio of around 30% (central government). On a relative basis, we have not experienced any lack of demand or difficulties carrying out the increased funding requirement during the pandemic.
Switzerland	As our government bonds are the most liquid and highest rated securities on the Swiss capital markets, we do not expect investor demand to be a significant problem. Even in the times of highest uncertainty, we were able to conduct successful auctions. As more than three quarter of our bonds are held by domestic investors, we have found that the demand for our bonds has been stable even in times of geo-political turbulences.
Turkey	We are closely monitoring monetary policies and tapering plans of central banks and its impacts over the domestic market as well as any ongoing risks related to the pandemic.
United Kingdom	

Table A.31. Q16 Following the pandemic which operations do you now plan to carry out remotely (including at least partially) as standard that you did NOT do remotely prior to the pandemic?

	Payments/transactions	Cash management	Auctions	Derivative operations	Syndications, private placements or some other type of funding operations	Others
Australia	X	X	X		X	
Austria	X	X	X	X	X	
Belgium	X	X	X	X		
Canada						
Chile	X	X	X	X	X	
Colombia						
Costa Rica	X	X	X			
Czech Republic						
Denmark						
Estonia	X	X	X		X	
Finland						
France	X					Administrative tasks, research
Germany						
Greece		X	X		X	
Hungary						
Iceland						
Ireland		X			X	
Israel	X	X		X		

	Payments/transactions	Cash management	Auctions	Derivative operations	Syndications, private placements or some other type of funding operations	Others
Italy	X	X		X	X	
Japan						
Korea						
Latvia						
Lithuania	X	X	X	X	X	
Luxembourg	X	X				
Mexico (local market debt)				X		
Mexico (external market debt)				X		
Netherlands						
New Zealand						
Norway			X			
Poland		X	X		X	
Portugal	X			X		
Slovak Republic						
Slovenia	X	X	X	X	X	
Spain						
Sweden						
Switzerland						
Turkey						
United Kingdom						N/A
Total	**13**	**14**	**11**	**10**	**10**	**2**

Annex B. OECD 2021 Survey on Liquidity in Government Bond Secondary Markets

---

This annex belongs to the OECD Sovereign Borrowing Outlook 2022.
Thirty-seven of the 38 OECD countries responded to this survey.
Countries which responded to the survey but did not provide comments to a question may not appear in the table of answers. The requested date for a response to the survey was 15 October 2021.
Source: 2021 Survey on Liquidity in Secondary Government Bond Markets by the OECD Working Party on Debt Management.

Table of contents

Table B.1. Domestic currency bond lines 167
Table B.2. Q2 Do you believe it is necessary/important to maintain certain volumes in specific maturity segments in your country? 169
Table B.3. What has been the overall trend in the liquidity conditions of your domestic sovereign bonds -in terms of bid-ask spread, trading volumes etc.- over the last 12 months? 171
Table B.4. Q4 If you answered there was an improvement or a decline in Q3, please specify the main factors that might affect the changes in liquidity conditions? 174
Table B.5. Q4 If you answered there was an improvement or a decline in Q3, please specify the main factors that might affect the changes in liquidity conditions? 176
Table B.6. Q4 If you answered there was an improvement or a decline in Q3, please specify the main factors that might affect the changes in liquidity conditions – Country Notes 178
Table B.7. Q5 Have you observed changes in liquidity conditions of your foreign bonds over the last 12 months? 179
Table B.8. Q6 Have you observed changes in liquidity conditions of bond related derivate and repo markets over the last 12 months? 180
Table B.9. Q7 Do you have measures in place to motivate dealers to provide liquidity? 182
Table B.10. Q8 Do you undertake any other measures in order to enhance liquidity? 185
Table B.11. Q8b If yes to Q8, please specify the measures that you undertake to enhance liquidity 186
Table B.12. Q8b Other specified measures that you undertake to enhance liquidity measures that you undertake to enhance liquidity 188
Table B.13. Q9 Have you imposed new requirements on market-makers in their provision of liquidity over the last 12 months? 189
Table B.14. Q10 Have you made any changes to your market communication strategies since the pandemic? 190
Table B.15. Q11 How has the transition to alternative reference rates been proceeding in your country? 191
Table B.16. Q12 In your opinion, are market participants in your country generally ready for the transition? 193
Table B.17. Q13 Do you have any plans to issue securities linked to an alternative reference rate? 195

Table B.1. Domestic currency bond lines

	How many domestic currency bond lines exist	With between USD 5 billion and USD 10 billion on issue	With greater than USD 10 billion on issue
Australia	29 Nominals 7 Linker lines 5 zero coupon lines (short term Treasury Notes) 41 Total	Assuming AUD = 0.7498, USD$5b ~ AUD$6.66b 5 Nominal lines 2 Linker Lines 3 zero coupon lines 10 Total	Assuming AUD = 0.75, USD$10b ~ AUD$13.33b 24 Nominal Lines 0 Linker Lines 0 zero coupon lines 24 Total
Austria	30	8	17
Belgium	Total: 60 OLOs: 32 EUR EMTN: 28	8 OLO lines	24 OLO lines at EURUSD (exchange rate 1.185677)
Canada	53 bond lines are outstanding, covering the 2, 3, 5, 10, 30, and 50-year sectors.	17 bonds have between USD 5 billion and USD 10 billion outstanding (including inflation adjustments for real return bonds).	30 bonds have greater than USD 10 billion outstanding (including inflation adjustments for real return bonds).
Chile	16	5	none
Colombia	There are 4 lines of zero coupon bonds, 12 lines of nominal bonds and 8 lines of linked bonds in local currency.	There are 8 lines of nominal bonds and 1 line of linked bonds in local currency between USD 5 billion and USD 10 billion on issue.	There are not lines with greater than USD 10 billion on issue.
Costa Rica	It´s 79 lines of nominal bonds: 4 lines zero coupon bonds, 20 lines of floaters, 44 lines of indexed rate and 11 lines of fixed rate.	The amounts of all lines or series are less than 5 billion.	The amounts of all lines or series are less than 5 billion.
Czech Republic	Bond lines as of 30. 06. 2021 Czech Republic government bonds denominated in CZK T-bonds: 24 bonds (3 lines of floaters, 2 line of zero coupon bond and 19 lines of fixed-rate bonds) T-bills: 4 lines Retail bonds: 22 lines (8 lines of inflation-linked retail bonds, 14 lines of fixed-rate retail bonds) Czech Republic government bonds denominated in foreign currency 1 line of fixed-rate Eurobond denominated in EUR 2 lines of zero coupon government bonds denominated in EUR issued on domestic market under Czech law 1 line of fixed-rate bond denominated in Yen – private placement	11 bond lines, all denominated in domestic currency	0 bond lines
Denmark	13	6	4
Estonia	2 (1 Treasury Bill and 1 Eurobond)	None	None
Finland	22	16	0
France	71 lines	8 lines	58 lines
Germany	82 lines: 62 nominal bonds, 5 inflation linked bonds, 3 green bonds, 12 bills	7 lines	73 lines
Greece	49 lines of nominal bonds 3 lines of inflation-linked bonds		
Hungary	30 lines of wholesale bonds, and 142 lines of retail bonds	none	none
Iceland	Total of 10 lines (7 nominal bonds and 3 linkers)	None	None
Ireland	31 (19 fixed, 10 amortising, 2 floating)	14	5
Israel	Total lines:36 Usd/ILS = 3.26	24	0
Italy	147 lines: 18 lines of bills, 90 lines of nominal bonds, 4 lines of zero-coupon bonds, 10 lines of floaters, 13 lines of linkers, 9 lines of linkers tailored to retail investors and 3 lines of nominal bonds tailored to retail investors	30 lines: 18 lines of bills, 2 line of nominal bonds, 2 lines of linkers, 5 lines of linkers tailored to retail investors and 3 lines of nominal bonds tailored to retail investors	116 lines: 88 lines of nominal bonds, 4 lines of zero-coupon bonds, 10 lines of floaters, 11 lines of linkers, 3 lines of linkers tailored to retail investors.
Japan	534 lines(As of end of June,2021)	50 lines(As of end of	277 lines(As of end of

	How many domestic currency bond lines exist	With between USD 5 billion and USD 10 billion on issue	With greater than USD 10 billion on issue
		June,2021)	June,2021)
Korea	60 lines of nominal bonds , 5 lines of inflation linkers (in terms of maturity, 7 lines of nominal bonds, one line of inflation linker)	21 lines of nominal bonds	34 lines of nominal bonds
Latvia	EUR is a currency used for both the Eurobond (XS ISIN under English law) issuances and domestic T-bonds (LV ISIN under Latvian law). Together there are 18 lines as of 01.01.2022, of which: 7 lines of domestic T-bonds (LV ISIN) 11 lines of Eurobonds (XS ISIN)	No line.	No line
Lithuania	Domestic market: 21 bond (5 of which are on-the-run bonds), 31 retail bond (none on-the-run). International markets (only in euros): 11 nominal bonds	0 (zero)	0 (zero)
Luxembourg	10	None	None
Mexico	15 lines of nominal bonds, 9 lines of nominal inflation linked bonds, 27 lines of zero coupon bonds and 54 lines of floaters.	7 lines, 2 cero coupon bond, 2 nominal bonds and 3 inflation linked bonds.	16 lines, 11 nominal bonds and 5 inflation linked bonds.
Netherlands	23	4	19
New Zealand	13 nominal bond lines and 4 inflation-indexed bond lines.	7 nominal bond lines (note this includes holdings by the Reserve Bank of New Zealand)	1 nominal bond line (note this includes holdings by the Reserve Bank of New Zealand)
Norway	9	5	0
Poland	33 domestic currency marketable bond lines 345 lines in 7 types of bond on the retail market	19 lines	3 lines
Portugal	We have 27 domestic currency bonds. 17 lines of nominal bonds, 6 lines of floaters and 4 retail bonds.	On the issue date, one line (a nominal bond).	On the issue date, none of them.
Slovak Republic	24	0	0
Slovenia	There are 21 domestic currency bonds.	None.	None.
Spain	61 domestic currency bond lines in total. 52 nominal bonds. 9 linkers (inflation-linked bonds).	4 bonds. 2 linkers and 2 nominal bonds	53 bonds. 4 linkers and 49 nominal bonds.
Sweden	18	6	2
Switzerland	23	1 (around USD 6 billion)	0
Turkey	79	None	None
United Kingdom	There are 53 nominal lines and 31 inflation-linked lines, totaling 84.	Two inflation-linked lines. Calculations exclude DMO holdings.	53 nominal and 28 inflation-linked gilts (ILG). One inflation-linked gilt, 0⅛% ILG 2051, launched in April 2021, has an amount outstanding of less than USD 5 billion. The largest respective nominal and inflation-linked lines are 0⅞% 2029, which has nearly £41.6bn (nominal) in issue, and 1⅛% ILG 2022, which has £22.8bn (uplifted nominal) in issue. Calculations exclude DMO holdings.

Table B.2. Q2 Do you believe it is necessary/important to maintain certain volumes in specific maturity segments in your country?

	Yes	No	Comment
Australia	X		Look to maintain sufficient line sizes particularly in the 3yr, 5yr, 10yr and 20yr parts of the curve to support the futures contracts.
Austria	X		A certain minimum size in the main benchmark bonds is important in order to support secondary market liquidity.
Belgium	X		In order to create and maintain a sufficiently liquid full curve, volumes issued in all lines should reach sufficient levels.
Canada	X		Benchmark size ranges for each sector are announced in the annual Debt Management Strategy. For fiscal year 2021-22, benchmarks in core sectors will be lower in many sectors relative to fiscal year 2020-21, reflecting the decreased overall issuance in bonds. Due to much higher issuance levels in core sectors, particularly in 10-year and 30-year bonds, the benchmark bond target ranges were increased in fiscal year 2020-21 relative to fiscal year 2019-20. In pursuing much higher bond issuance and help smooth the cash flow profile of upcoming maturities, in fiscal year 2020-21 the government added a new December 1st maturity date in the 10-year sector and two new maturity dates in the 3-year bond sector, April 1st and October 1st, by promoting the 3-year bond sector to its own maturity dates (previously fungible with 5-year bonds). As of fiscal year 2021-2022, (in CAD) these benchmark size ranges were (as per Table A2.5): https://www.budget.gc.ca/2021/report-rapport/anx2-en.html 2Y: $16 Billion to $22 Billion for February, May, August, and November maturity dates 3Y: $16 Billion to $20 Billion for April and October maturity dates 5Y: $22 Billion to $26 Billion for March and September maturity dates 10Y: $38 Billion to $44 Billion for June and December maturity dates 30Y: $46 Billion to $58 Billion for December maturity dates RRB: $8 Billion to $12 Billion for December maturity dates (including inflation adjustments)
Chile	X		The issuance policy established by the DMO consider the issuance of benchmarks, which are reopened until they reach an amount that is considered reasonable to make a bond liquid.
Colombia	X		We believe it is important to maintain high volumes all along the yield curve not only to keep liquidity in secondary market but in order to have benchmarks in the different sections of the curves.
Costa Rica	X		Benchmark: 3, 5 7 and 10 years. USD 160 million for CRC zero coupon bonds, USD 1.100 million for CRC fixed rate, USD 800 floating and USD 600 for indexed rate bonds. The Ministry of Finance of Costa Rica maintains volumes in certain segments or focal dates allows better price formation, which impacts the liquidity of the issues, allowing the placement of debt in better conditions.
Czech Republic	X		Ministry of Finance tries to keep sufficient outstanding amount of T-bonds along the whole yield curve so market participants may benefit from the market liquidity.
Denmark	X		Strategy is aimed at building up liquid benchmark series in key maturity segments. Focus on 2- and 10-year bonds, which in recent years, have been build up to a minimum of respectively around 8 USD bn. and 12 USD bn. However, volumes were higher in 2020 due to an increased financing requirement as a result of the covid-19 pandemic.
Estonia		X	
Finland	X		
France	X		It is important for us to maintain large volumes on all segments of our market. Nonetheless, we are demand-driven and would lower volumes issued if demand was weak on a particular segment. Our auction system (bill auction every week, long term nominal bonds, medium term nominal bond and inflation-linked bond every month) makes it easy to issue on every segment.
Germany	X		We perceive the traditional Bund segments of 2, 5, 10 and 30 years as well as Bills and Inflation-linked bonds to be of high importance for market participants.
Greece	X		
Hungary	X		We have regular and frequent benchmark auctions with maturities from 3 months up to 20 years. In 2021 we have introduced a new 30-year Green Bond, which is also auctioned regularly (quarterly). Issuing at several maturities ensures us a balanced maturity profile. Bond series are reopened several times, which helps to build up sufficiently large volumes. The targeted sizes are usually around USD 3 billion equivalent, the largest bond series are over USD 4 billion equivalent.
Iceland	X		It's very important to maintain liquidity in most segments on both our nominal and inflation-indexed curves, especially in 2, 5 and 10 years lines with regular issuance. A certain pre-announced minimum size in benchmark series is important to support secondary market liquidity.
Ireland	X		It is important to maintain liquidity throughout the curve. In general, the 5yr and 10yr and increasingly the 15 and 30 year points are viewed as key maturity segments and are usually the most active.
Israel	X		One of our primary focuses is on maintaining certain liquidity levels which support tradability, and vice versa. This is also a main goal for the primary dealership model (nonetheless, due to market conditions and structure some segments are known to be less liquid). Primary dealers (PDs) are obligated to quote bonds in both New Israeli Shekel (NIS) denominated Consumer Price Index (CPI)-linked and nominal bonds, including On-the-run bonds. Most bonds are quoted with a maximum spread of 3-4 bps, except for the 10 years On-the-run bond which is quoted with a maximum spread of 2 bps.

	Yes	No	Comment
Italy	X		This is a key pillar that we have in mind when define our issuance strategy. For each instrument and for each maturity we set a minimum outstanding volume to be issued before launching a new bond. Having an outstanding large enough for each bond is extremely important in order to guarantee a sufficient liquidity of the bond on the secondary market.
Japan		X	A breakdown of the JGB market issuance by maturity is determined with market needs and trends taken into account, covering a wide range of maturities from the short term to the super long term, based on government debt management policy requirements.
Korea	X		10 year maturity (benchmark)
Latvia	X		Liquidity is important regardless of maturity segment and is beneficiary for both primary and secondary market.
Lithuania	X		It is important to issue regularly at the longer end – 7-12 years, to ensure liquidity of the bonds. Volumes are not particularly important as longs as the issuance is regular.
Luxembourg	X		Liquidity is certainly important but the Luxembourg bonds lack volume in each maturity segment.
Mexico	X		Local Market Debt On the run bonds, are fundamental for portfolio duration management and for market makers to provide enough liquidity to the secondary market. This allows the correct development for local and foreign investors. Duration management is important to give flexibility to investors due to perspectives on market conditions or to specific investment objectives. For on the run bonds new issuances, we attempt to have an outstanding value of at least 5 billion dollars. The time to reach the 5 billion dollars outstanding in the short-term bonds is a year, for middle and long term is between 2 - 3 years. External Market Debt This is an aspect to which the Federal Government gives a lot of attention regarding its foreign denominated bonds. It's absolutely very important for bonds at specific tenors to comply with all the necessary characteristics in order to be consider as real benchmarks and size is one critical characteristic as it relates directly to liquidity (size it also a very important criteria for bonds to be included in global indexes which also enhance the instrument's liquidity). Here I's important to mention that bonds are consider as liquid benchmarks depending on the market where they are issued; for example, in the US dollar market Mexico's typical benchmarks are 10 and 30 years for notional amounts of at least 2 billion while in the euro market most typical benchmarks are 7 years (a notional amount of 750 million its more than enough) and 10, 12 and even 20 years (for these tenors in euros Mexico considers at least 1 billion as the proper benchmark size). As a sovereign issuer Mexico has the responsibility to establish true benchmarks in international financial markets as this will both enhance and facilitate the price discovery process of other Mexican issuers (either from the private or public sector).
Netherlands	X		All bonds <= 10 years (y) have a target of around 12 billion (bn). All bonds > 10 years (y) have a target of at least 10 billion (bn)
New Zealand	X		We target quickly building volume in newly syndicated 'benchmark' 10y and 20y (and now 30y) lines to a minimum of circa NZ$4b, in order to promote liquidity in these lines that we see as important points on the curve for offshore investors. We have a 'cap' on individual nominal and inflation-indexed bond lines of NZ$18b and NZ$6b respectively. These caps are designed to balance the need for liquidity in each line against building out a full New Zealand Government Bond (NZGB) curve and mitigating refinancing risk.
Norway	X		Norway has a policy of limiting the number of bond lines in order to build up the volume in existing lines to ensure liquidity. We issue a new 10-year bond every year in order to maintain the yield curve up to 10 years. The policy is to build the new 10-year bond up to a volume that constitutes nearly half of the borrowing requirement in each year. There is however large uncertainty about which volumes are necessary to reach satisfying liquidity in the specific segments.
Poland	X		In order to enhance market liquidity it is important to build large issues of benchmark bonds. In case of medium- and long-term domestic fixed rate bonds the desired amount outstanding is at least PLN 25bn (about USD 6.25bn).
Portugal	X		We believe it is important to maintain good levels of liquidity in all segments of our curve, in particular in 5y and 10y buckets. In those segments (5y and 10y), it is important to have at least an outstanding amount of USD 5 bln per bond. In steady state, we believe that the outstanding volume per bond should hover USD 10 bln.
Slovak Republic	X		We have goals stemming from the Debt Management Strategy that require us to meet refinancing and refixing risk criteria. It is up to DMO what mix of maturities will lead to fulfilling this criteria. We have to issue what market wants and what is risk and cost efficient within the Strategy boundaries
Slovenia		X	In the past Slovenia tended to issue "smaller" sizes of bonds in comparison to other Eurozone countries (around €1bn). For the past couple of years or so the policy has been to tap existing EUR bonds and thus increasing their original issue size up to €3bn. For the Republic of Slovenia, as a smaller issuer, is therefore liquidity wise not so necessary/important to maintain certain volumes in specific maturity segments than it is to ensure bigger issue size per bond.
Spain	X		Given our size as a sovereign issuer, our issuance plays a key role in financial markets. In order to maintain stability, predictability, and the liquid status of our issuance, we must make sure to maintain liquidity throughout all of our main maturity segments. Specifically, we try to maintain liquidity throughout all of the main points of our yield curve. To achieve this, we use benchmark programs, trying to keep liquid benchmarks with large volumes that represent each of the main points of our yield curve, such as the 5, 10, 15, 20, 30 and 50 year points. As time goes by and these benchmarks no longer correctly represent the intended maturity segment, they are replaced with a new benchmark.

	Yes	No	Comment
Sweden	X		Our bonds will be classified as benchmark once they become larger than 20 BN SEK
Switzerland	X		In our view, it is important to cover maturities of 1 to 13 years with liquid T-bonds. Additionally in the case of longer maturities, intermittent anchor points with individual bonds may complete the government yield curve. The yields on T-bonds constitute a key benchmark and therefore help to ensure an attractive and efficient Swiss capital market that functions well. As the Federal treasury finances itself exclusively via the domestic market, an efficient market is important to ensure beneficial financing conditions for the government. We are aiming for a maximum volume at maturity of around CHF 4 billion. This helps us to ensure that our relatively small debt volume (around USD 70 billion) is somewhat evenly distributed among the individual bonds.
Turkey	X		It is important to maintain a certain amount of liquidity for 2, 5 and 10 years benchmark bonds in order to meet the different duration needs of the investors as well as to form a solid long-term yield curve that will be treated as a reference rate in bond and money markets.
United Kingdom	X		Even though there are no specific volume targets in place, we believe that regular issuance at key benchmark maturities supports more efficient price discovery/price adjustment and, therefore, contributes to smooth functioning of the gilt market. To this end, we focus issuance of conventional (i.e. nominal) gilts particularly at the 5-, 10-, 20- and 30-year benchmark maturities with successive re-openings of relevant bonds until they reach benchmark size. The range of benchmark maturities to be supported and the volumes that are appropriate to target will vary over time according to the overall size of the debt programme and of the debt stock. For nominal gilts at present this is typically up to at least £30bn, with some lines reaching over £40bn. In the case of inflation-linked gilts, issuance takes place particularly at 10-, 20- and 30-year maturities with sizes typically built to around £15 to £20bn. Currently, the longest dated gilts are 1⅝% 2071 (nominal gilt) and 0⅛% 2068 (inflation-linked gilt), with approximately £21.6bn and £15.5bn nominal in market hands respectively.
Total	**34**	**3**	

Table B.3. What has been the overall trend in the liquidity conditions of your domestic sovereign bonds -in terms of bid-ask spread, trading volumes etc.- over the last 12 months?

	Trend	Comment
Australia	Decline	
Austria	No change	In the first nine months of 2021 (Jan-Aug), we have seen a decline in secondary market turnover in RAGBs (Republic of Austria Government Bonds) vs. the same period in 2020 of around 13%. However, in 2021YTD*, bid-ask spreads have tightened significantly compared to the last year and are back to pre-crisis levels. E.g., for the 10-year benchmark bonds the average bid-ask spread (on price basis) is as follows: 2017 16 ct 2018 18 ct 2019 14 ct 2020 26 ct 2021* 16 ct * until September 30, 2021
Belgium	Decline	Liquidity conditions are back to normal. We see a strong reduction in the use of our repo facility, which would indicate that interbank repo markets are functioning well. Secondary market volumes excluding the purchase programs by the ECB are down, both in activity by customers as in interdealer activity.
Canada	No change	Government securities markets in Canada were exhibiting good liquidity conditions entering the COVID-19 pandemic. Bid-ask spreads are generally low and trading volumes were strong across the curve. Investors exhibited good demand for Government securities including a significant proportion of foreign investors (non-residents). As global uncertainty increased at the beginning of 2020, investor confidence was disrupted and high levels of volatility caused a global flight from risk. Financial markets in Canada began to show signs of impairment with a deterioration in liquidity conditions. Market makers became reluctant to facilitate trades and some market participants rushed to sell assets to increase cash holdings. During this time, pricing of Canadian treasury bills and Government of Canada bonds became more uncertain, making it harder to price other assets (i.e. spread products) in the Canadian fixed income market. Higher bid-ask spreads and price-impact were observed for a few weeks during the months of March and April 2020, they have since reduced to lower levels (please refer to: https://www.bankofcanada.ca/2020/05/financial-system-review-2020/). Several policy actions were introduced by the Bank of Canada to help alleviate impaired market liquidity in Canada. A range of liquidity facilities and large-scale asset purchase programs were introduced in March and April 2020 to help restore market functioning and ensure that financial institutions have adequate liquidity. These programs have helped to improve liquidity conditions and market functioning across a wide range of markets. The overall trend in the liquidity conditions of Canadian domestic sovereign bonds is unchanged throughout most of 2021, as liquidity is back to normal levels since at least May 2020 (after its decline in March/April 2020). Furthermore, there has been increased participation from investors in Government of Canada securities.
Chile	Decline	The local market has experimented a downward in the liquidity trend, explained by the internal discussion derived from the pension management system and the withdrawals from individual account of pension funds, authorized by Law.
Colombia	Improvement	Over the past 12 months we've seen the overall trend has been improving particularly the first quarter of the year with a daily trading average of USD 600 million. Second and third quarters of the year were USD 450 million on average. 2021 has been better in terms of trading volumes than 2020. In terms of Bid-ask spread, 2021 has

	Trend	Comment
		had a better performance since we didn't observe peaks of 50-80bps as it was in March of 2020. During 2021, we've seen a bid-ask spread average of 4bps in nominal bonds and Bid-ask spread of 12bps in linked bonds.
Costa Rica	Improvement	The traded volume of government bonds in the secondary market is increased in 14%. The recent negotiations with the IMF and the application of the fiscal reform, have generally allowed improvements in market conditions because the confidence of the participants has increased.
Czech Republic	No change	Bid-ask spreads in last 12 months are relatively stable without any significant changes.
Denmark	No change	Overall there has been no specific trend in the liquidity conditions. During the period there has been some variation in the liquidity, primarily due to spill-over from the mortgage market where the duration of convertible bonds has increased significantly in periods.
Estonia	No change	Securities issuance was set up only in 2019 when Treasury Bills were first introduced. In 2020, Estonia reentered the international capital markets after 18 years by issuing a Eurobond (EUR 1.5 billion), which has been rather illiquid in the secondary market. There is no regular issuance calendar in place.
Finland	No change	
France	Improvement	Average volumes for 2021 back to 2019 levels after a decline in 2020. Bid-ask spreads have also normalized.
Germany	No change	Liquidity conditions in German Federal securities remain very good.
Greece	Improvement	
Hungary	Decline	The HGBs secondary market liquidity is lower compared to 2019, partly due to the central bank's QE programme. The traders' willingness to take risk is low, and the investors wait and most often follow the movements of the core (EUR, USD) markets with their decisions. Concerning the spreads it can be said that Primary Dealers (PDs) show a narrow spread for investors, there are already slightly wider spreads in the OTC market, and often the maximum spread is applied - especially if volatility increases - on the MTS Hungary market, which is the official platform of PDs' mandatory market making for HGBs.
Iceland	No change	Bid–ask spread and average ticket size have remained on average stable in recent years. Secondary market turnover is similar over the last two 12 month periods.
Ireland	No change	Bid-ask spreads have been relatively stable. Volumes fluctuate throughout the year and are higher around issuance windows
Israel	No change	The average daily volumes have remained about the same as in 2020, which increased volumes comparing with previous years. Nonetheless some months in the past year were characterized by lower volumes. We can add that although the CB quantitative easing program did reduce some liquidity, overall there wasn't a major change in liquidity measures.
Italy	Improvement	Over the last twelve months, the liquidity levels have been quite stable also thanks to the Central Banks' purchase programmes (APP and PEPP) that contributed to maintain low levels of volatility and favorable financial conditions through-out the year. Differently from the last quarter of 2020, during the first months of 2021 the volumes traded have increased significantly over all the segments of the Italian curve. Moreover, also for what concerns the bid-ask spread, it has reduced restoring the pre-pandemic levels. In terms of volumes traded on the main interdealer platform (MTS Italy), the positive trend reached its peak in the second quarter of 2021 keeping the levels of volumes traded stable during the recent months.
Japan	No change	
Korea	No change	
Latvia	Improvement	Active reopening of outstanding Eurobonds via Primary Dealer system in auctions in the domestic market has positively affected the trading in the secondary market
Lithuania	Mixed (Decline/No change)	The ECB's pandemic emergency purchase programme (PEPP) has decreased liquidity significantly and distorted the market even more than PSPP did.
Luxembourg	Don't know	
Mexico	Improvement	The Federal Government has witnessed a reduction in the bid/ask spread and an increase in volume, in addition to an increase of sensibility (DV01) in contrast with beginning of the COVID-19 pandemic.
Netherlands	No change	There has been little change in the overall trend in liquidity conditions. Secondary market turnover has been moving around the average of the last couple of years with ups around new issuances and re-openings and downs when issuance is lower and market participants are less active i.e. during August. Bid-ask spreads have been quite volatile from month to month but even from week to week or day to day. Bond markets have seen an overall increase in volatility, especially during the last couple of months, and therefore a slightly higher b/a-spread is only a function of market conditions and not necessarily due to trading conditions.
New Zealand	Decline	Primarily a function of personnel turnover at trading banks and lower risk appetite from price-markers.
Norway	Improvement	We use a liquidity index to monitor liquidity in the secondary market for government bond. The index is a composite of four indicators that are primarily price-based measures. The index shows signs that liquidity has gradually improved since 2012. However, owing to the market turbulence associated with Covid-19, the liquidity conditions declined sharply in early 2020. Since then, the liquidity situation has improved significantly again.

	Trend	Comment
Poland	Improvement	Quoted bid-ask spreads of 10-year benchmark bond were initially narrowing after their peaks in March 2020. Since the second half of 2021 they started to increase and at the end of September reached almost half of the maximum level noted in the beginning of the pandemic. Spreads of shorter benchmark bonds were quite stable over the last 12 months and stayed within the pre-pandemic levels. The upward trend in average quoted volumes was continued by the end of 2020 and then started to decline toward the levels noted at the beginning of the pandemic. Data from electronic market for secondary trading.
Portugal	No change	In 2020 and before the pandemic crisis, the liquidity in the secondary market was improving vs 2019 in terms of bid-ask spreads, but with lower volumes. After that, liquidity for Portuguese government bonds decreased considerably, particularly in the month of March of 2020, when new COVID-19 cases emerged in European countries: bid-offer spreads widened significantly and some Primary Dealers interrupted their market making activity motivated by increased overall uncertainty (there were days without any quotation). The ECB measures (namely with the introduction of the PEPP and the new PELTROs) contributed to the stabilization of the market and improve liquidity, which resumed pre-crisis levels. Bid-ask spreads also tightened again, returning to pre-Covid levels and remained unchanged during most of 2021. Only at the beginning of August 2021 have we seen a slight increase in spreads due to lack of liquidity during the holiday season.
Slovak Republic	No change	Spreads comparable with 2020 and less trades on MTS since the COVID-19 pandemic.
Slovenia	Improvement	In the last 12 months the bid-ask spread tightened comparing to the year before converging to the level in the period before pandemic. Correspondingly trading volumes increased.
Spain	Improvement	We have two main metrics to measure liquidity conditions in our secondary market. On the one hand we use an indicator we call the "VNC" which measures the turnover volume, the total time that price-quotes are displayed on the secondary market and the bid-ask spread. This VNC indicator depends positively on the total price-quote time, positively on the turnover volume and negatively on the bid-ask spread. It is therefore a good indicator to measure overall liquidity conditions in our secondary market. Overall, this VNC indicator has shown an improvement in the past 12 months, and is currently above its pre-pandemic levels for our Bonos y Obligaciones del Estado (instruments with a maturity between 3 and 50 years). Going back to the start of 2020, we saw a sharp fall in March and April, followed by a strong recovery. However, for the past 12 months, there has been a continued upward trend in liquidity conditions. Looking at our Letras del Tesoro, with 3/6/9/12 month maturities, their liquidity conditions also declined after the pandemic, and have shown a strong recovery. However, in this case, the liquidity conditions have returned to pre-pandemic levels and stayed relatively stable at this level.
Sweden	Decline	Reduced borrowing need after initial increase due to pandemic. Also reduced liquidity due to QE from the central bank.
Switzerland	Improvement	After the market turbulences at the beginning of the pandemic, the Swiss capital market quickly normalized. At the end of the summer of 2020, liquidity conditions were mostly back to normal. The further waves of the pandemic had no pronounced impact on the liquidity conditions of our bonds. As in all years, there were some seasonal differences in terms of market liquidity (e.g. less activity in the summer months), but those are not specific to our sovereign bonds. The main contributor to a slightly improved secondary market liquidity of our sovereign bonds was the higher issuance volume of the Swiss Confederation caused by the elevated financing needs of the Confederation's Covid-19 measures. We expect the market liquidity to return to pre-pandemic levels once the issuance activity of the Confederation normalizes.
Turkey	Decline	Domestic bond trading in the last 12 months (October 2020-September 2021) in Borsa Istanbul's organized Outright Purchases and Sales Market shows fluctuations with an average of 3 billion USD per month. While in the first quarter of year 2021 there was strong increasing trend in bond trading, this has decreased over the summer. On the other hand, comparing the first nine months' trading volumes of year 2020 and 2021, there is a decrease in 2021 (47.75% decrease in USD terms and 36.50% decrease in TRY terms.
United Kingdom	Improvement	Data available to us suggest that bid offer spreads of 10-year gilts were largely unchanged in September 2021 when compared to September 2020. Bid-offer spreads exhibited higher volatility in the September 2020 to March 2021 period; from April 2021 onwards, the trading range has narrowed. With respect to 30-year gilts, bid offer spreads have decreased over the past year. In the September 2020 to April 2021 period though, the trading range was more volatile than it has been recently; two short-run spikes were recorded (in the second half of December 2020 and around the end of February and beginning of March 2021).
Total: Improvement	13	
Total: Decline	8	
Total: No change	17	
Total: Don't know	1	

Table B.4. Q4 If you answered there was an improvement or a decline in Q3, please specify the main factors that might affect the changes in liquidity conditions?

In the LAST 12 months

	COVID-19 pandemic on a global basis	COVID-19 pandemic on a national basis	Monetary policy developments	Issuance strategies	Design of borrowing instruments	Market microstructure (e.g. electronic trading)	New regulations	Changes in investor base	Changes in investor sentiment	Others
Australia	X	X	X			X		X		
Austria										
Belgium			X	X						
Canada										
Chile	X						X			
Colombia	X	X		X	X	X	X	X	X	
Costa Rica	X	X			X				X	Level of interest rates
Czech Republic										
Denmark										
Estonia										
Finland										
France	X	X	X						X	
Germany										
Greece	X	X	X	X				X	X	
Hungary	X	X	X	X						
Iceland										
Ireland										
Israel										
Italy	X		X	X		X		X	X	
Japan										
Korea										
Latvia			X	X	X				X	

	COVID-19 pandemic on a global basis	COVID-19 pandemic on a national basis	Monetary policy developments	Issuance strategies	Design of borrowing instruments	Market microstructure (e.g. electronic trading)	New regulations	Changes in investor base	Changes in investor sentiment	Others
Lithuania			X						X	
Luxembourg										
Mexico	X	X	X	X				X	X	Fiscal balance
Netherlands										
New Zealand			X						X	Personnel changes at trading banks.
Norway	X	X		X						
Poland	X	X	X					X	X	
Portugal										
Slovak Republic										
Slovenia	X		X							
Spain			X	X					X	
Sweden			X							
Switzerland	X	X	X	X						
Turkey	X	X	X							
United Kingdom	X	X	X	X						
Total	15	12	17	11	3	3	2	6	11	3

Table B.5. Q4 If you answered there was an improvement or a decline in Q3, please specify the main factors that might affect the changes in liquidity conditions?

In the NEXT 12 months

	COVID-19 pandemic on a global basis	COVID-19 pandemic on a national basis	Monetary policy developments	Issuance strategies	Design of borrowing instruments	Market microstructure (e.g. electronic trading)	New regulations	Changes in investor base	Changes in investor sentiment	Others
Australia	X	X	X				X			
Austria										
Belgium			X							
Canada										
Chile							X			
Colombia			X							
Costa Rica			X	X				X	X	
Czech Republic										
Denmark										
Estonia										
Finland										
France	X	X	X						X	
Germany										
Greece	X	X	X	X				X	X	
Hungary	X	X	X	X						
Iceland										
Ireland										
Israel										
Italy	X		X	X		X		X	X	
Japan										
Korea										
Latvia			X	X	X				X	
Lithuania			X						X	

	COVID-19 pandemic on a global basis	COVID-19 pandemic on a national basis	Monetary policy developments	Issuance strategies	Design of borrowing instruments	Market microstructure (e.g. electronic trading)	New regulations	Changes in investor base	Changes in investor sentiment	Others
Luxembourg										
Mexico	X	X	X	X	X			X		
Netherlands										
New Zealand			X	X					X	
Norway	X			X						
Poland	X	X	X					X	X	
Portugal										
Slovak Republic										
Slovenia	X		X							
Spain										
Sweden										
Switzerland	X	X	X	X						
Turkey	X	X	X							
United Kingdom	X	X	X	X		X	X	X	X	
Total	**12**	**9**	**17**	**10**	**2**	**2**	**3**	**6**	**9**	**0**

Table B.6. Q4 If you answered there was an improvement or a decline in Q3, please specify the main factors that might affect the changes in liquidity conditions – Country Notes

Australia	
Austria	
Belgium	Given the increased issuance and the interventions of central banks, the market has been (and may continue to be) much more focused on primary transactions than on secondary positioning.
Canada	Not applicable (N/A)
Chile	See last comment
Colombia	
Costa Rica	
Czech Republic	
Denmark	
Estonia	
Finland	
France	
Germany	
Greece	
Hungary	
Iceland	
Ireland	
Israel	
Italy	
Japan	
Korea	
Latvia	
Lithuania	
Luxembourg	
Mexico	
Netherlands	
New Zealand	
Norway	
Poland	
Portugal	
Slovak Republic	
Slovenia	
Spain	We could highlight two main factors behind the improvement in liquidity conditions. On the one hand, the stable issuance strategy carried out by the Spanish Treasury is an important contributor to liquidity in our secondary markets. This is because it gives Primary Dealers a stable framework that they can count on, and therefore more incentives to continue to participate in providing liquidity in secondary markets. On the other hand, the favorable market conditions brought about by the ECB's monetary policy response to the pandemic. This response could be one of the factors behind the improvement in liquidity.
Sweden	
Switzerland	The pandemic led to higher debt levels and higher issuance activity. Both had a positive effect on liquidity conditions. Over the next 12 months, there could also be some monetary policy developments (tapering, interest rates) that could influence the capital markets and the liquidity conditions of our bonds.
Turkey	
United Kingdom	

Table B.7. Q5 Have you observed changes in liquidity conditions of your foreign bonds over the last 12 months?

	Change	Comment
Australia	Not applicable	
Austria	No change	Liquidity in our foreign currency issues under the Euro Medium Term Note (EMTN) programme has always been relatively limited. We have not received any indications that this has changed.
Belgium	No change	We do not impose quoting obligations on our foreign currency bonds and do not track liquidity conditions.
Canada	Decline	Canada issues foreign global bonds denominated in both USD and in Euros. Regarding foreign bonds issued in USD, these are typically issued to buy and hold investors, and, as such, are not actively traded. When investors want to sell, they are often able to find dealers who are willing to make markets for these bonds. Foreign USD bonds are typically issued through a syndication process. To be considered for the syndicate, dealers must meet eligibility criteria, including the provision of market-making services for these Foreign USD bonds. There has not been a large change in the past year in terms of liquidity for these instruments. Although, over the last few years, bid-ask spreads have generally widened, and dealers are less willing to warehouse excess inventory due to balance sheet constraints. There has also been an increase in crowded trades and herding behavior, as dealer positions have become more similar. Oftentimes, the market tends to trade in the same direction, as the underlying factors driving dealer behaviour reflect similar macroeconomic and technical factors. Euro and USD medium-term notes can also be issued through a private placement process. In general the liquidity of MTNs, especially non-structured MTNs, have deteriorated.
Chile	No change	
Colombia	Don't know	
Costa Rica	Don't know	
Czech Republic	Don't know	Since 2012, Ministry of Finance of the Czech Republic has not entered the Eurobond market and relied only on the domestic market. As of 30 June 2021, there is only 1 issue of Eurobond (due in 2022) outstanding.
Denmark	Don't know	Bonds in foreign currency are not issued on a regular basis.
Estonia	Not applicable	
Finland	Don't know	
France	Not applicable	
Germany	Not applicable	
Greece	Not applicable	
Hungary	No change	These bonds are rather illiquid.
Iceland	No change	Liquidity in our foreign bonds issued under EMTN program has almost always been limited. Investors seem to buy and hold our foreign bond issues.
Ireland	Not applicable	
Israel	No change	
Italy	Improvement	Relatively more secondary trades in the first part of the year, due to changing market rates expectation in the second half. Emission of longer dated bonds to give more depths and improve liquidity in the curve. Overall improve of liquidity in the foreign sovereign curve by becoming a frequent issuer in the USD market.
Japan	Not applicable	
Korea	Don't know	
Latvia	Improvement	Taking into account that borrowing volumes (because of Covid-19 pandemic impact) have increased, the Treasury has been able to issue larger benchmarks in syndications in the international markets and then TAP those bonds in domestic market. Active reopening of outstanding Eurobonds via Primary Dealer system in auctions in the domestic market has positively affected the trading in the secondary market.
Lithuania	Decline	
Luxembourg	Not applicable	
Mexico	Improvement	From September 1st, 2020 to September 29th, 2021 Mexico's foreign denominated bonds have shown an improvement in liquidity (measured through the difference in their bid/ask prices). During that period, US dollar denominated benchmarks (5, 10 and 30-year bonds) improved their average liquidity from 0.35 to 0.28 while euro denominated benchmarks (5, 10, 20 and 25-year bond) improved their average liquidity from 0.51 to 0.39.
Netherlands	Not applicable	
New Zealand	Not applicable	
Norway	Not applicable	
Poland	Don't know	
Portugal	No change	We have only one foreign bond that is actively traded in the market, and we have not experienced any relevant change in the liquidity of this bond. IGCP carried out a buyback auction in July 2021, that reduced the outstanding of the bond and may have affected liquidity, but so far, we do not have strong evidence of changes

	Change	Comment
		in liquidity conditions in this market.
Slovak Republic	Don't know	No foreign bond are being traded on MTS. These issues are smaller mostly in hands of buy and hold investors. We have very limited information about liquidity of these bonds. this has changed.
Slovenia	No change	
Spain	No change	Our bonds with a foreign currency denomination are a marginal element of our outstanding debt portfolio, and do not play a significant role in the Spanish Treasury's current DMO strategy.
Sweden	No change	
Switzerland	Not applicable	The Federal Treasury has never issued foreign currency bonds and is not planning to do so.
Turkey	Not applicable	No bonds which are issued by foreign institutions are currently traded in our Markets.
United Kingdom	Not applicable	The UK DMO issues only sterling denominated bonds.
Total: Improvement	**3**	
Total: Decline	**2**	
Total: No change	**10**	
Total: Don't know	**8**	

Table B.8. Q6 Have you observed changes in liquidity conditions of bond related derivate and repo markets over the last 12 months?

	Change	Comment
Australia	Decline	The Reserve Bank of Australia began conducting bond purchases (at a faster rate than AOFM is issuing) this has meant that the physical bonds now trade expensive to the futures contracts. This has reduced demand from some participants who historically took advantage of the arbitrage available from the bonds trading cheap vs the futures (they had specific requirements to be long bonds so can't participate to the same extent now). The RBA also targeted the yield on a 3yr bond at 10 basis points. This bond was in the 3 year futures contract (has fallen out in the September roll). This meant that the 3 year contract did not behave as well as a hedging or speculating instrument as it would have historically and consequently demand was reduced. The new 5 year contract has not yet (and may not) filled this gap. Liquidity in the 10 year contract remained high. AOFM provides a Securities lending facility (a facility of last resort). Usage of this facility has been elevated. In addition the RBA set up a separate facility in 2020 to lend bonds which has also seen high usage.
Austria	No change	
Belgium	Improvement	There was less demand for the repo facility we offer (cf 3)
Canada	No change	Liquidity varies across term types in the futures market. When comparing different terms to maturities, liquidity has often been the highest for old 10-year securities. Furthermore, in the 10-year sector, bond futures have been more liquid than the cash market. Liquidity in the futures market for the 2–year and 5-year sectors remains subdued. In the last few years, repo markets have been functioning well with good levels of liquidity and no repo tightness.
Chile	Not applicable	
Colombia	Improvement	Repo market in Colombia has been improving in 2021 since Central Bank increased the Open Market Operations (OMOs) from a daily average of USD 1 billion in 2020 to USD 1.7 billion on average in 2021. Repo market between primary dealers keep unchanged with a daily average of USD 1.2 billion.
Costa Rica	Decline	The traded volume of government bonds in the related repo markets declined in 33%.
Czech Republic	Don't know	
Denmark	No change	Seems more or less unchanged.
Estonia	Not applicable	
Finland	Not applicable	
France	Improvement	Repo outstanding has been growing steadily during the past 12 months
Germany	No change	During the last 12 month the repo market for German government securities was very liquid. Even on crucial quarter end dates there has always been enough liquidity and therefore no squeezes occurred. Against this background the future market has at least maintained its pivotal role for the liquidity conditions in the EGB market.
Greece	No change	
Hungary	Improvement	Repo transactions for security lending purposes declined, but the much higher volume cash management repos increased as they were restarted by the Debt Management Office (DMO) in 2021 after their suspension in April 2020.
Iceland	Not applicable	

	Change	Comment
Ireland	No change	
Israel	Not applicable	
Italy	No change	Overall volumes have been rather stable in 2022 versus 2021 but while we have observed less interest on Repo General Collateral, there was an important increase in the Special Repo segment. We have observed for quarter-end and especially for year-end a notable squeeze of rates, more relevant than the previous years.
Japan	No change	
Korea	Don't know	
Latvia	Not applicable	
Lithuania	Don't know	
Luxembourg	Not applicable	
Mexico	Decline	In general, liquidity in the local market has decreased considerably due to volatilities in developed and emerging markets. Risk-averse conditions have skewed the market to one side since February of this year. This has equally affected both the repo market and the derivatives market with underlying government bonds.
Netherlands	Don't know	
New Zealand	Decline	Interest rate swap and repo markets have experienced similar liquidity challenges for the reasons outlined in question 3.
Norway	No change	
Poland	Improvement	Over the last 12 months values of bond transactions (repo and buy-sell-back) were fluctuating. The average monthly value of transaction in this period amounted to ca. PLN 480bn, however an upward trend was visible – in September 2020 the value of those transactions was ca. PLN 412bn, while in August 2021 it was PLN 602bn.
Portugal	Not applicable	
Slovak Republic	Not applicable	We use only CCIRS for foreign currency bonds. We haven't issued any new foreign currency bonds since 2014 and didn't have to initiate any new derivatives.
Slovenia	No change	
Spain	No change	
Sweden	Improvement	More interest rate adjustments are nowadays being done via derivatives than cash market.
Switzerland	Don't know	There is a sovereign bond futures market (CONF Futures), however due to the lack of involvement in this market we are not aware of any changes in liquidity conditions. We are also not aware of any changes in the share of repo transactions which were collateralized with bonds of the Swiss Confederation.
Turkey	Decline	The trading volumes in repo markets has shown a smoother declining trend when compared with outright purchases and sales markets (35% decrease in USD terms and 23% decrease in TRY terms when compared the first nine months of year 2021 and 2020). Bond related derivatives are not traded in Borsa Istanbul markets at the moment.
United Kingdom	No change	The UK DMO's Dealing Desk has not seen a marked change in liquidity conditions over the past year. trading/liquidity is concentrated in overnight or next day repo transactions. According to Bank of England data, liquidity in the sterling repo markets has deteriorated in overnight repo (i.e. where a financial institution sells securities and agrees to buy them back the following day), but has remained the same in tomorrow/next day maturities (a transaction that spans two consecutive business days – tomorrow and the following day – that enables traders to roll over their positions).
Total: Improvement	**6**	
Total: Decline	**5**	
Total: No change	**12**	
Total: Don't know	**5**	

Table B.9. Q7 Do you have measures in place to motivate dealers to provide liquidity?

	Yes	No	Comment
Australia		X	
Austria	X		According the General Primary Dealer Agreement, primary dealers have to take care of the market for all RAGB during trading hours. The bid/offer spread needs to be reasonable and bid/offer sizes shall allow for bigger tickets, too. The secondary market performance of primary dealers is monitored and part of the overall primary dealer performance ranking.
Belgium	X		We rank our dealers in order to determine who qualifies for joint lead management roles in syndicated issues and what syndication fees are paid to each of the banks. This ranking is based on a number of quantitative and qualitative elements, among which liquidity provision and activity with investors. Non-competitive offers are granted on the basis of auctions participation and we reward the performance of primary dealers on our selected e-platforms BtoB in a second round of non-competitive offers.
Canada	X		The dealer model used in Canada creates incentives for dealers to provide liquidity to the market. To participate as a dealer in the Government of Canada primary market, entities must meet specific criteria: • Dealers must maintain certain levels of domestic fixed-income trading activity • Dealers must demonstrate adequate levels of participation at auctions Once an entity has obtained its dealer status, it benefits by having direct access to the primary market. Customers must bid through dealers and don't have access to the primary market directly. Dealers may benefit from being able to observe customer order flow. The government also conducts operations that benefit dealers. One such operation is the switch buyback, which improves the dealer's access to building benchmarks. Other benefits for dealers may include increased visibility and recognition, along with the potential to attract more clients for its business. Government securities distributors (GSDs, i.e., dealers) are encouraged to provide liquidity. Bidding limits for Government of Canada bond and treasury bill auctions are calculated based on the GSD's trading activity in primary and secondary markets. A GSD may be granted a primary dealer (PD) status when its calculated bidding limit reaches a threshold level of 10 per cent based on its primary and secondary market share, and buyback activity. Having achieved PD status, a GSD is allowed a higher bidding limit and thus a larger presence (compared to GSDs) in the primary auctions. Further, PDs themselves have different bidding limits dictated in part by their secondary market activity and their participation in buyback activities. PDs must maintain a minimum level of activity in primary and secondary markets, must participate for a minimum amount within a certain price threshold at every auction, and are expected to make two-sided markets for GoC securities under normal market conditions. PDs must also have their core domestic fixed-income market trading and sales operation for GoC securities reside within Canada. In return for these obligations, PDs have greater access to the GoC securities auctions both for their own account and on behalf of their customers, as well as the ability to gather information from customer order flow at auctions. PDs are also eligible to participate in the following Bank of Canada (BoC) operations: overnight repos and reverse repos, term repos, securities lending, and overnight standing repo facility. They are also eligible to participate in the morning auctions of Receiver General cash balances. The Government of Canada employs an open and collaborative approach for its debt management function. Actions such as engaging in market consultations and also incorporating dealer feedback into the decision-making process have been effective. This approach has helped to ensure the well-functioning of the Government of Canada markets and favourable conditions for market liquidity in both the primary and secondary Government of Canada securities markets as well. Being open and transparent in the communication strategy with dealers has also been an effective approach to motivating dealers to provide liquidity to the market. The following are two examples of our transparency in communication with financial market participants: • Publication of the quarterly bond schedule prior to the start of each quarter in advance of auctions • Publishing details for each operation in a call for tender a week prior to the auction
Chile		X	
Colombia	X		During 2021 we have maintained some of the policies applied in 2020 to provide liquidity to the secondary market for example we still have 3 maturity segments in long term auctions, we kept parameters for over-allotment in auctions for example for Bid to cover ratio higher than 2 times we allocated 30% additional to the initial amount offered and for Bid to Cover ratio higher than 2.5 times we allocated 50% additional to the initial amount offered. In 2021 we increase the number of market-makers from 13 to 14 which not only has improved liquidity but also has extended our investor base.
Costa Rica	X		A market maker project is planned to be carried out in the following months, which will improve the price formation and liquidity of the securities.
Czech Republic	X		Tools applied for secondary market liquidity: Issuing calendar publishing and sufficient outstanding amount of benchmark bonds. Quoting obligation of benchmark government bonds and subsequent evaluation of Primary dealers. Primary dealer's access to Ministry of Finance lending facilities (repos and loans of securities available for Primary dealers) Buy-back of short term illiquid bonds and their replacement by benchmark bonds (exchange operations available for Primary dealers).
Denmark	X		To support the primary and secondary markets, the central government has entered into primary dealer contracts with a number of regional and international banks.
Estonia		X	
Finland	X		Fee-producing business allocated according to performance measurement, where liquidity provision (both end-

	Yes	No	Comment
			investor and interbank) are used as inputs
France	X		The most effective measures are : a responsive auction system, reducing the risk of protracted short positions for dealers providing liquidity, the obligation for dealers to provide the market making of our bonds under set metrics on MTS France and Brokertec that are monitored, the consideration of volumes traded on the secondary market in the ranking of primary dealers. In addition, we have a security lending facility to help dealers in case of delivery issues and we also run a buyback programme for OAT exiting the medium and long-term market (0-2 years of remaining maturity).
Germany		X	
Greece	X		
Hungary	X		• Primary Dealers (PDs) are required to buy at auctions a minimum share of Bonds and 1-year T-Bills in every calendar half-year period. • The names of the 5 best PDs in both Bond and T-Bill auctions are published on our website at the end of every half year. • Primary dealers are required to quote two-way prices with minimum amounts and maximum spreads set. Failing to meet these requirements results in sanctions. • Best price quotation data (with the PD's name who quoted the best bid or offer price for the given security) is published together with a benchmark fixing. • The Debt Management Office (DMO) supports PDs' price quotation by a stand-by repo facility, where PDs can ask the DMO for government securities to a limited amount. • In 2012, MTS Hungary was introduced and PDs' price quotation was moved to this platform. Some other functionalities of this platform can be attractive to PDs. Mid-price crossing function was introduced in 2016 in order to generate higher trading volume on the MTS Hungary platform. • Every year the best PDs are awarded (based on auction participation, secondary market share, buy-backs, repos with the DMO) and the first 3 in each category is published.
Iceland	X		PDs have exclusive access to the primary auctions and have the option to buy additional 10% at the accepted price 2 business days after the day of the auction. They also have exclusive access to securities lending facility offer and other privilege offered by DMO. The Treasury pays two kinds of commission to the PDs, first for participation in primary auctions (% of accepted bids) and secondly a fixed amount, paid every 6 months, that is divided between PDs relative to their secondary market turnover.
Ireland	X		Dealers are required to make two-way prices in Irish government bonds for 5 hours a day in €5m size. They are also incentivised through rankings to quote tighter spreads. The NTMA also offers repos and switches to assist Primary Dealers in market-making
Israel	X		The main measure is the primary dealership program. We require primary dealers to comply with several obligations in both primary and secondary markets, and in return grant several exclusive benefits such as: exclusive auctions, green-shoe, access to the government bond lending facility and the title of 'Primary Dealer in Israeli Government Bonds. In addition, only PDs are nominated as underwriters in global issuances and are considered as exclusive counterparties for hedging transactions. In our experience financial incentives are the most effective as long as the cost of the current activity is not significantly higher. Continuous communication with the market – PDs as well as other type of investors – also contributes, as well as providing transparency to market participants
Italy	X		Our Evaluation Criteria of Specialists in Government Bonds provide a detailed and systematic set of parameters to measure the contribution of each market maker to trading and quoting activity, both in the cash and in the repo markets. These parameters are changed in the medium term according to market conditions and public debt management objectives. These changes are therefore introduced when the evolution of market conditions makes some parameters less effective in motivating market makers to bring enough liquidity on the market or when the DMO updates its debt management goals (for example by changing emphasis on issuance activity from some products to others), which may require a consistent re-orientation of market makers' efforts. The Evaluation Criteria of the last decade (and even more) can be found on the Treasury Public Debt website (www.publicdebt.it). For 2021, the Treasury has considered opportune to keep the 2020 Evaluation Criteria mostly unchanged, considering the efficiency of the measures foreseen in 2020 in motivating dealers to provide liquidity. Minor amendments have been made in order to rewards the dealers which provide liquidity to the market with respect those approaching the market with a more opportunistic attitude. However, we monitor closely the evolution of the market to react in a timely manner in case of need of any amendment to our Evaluation Criteria, even during the course of the year.
Japan	X		Although it is difficult to compare the effectiveness of each policy, Liquidity Enhancement Auctions have been one of the most major policies for providing liquidity in the Japanese Government Bond (JGB) market.
Korea	X		
Latvia	X		Regular auctions in domestic market and new instruments/methods makes the market more attractive for investors and for dealers.
Lithuania		X	
Luxembourg		X	
Mexico	X		The market makers program motivates the daily pricing in the liquidity volume.
Netherlands	X		We have a (contractual) quotation obligation for dealers in place, which is incentivized by tying the auction non-comp eligibility to a dealers quotation performance.

	Yes	No	Comment
New Zealand	X		· Maximizing secondary market liquidity was one of the key objectives underpinning the introduction of our Primary Markets Access Framework that came into effect on 30 September 2019. The framework formalises the incentives and rewards for registered tender counterparties actively engaged in supporting liquidity in the NZGB market. This includes being considered for appointment to syndication panels, participation in roadshows and conferences, and other auxiliary financial markets transactional business.
Norway	X		Our performance based remuneration scheme provide the primary dealers with incentives to attract investors and maintain an active secondary market. Participation as lead managers when syndicating new bond series.
Poland	X		There are quality quotation index (introduced in October 2011) and value of outright transactions concluded on Electronic market (July 2019) that stimulate the liquidity on the TS market. The first one influences spreads narrowing at the same time. In April 2021, we introduced new requirement for dealers and dealers candidates - minimum share in outright transactions concluded on electronic market - in order to increase liquidity and efficiency of the market. All these measures are included in the quarterly assessment of the entities and encourage them to be more active on the market which gives higher scoring.
Portugal	X		We allocate 35% of the PD evaluation to liquidity related criteria: 17,5% to quoting criteria (divided into 3 categories) and 17,5% to turnover with end-investors (from HRF reports). Quoting Total points = 17,5% (divided into quoting obligation (mandatory), additional amount and time quoted (non-mandatory), and passive turnover (non-mandatory)) -Quoting obligations = 7,5% On the quoting criteria we ask PDs to quote the Portuguese Government bonds for a minimum of 5 hours, with 5 million each side and with a bid-ask spread that cannot be larger than the average of the bid-asks spreads of all PDs times 1.5; Bid-ask spreads quoted under a certain target are awarded twice as much. -Additional amount and time quoted = 5% We give additional points to PDs that quote with extra amount and extra time on top of the mandatory by the first criteria. -Passive turnover = 5% We award points to PDs that are quoting on our platforms and are more often the passive counterparty of a transaction when compared to being the active counterparty in a transaction. This measure incentivizes PDs to keep quoting on the electronic platforms, as now they are awarded for being "hit" by other PDs. Indirectly it creates a penalty for abusive dealers who only "hit" the platform as they are awarded 0 points. In addition to all of these, we multiply the daily score in the quoting obligation of each PD by a volatility factor that is added on special volatile days, giving extra points to the PDs that quote on those "volatile days
Slovak Republic	X		The evaluation of the EMAR (formerly HRF reports) is one part of overall evaluation of PDs. The other part is MTS quoting evaluation. The MTS quoting represents 20% of overall evaluation and EMAR trades 10%.
Slovenia	X		Evaluation of dealers' daily and monthly market making performance by the following categories bid-ask spread, volume of exposure and traded volumes.
Spain	X		Our Primary Dealer Network has a carefully calibrated incentive scheme, with points assigned to Primary Dealers for various actions, including secondary market liquidity. These points have direct effects on the assigning of syndication Joint-Lead Manager roles. In our experience, this method has proved very effective for providing incentives to our Primary Dealers' behavior.
Sweden	X		Provisions based on primary and secondary mkt share.
Switzerland	X		By selling so-called "own tranches" directly to investors on demand and at market prices, the Treasury is able to bridge temporary illiquidity in certain bond lines.
Turkey	X		In order to help to ensure a sustainable secondary market liquidity, according to the primary dealership contract the primary dealers are obliged to give quotations in a regular manner for the benchmark securities determined by the Treasury and selected by the PDs.
United Kingdom	X		The DMO does not mandate bid/offer spreads or specify minimum bid or offer sizes; however, one of the criteria that needs to be met by primary dealer firms is a commitment to make continuous and effective two-way prices to their clients, in all gilts for which they are recognised as a market maker. The DMO monitors the secondary market turnover share of each primary dealer and has regular contact with primary dealer firms about their performance. Measures to motivate primary dealers include the recognition formally as a GEMM which carries privileges such as participation in consultation meetings, direct access to auctions, access to our standing repo facility and the opportunity to win lead manager mandates at our syndicated offerings. Primary dealer firms highly value undertaking lead manager roles on these transactions. Selection for these roles takes into account many factors including the extent to which individual firms are actively participating in the gilt and Treasury bill primary markets (including regular bidding participation in auctions) and activities as a DMO cash management counterparty, as well as market share and liquidity provision in the secondary market.
Total	**31**	**6**	

Table B.10. Q8 Do you undertake any other measures in order to enhance liquidity?

	Yes	No
Australia	X	
Austria	X	
Belgium	X	
Canada	X	
Chile	X	
Colombia	X	
Costa Rica	X	
Czech Republic	X	
Denmark	X	
Estonia		X
Finland	X	
France	X	
Germany	X	
Greece	X	
Hungary	X	
Iceland	X	
Ireland	X	
Israel	X	
Italy	X	
Japan	X	
Korea	X	
Latvia		X
Lithuania	X	
Luxembourg		X
Mexico	X	
Netherlands	X	
New Zealand	X	
Norway	X	
Poland	X	
Portugal	X	
Slovak Republic	X	
Slovenia	X	
Spain	X	
Sweden	X	
Switzerland	X	
Turkey	X	
United Kingdom	X	
Total	**34**	**3**

Table B.11. Q8b If yes to Q8, please specify the measures that you undertake to enhance liquidity

	Benchmark bond programme	Re-opening auctions	Tap sales	Frequency and size of auctions	Primary dealer models	Buy backs of illiquid lines	Strips programme	Security lending facility and repos	Secondary trading operations	Others
Australia	X	X	X	X		X		X		
Austria	X	X	X	X	X		X		X	
Belgium		X		X		X		X		X
Canada	X	X		X	X	X		X	X	6
Chile					X			X		
Colombia	X			X	X			X	X	
Costa Rica	X	X		X		X				
Czech Republic	X	X	X	X	X	X		X	X	
Denmark	X	X	X	X	X	X		X	X	
Estonia										
Finland	X	X			X					
France	X	X		X	X		X	X	X	
Germany	X	X		X			X	X	X	
Greece	X	X	X		X	X				
Hungary	X	X		X	X	X		X		
Iceland	X	X		X	X	X		X		X
Ireland	X		X	X	X			X	X	
Israel	X		X	X	X			X		
Italy	X	X	X	X	X	X	X	X		
Japan		X		X	X	X				
Korea		X	X	X	X	X	X	X	X	
Latvia										
Lithuania	X	X	X	X						
Luxembourg										
Mexico	X	X		X	X	X		X		X
Netherlands	X	X	X	X	X		X	X		X
New Zealand	X			X	X	X				

	Benchmark bond programme	Re-opening auctions	Tap sales	Frequency and size of auctions	Primary dealer models	Buy backs of illiquid lines	Strips programme	Security lending facility and repos	Secondary trading operations	Others
Norway	X	X		X	X			X		
Poland	X	X	X	X	X			X		
Portugal	X	X	X	X	X	X		X	X	
Slovak Republic	X	X	X	X	X	X			X	
Slovenia	X		X			X				
Spain	X	X	X	X	X		X			
Sweden	X	X	X	X	X	X		X		
Switzerland		X		X						
Turkey	X	X		X	X		X	X		X
United Kingdom	X	X		X	X			X		
Total	**29**	**28**	**17**	**30**	**27**	**18**	**8**	**23**	**11**	**11**

Table B.12. Q8b Other specified measures that you undertake to enhance liquidity measures that you undertake to enhance liquidity

Australia	
Austria	
Belgium	Optional Reverse Inquiries; a facility to tap bonds on demand (in limited size)
Canada	(i) Government Bond Purchase Program (GBPP). (ii) A debt management program that is based on the pillars of transparency, regularity, liquidity, and prudence. (iii) Minimum bidding requirements and maximum bidding limits for government securities distributors and customers -> auction rules. (iv) The posting of a quarterly bond auction schedule prior to the start of each quarter. (v) Being a transparent and predicable issuer helps the Government of Canada to reassure investors that the bonds they wish to purchase will be available, and it also allows investors to plan out their investment strategy. A combination of these measures helps to boost investor confidence, which contributes towards enhancing market liquidity. (vi) Benchmark target range sizes are planned and announced at the beginning of the fiscal year as part of the Debt Management Strategy.
Chile	
Colombia	
Costa Rica	Liability Management Operations
Czech Republic	
Denmark	
Estonia	
Finland	
France	
Germany	
Greece	
Hungary	
Iceland	Switch auctions
Ireland	
Israel	
Italy	
Japan	
Korea	
Latvia	
Lithuania	
Luxembourg	
Mexico	Switch with lending facilities
Netherlands	Buybacks of bonds with maturity <= 24 months
New Zealand	
Norway	Buy back program of bonds maturing within 1 year
Poland	
Portugal	
Slovak Republic	
Slovenia	
Spain	
Sweden	
Switzerland	
Turkey	Switch auctions
United Kingdom	

Table B.13. Q9 Have you imposed new requirements on market-makers in their provision of liquidity over the last 12 months?

	Yes	No	Comment
Australia		X	
Austria		X	
Belgium		X	
Canada		X	N/A
Chile		X	We don't have market makers. There is a plan to study the feasibility to have market makers for the Treasury securities.
Colombia		X	We haven't imposed new requirements, we still have requirements of maximum bid ask spread of 30 bps for nominal bonds and 40 bps for linked bonds in local currency to score in the Market-Maker Program.
Costa Rica		X	There are currently no market makers in Costa Rica.
Czech Republic		X	
Denmark		X	
Estonia		X	
Finland		X	
France		X	
Germany		X	We do not impose any requirements on market makers.
Greece		X	
Hungary		X	
Iceland		X	
Ireland		X	
Israel		X	
Italy		X	Please refer to the answer to the question n°7.
Japan		X	
Korea	X		More requirement on bid-ask, less requirement on market making
Latvia		X	
Lithuania		X	
Luxembourg		X	
Mexico		X	The Ministry of Finance has not made any modifications to the market-makers program.
Netherlands		X	
New Zealand		X	
Norway		X	
Poland	X		We introduced the new requirement in April 2021 (it was described in the answer to the question number 7).
Portugal		X	Due to a well-functioning Portuguese market and after consulting the Primary Dealers, IGCP decided not to change requirements in 2021.
Slovak Republic		X	
Slovenia		X	
Spain		X	Our requirements and incentive scheme for primary dealers in terms of their provision of liquidity has remained very similar over the past 12 months.
Sweden		X	
Switzerland		X	We do not rely on a primary dealer system
Turkey	X		We have added the TLREF-indexed bonds to the benchmark securities portfolio from which the PD banks are obliged select the bonds that they are obliged to give quotations in the secondary market.
United Kingdom		X	
Total	**3**	**34**	

Table B.14. Q10 Have you made any changes to your market communication strategies since the pandemic?

	Yes	No	Comment
Australia	X		We make announcements (in general) after Budget (and updates) but the focus is now on the next 6 months rather than annual guidance which may have been provided previously. We are less prescriptive in our guidance, in particular dropping any reference of a weekly issuance rate (we still publish our annual expected volume). This has been to increase our flexibility to respond to changes in funding requirements and market conditions. https://www.aofm.gov.au/program/issuance-program
Austria	X		
Belgium		X	Not really, the greater uncertainty surrounding financing needs is of course discussed with investors, but this is well understood by the investor community.
Canada		X	The Government of Canada employs an open and collaborative approach for its debt management function. Actions such as publishing market notices, which act as information communiques containing operational details, and/or new program announcements, have been effective. Senior government officials have also effectively communicated changes in funding needs and information on programs and operations during public appearances/speeches. This approach has helped to ensure the well-functioning of the Government of Canada markets and favourable conditions for market liquidity in both the primary and secondary Government of Canada securities markets. In addition, new programs and changes to existing programs that have been announced by the Government to support key financial markets to ensure that they continue to function properly, have been well received by market participants and primary dealers (PDs). Given the government's unprecedented borrowing requirements due to COVID-19, Government officials have also communicated directly to PDs in order to reinforce PDs significant role in Government of Canada Debt Distribution Framework (DDF) in helping to manage the huge increase in Government issuance and providing secondary market liquidity to the GoC market. Being open and transparent in the communication strategy with PDs has also been an effective approach to motivating dealers to provide liquidity to the market and to support primary market issuance. Overall, market communication strategies have remained consistent and similar prior to the pandemic and since the onset of the pandemic.
Chile	X		More frequent information, in special regarding ESG issues.
Colombia		X	Before and during pandemic we have kept our dialogue with investors and market participants. We have continued to participate in forums and investor webinars and we publish in our web page debt statistics, presentations and relevant information for investors.
Costa Rica		X	
Czech Republic		X	Ministry of Finance transparently communicates its funding strategies and operations (including changes) via Primary Dealer Committees meetings as well as per individual consultation with market participants. Apart from the regular publication of the Czech Republic Funding and Debt Management Strategy in December and its update for the second half of the year in June, the Ministry published an extraordinary update of Strategy in April in connection with an approval of new act on state budget which significantly increased planned budget deficit for 2021.
Denmark		X	
Estonia		X	Usual communication through the press.
Finland	X		A new process for selecting bonds to be auctioned, including requesting recommendations
France		X	
Germany	X		We established analyst/investor calls on the publication dates of our annual issuance outlook and its quarterly updates.
Greece			All changes were communicated to the market and its participants during non-deal road shows that took place remotely, through conference calls and video conferences.
Hungary	X		The Debt Management Office (DMO) started to publish on its website an Investor Presentation in 2020, which is updated quarterly, providing details of the financing plan, among other information. We have also held online discussions with market participants, primary dealers.
Iceland		X	
Ireland		X	
Israel		X	
Italy		X	
Japan		X	We continuously hold careful dialogues with market participants through dialogue sessions with same strategies as before. Also, we communicate with JGB Market Special Participants and JGB Investors more than ever.
Korea	X		
Latvia		X	We publish updates of investor presentation on a monthly basis as before, including description of approved and actual COVID-19 measures, their impact to the budget balance. For the total financial necessity section in the presentation we maintain the disclaimer for investors that borrowing volumes may change.

	Yes	No	Comment
Lithuania	X		Wouldn't say this was done directly because of the pandemic, but we have increased the frequency of meetings with the primary dealers.
Luxembourg		X	
Mexico	X		Local market debt changes only: The Federal Government has undertook a more proactive approach with more frequent calls and reunions with the central bank and participants of the financial markets.
Netherlands		X	
New Zealand	X		We have continued to maintain regular engagement with investors and intermediaries and have done so via a series of virtual investor meetings. We have also introduced a monthly 'E-newsletter' to keep market participants informed about developments in New Zealand and recently started publishing NZDM Insights – detailed research notes on topics of interest.
Norway		X	
Poland		X	Our funding plans are published before coming months and quarters. Prior to announcing the plan, we contact our primary dealers to present our ideas and ask for their opinions. Our communication strategy was basically unchanged.
Portugal		X	During 2021 there were no changes to the initial budget and IGCP resumed the market communications strategies used before the pandemic, with the usual quarterly update of the funding programme.
Slovak Republic		X	Regular communication with Primary dealers. No specific communication with participants outside of Primary dealers.
Slovenia		X	
Spain		X	We continue to put special emphasis on predictability, transparency and communication with our primary dealers and investors. However, this was already important before the pandemic, and continues to be so afterwards.
Sweden		X	
Switzerland		X	We publish our issuance calendar for the following year at the beginning of December. This calendar shows the auction dates and the planned total issuance volume for the whole year. If there is a material change away from this issuance goal, we inform the markets with a press release as well as on Bloomberg and Reuters. This strategy has proven to suit the needs of our counterparties and to allow us to maintain the necessary flexibility to adjust the funding plan if needed. The only effect of the pandemic was, that due to the high uncertainty we updated our issuance goal more frequently than usual.
Turkey	X		In addition to the existing formal communication channels, we have started to use informal ad-hoc channel more actively and frequently.
United Kingdom		X	Our communication strategy has not changed. However, with respect to green gilts, we have had a greater level of investor engagement than is typical for a standard gilt transaction, around publication of the UK Government Green Financing Framework on 30 June 2021, and in the run-up to the inaugural green gilt issue in September 2021.
Total	**11**	**25**	

Table B.15. Q11 How has the transition to alternative reference rates been proceeding in your country?

Australia	
Austria	As the Republic of Austria has no outstanding non-USD LIBOR-linked instruments, we are at the moment not affected by the transition to alternative reference rates.
Belgium	/
Canada	In Canada, benchmark reform efforts are being led by the Canadian Alternative Reference Rate Committee (CARR), a group of financial sector firms and public sector institutions including the Bank of Canada. CARR's mandate includes promoting the use of the Canadian Overnight Repo Rate Average (CORRA) as a key risk-free interest rate benchmark in Canada. This transition to alternative reference rates has been proceeding well and has been a multi-year effort involving multiple stakeholder groups in Canada. Canada's national benchmark reform working group is working to develop conventions for the cash market and to improve the liquidity of products tied to CORRA, although this work is in its early stages. Although liquidity remains concentrated in products linked to CDOR, we expect this to change over time as Canada's market shifts towards CORRA-referencing products. Another impediment is the existence of multiple benchmark rates (even if one is a credit-based benchmark, thus, in principle, requiring two liquid markets). CORRA is a robust, transaction-based benchmark that reflects billions of dollars in daily overnight repo transactions. It meets global benchmark standards and is similar to other global risk-free rates (RFRs). While the Canadian Dollar Offered Rate (CDOR), Canada's other main interest benchmark, is not anticipated to immediately go away, we expect its relevance to decline, like other credit-based benchmarks, as markets globally move to RFRs. As a voluntary, survey-based measure, CDOR may ultimately be discontinued. The national working group expects that, over time, CORRA will potentially become the primary benchmark rate in the Canadian financial system, thus generating demand from a wide variety of market participants.

Chile	There has been no big impacts.
Colombia	The public debt office started reducing its exposure to libor in 2019. We had closed 89 operations between July 2019 and August 2021 to change loans from libor to fixed rate. These operations are for a total amount of USD 17.5 billion and EUR 3 billion.
Costa Rica	A lot of financial institutions (for example BID, BCIE, Banco Mundial) made a great work in this topic, for that reason the country is ready.
Czech Republic	Most of variable-rate state debt instruments are linked to PRIBOR (Prague Interbank Offered Rate) and transitions from LIBORs to new alternative reference rate are not relevant for the Ministry of Finance as no debt instrument is linked to LIBOR.
Denmark	Danmarks Nationalbank took over the administration of the new proposed reference rate DESTR I 2020. The first publication of DESTR is foreseen in Q1 2022. Recently a private sector working group suggested to phase out the existing short-term reference rate Tom/next in favor of DESTR. For CIBOR no changes are foreseen at the moment. A private sector working group is working on preparing solid fall-backs for CIBOR based on DESTR.
Estonia	As Estonia is a member of the Eurozone, the primary reference rates in use are Euribor and Eonia which are not subject to any transition. The MoF of Estonia does not have any loans or derivatives linked to LIBOR rates.
Finland	Not applicapble for cash bonds for the DMO, good progress with derivative portfolios
France	France does not issue variable rate instruments hence a limited impact on our sovereign issuances. The orderly transition is supervised by market authorities both at a national and European level.
Germany	We can only comment on our own activity and for us the transition has went very smoothly without any frictions.
Greece	
Hungary	As the Hungarian Debt Management Office (DMO) has exposure only to EUR benchmark rates, and EURIBOR does not fall under the RFR transition, the only change we have to make is to change EONIA to ESTR (or ESTR + 8.5 basis points) in our ISDA CSAs. This might be facilitated by adhering to the respective ISDA Protocol.
Iceland	Is proceeding according to plan. The goal is that the transition will be implemented beginning of next year (2022).
Ireland	
Israel	Financial entities as well as the government and CB have started to assess the potential implications and if required to amend existing contracts as well as prospectus.
Italy	Quite smoothly. Euribor rates will still be published, and this reduces the operational risk/impact of the overall switch for institution entities as well as households. €STR quotation has become more and more liquid. For regulated deals the RFR switch and relative compensation amount has been put in place by the Central Counterparty Clearing House (CCP), while for the OTC deals managed outside the CPP the compensation and switch should be agreed bilaterally. Being the publication of LIBOR not guaranteed beyond 2021, to address the risk that one or more LIBORs or benchmarks are discontinued while market participants continue to have exposure to that rate, financial institutions and clients have adopted contractual fallback provisions using Alternative Reference Rates as replacement rates. Furthermore, market participants are trying to ensure that the contracts align as closely as possible to the original agreement after the fallback kicks in, resulting in a rate that is predictable, transparent and fair.
Japan	Answer as one of the swap market participants, regarding JPY LIBOR, Bank of Japan has taken the lead in establishing the Cross-Industry Committee on Japanese Yen Interest Rate Benchmarks, and the committee has been the process of considering the transition to alternative reference rates.
Korea	
Latvia	There are market guidelines available for all in order to make the transition process more structured and smooth. However the Treasury cannot provide comment on the whole market participants.
Lithuania	Slowly
Luxembourg	Not the case for Luxembourg
Mexico	The transition to new reference rates in the local market has been gradual. On October 5th of this year, the new BONDES F were launched, referred to the new TIIE Fondeo. Through swaps, the aim is to replace BONDES D by BONDES F. Having a government instrument at this new rate will generate greater dynamism in new placements and the construction of curves for derivative instruments. At the same time, this gradual change will allow more time for the market to be operationally prepared for the necessary changes.
Netherlands	No impact on Dutch government bonds (all bonds are fixed rate).
New Zealand	Transition arrangements are progressing well, local authorities have agreed fallback rates for domestic benchmarks and ISDA have announced these will be included in an upcoming protocol. Domestic price-makers are working with clients around impacted trades for other IBOR related products and the process around transitioning these transactions and/or terminating them.
Norway	The Norwegian Overnight Weighted Average (Nowa) was recommended as the alternative reference rate in NOK in September 2019. Last year the working group presented recommended market conventions for Nowa and has since worked to incorporate these into contracts for bonds, derivatives and credit agreements. There has also been good progress towards establishing a derivative market based on Nowa and brokers have started to publish prices for some Nowa derivatives. The activity in this market is expected to pick up when LCH is ready with clearing in the first half of 2022. A well-functioning interest rate derivative market will help to increase the use of Nowa as a reference rate going forward.

Poland	The working group of the financial sector which acted under auspices of the Ministry of Finance has recommended two possible alternative risk free rates: WRR (Warsaw Repo Rates) based on overnight secured transactions and WIRD (Warszawski Indeks Rynku Depozytowego) based on overnight unsecured transactions. Both rates are being developed by GPW Benchmark, the administrator of the current main rate WIBOR, which is an-IBOR type rate. GPW Benchmark indicates that it will also consider WIRF (Warszawski Indeks Rynku Finansowego) which would be an overnight version of WIRD rate, excluding corporate deposits. The risk free rates should be delivered in 2022.
Portugal	IGCP has no products linked to IBORs and has not been actively involved in transition discussions
Slovak Republic	We have no floating securities issued linked to reference rates.
Slovenia	The Ministry of Finance takes reference rates into account when processing relevant deals. Should the reference rate change, the reference rate for our deals will be changed accordingly. Fixed rate EUR denominated reference bonds have been and remain the primary funding instrument. The outstanding state budget debt is based on EUR fixed rate. Should any FRN debt issuance be envisaged we would use the reference rate applicable or predominantly used in the market at the time of issuance and would include relevant fallback rates and trigger events in the issuance documentation.
Spain	Given that we are part of the Eurozone, we have seen a very smooth transition in regards to new reference rates. The transition to STR from EONIA has been not posed problems. Given the size of Euro-area financial markets and the size of the main financial actors in these markets (large commercial banks and investment banks, among others), this transition was easy to carry out.
Sweden	Central bank has started to publish the new SWESTR since Sept 1.
Switzerland	A large fraction of the cash market already transitioned to the new Swiss reference rate SARON but some market participants still need to accelerate their reduction of legacy LIBOR contracts. Furthermore, the Swiss Financial Market Supervisory Authority (FINMA) emphasized that it is important to timely meet the deadlines of the FINMA guidance. Since 30 June 2021, new contracts should in general be based on alternative reference rates (e.g. SARON and SOFR). FINMA reminded members that full operational readiness is required by 31 December 2021.
Turkey	Turkish Lira Reference Rate (TLREF) has been calculated and published daily by Borsa Istanbul, derived from repo transactions in Repo-Reverse Repo Market since the end of 2018. There is also TLREF Index published on a daily basis. There are government as well as private sector debt securities using TLREF index for coupon payment.
United Kingdom	The Financial Conduct Authority (FCA) announced on 29 September 2021 further arrangements for the orderly winding down of LIBOR at the end of 2021. The announcement has confirmed the methodology for 'synthetic LIBOR', based on term risk-free rates, for the duration of 2022. The FCA will decide and specify before year-end which legacy contracts are permitted to use synthetic LIBOR rates, and is currently holding a consultation in order to provide market participants with the opportunity to provide input.

Table B.16. Q12 In your opinion, are market participants in your country generally ready for the transition?

	Yes	No	Comment
Australia			
Austria	X		
Belgium	X		We have no trades referring to libors that will cease publication in 2022; most of our counterparties have indicated that they are ready for the transition.
Canada		X	Yes, as Canada's domestic working group for financial benchmark reform helps develop a market for CORRA-linked cash products, we expect Canada's market will potentially move to primarily referencing CORRA. This has been a multi-year process, and market participants have been preparing for this transition and have been consulted and involved in the development of the alternative reference rate market in Canada. Overall, readiness amongst market participants for the transition is generally good. However, there are several challenges and costs of adapting to the benchmark reform that could impede readiness of market participants. These include: Developing internal capability to transact in the new RFR instruments and do proper valuation and risk/performance attribution under a new RFR-based discounting regime. Managing the existing LIBOR derivatives to mitigate risks. Understanding and preparing for the underlying economic impact this reform might have on participants derivatives linked funding in general.
Chile	X		
Colombia		X	
Costa Rica	X		Yes, they do. The market participants are ready.
Czech Republic			
Denmark	X		
Estonia	X		We believe commercial banks and largest corporates that might use LIBOR-based product are generally ready for the transition.
Finland	X		

	Yes	No	Comment
France	X		
Germany			We do not have an overview therefore are not able to comment
Greece			
Hungary	X		We do not have enough information on the situation of other local market participants, but negative information has not come to our knowledge.
Iceland	X		
Ireland	X		
Israel	X		
Italy			The path of the transition away from LIBOR is complex. Transition has affected both new and existing products and in different ways. The consequences of reform are unpredictable and may have an adverse impact on any financial instruments linked to the interest rate benchmarks. Whilst global regulators and industry bodies are trying to minimise value transfer in the transition process, this cannot be entirely eliminated, and contracts linked to LIBOR are at risk of economic impact as they are transitioned to the new reference rates.
Japan	X		The Cross-Industry Committee on Japanese Yen Interest Rate Benchmarks has taken the lead in recommending to cease the initiation of new transactions of interest rate swaps referencing JPY LIBOR by the end of September 2021 at the latest, and that TONA should be the main alternative interest rate benchmark for transactions in the JPY interest rate swaps market ("TONA First"). The Committee that includes market participants has been working on the transition to alternative reference rates.
Korea			
Latvia			The Treasury cannot provide comment on the whole market participants.
Lithuania	X		
Luxembourg			
Mexico		X	Although most of the participants are ready for the BONDES F floating instrument, most are not yet ready to implement the valuation of the new TIIE Fondeo in their derivatives system. Similarly, there are institutions that are still awaiting approval for the derivative market instruments by their investment committee.
Netherlands			Don't know
New Zealand	X		We understand there are several issues associated with the domestic fund management community and corporates that are still to be worked through around tax implications, cost attribution and hedge accounting/effectiveness, but we are not that close to these issues.
Norway	X		Our impression is that banks with exposure to Libor seems to be well prepared for the cessation by end of 2021. Regarding Nibor there is no prospect of a Nibor cessation, and Nibor is set to coexist together with Nowa, the alternative reference rate in NOK.
Poland			The market participants put in place contingency plans in case of cessation of the main rate which are transposed to the contractual relations with clients. Nevertheless the proper preparations will take place once the risk free rates are available.
Portugal	X		The IBORs transition has not been a topic in discussions IGCP has had with market participants and for this reason we assume they are generally ready for the transition. Otherwise, we had already been informed by them.
Slovak Republic	X		
Slovenia	X		Slovenia follows the EU directives in this respect.
Spain	X		Spain enjoys a strong financial market, with large banks that are players on a global scale. This means that our financial system has enough resources to easily adapt to the new transition. Of course, it will take some time to get used to the transition, but we expect it to be smooth.
Sweden		X	
Switzerland	X		See Q11
Turkey	X		It is already used for some bond issues.
United Kingdom	X		The FCA has encouraged market participants to continue actively to transition away from LIBOR wherever practicable. The market has been well-aware of the transition for some time now and should be prepared to adapt in 2022.
Total	**24**	**3**	

Table B.17. Q13 Do you have any plans to issue securities linked to an alternative reference rate?

	Yes	No	Comment
Australia			
Austria		X	
Belgium		X	We mainly issue fixed rate securities.
Canada		X	No impact on domestic debt program. At the current moment there are no plans for the domestic debt program of Canada to support the development of alternative reference rate market. Canada does not use IBOR-linked products for the domestic debt program. Reserves The Foreign Reserves are managed under an asset-liability matching principle. Derivatives and medium-term notes linked to LIBOR are used in support of funding, and FRNs linked to LIBOR are held in the Reserves. To the extent that reserve management actions can further facilitate liquidity in these markets, the Bank of Canada may work on reserve management activities to transact in SOFR as needed, and this may provide support to the development of the alternative reference rate market on the margin. We are assessing whether it is appropriate to replace legacy LIBOR derivatives with SOFR-linked derivatives. In the future, derivatives linked to SOFR could be used as part of Reserves funding, and investments linked to SOFR could be held in the Reserves.
Chile		X	
Colombia		X	
Costa Rica		X	
Czech Republic		X	The last floater line (CZGB VAR/31) was issued on 30 April 2021. The reference interest rate in relation to the respective interest period for the purposes of the issuance terms and conditions is PRIBOR. If the interest rate PRIBOR is no longer used in the market of interbank deposits in general or in consequence of the Czech Republic's transition to other legal currency, an interest rate used in the market of interbank deposits in the Czech Republic instead of the PRIBOR will be used for the purposes of the average reference interest rate determination.
Denmark		X	We currently consider how best to support the launch of DESTR, this could include conducting swaps based on DESTR or other ways.
Estonia		X	
Finland		X	
France		X	
Germany		X	
Greece			
Hungary		X	
Iceland		X	
Ireland		X	
Israel		X	
Italy			Among Italian Government bonds the only instrument linked to a benchmark interest rate is CCTeu, which is linked to 6months EURIBOR (The Euro Interbank Offered Rate). At the time being, no potential cessation date has been set for EURIBOR, which completed reforms of its methodology in Q4 2019. The European authorities believe reformed EURIBOR can exist beyond 2021 and no indication has been given that EURIBOR is likely to cease anytime soon. However, we are currently evaluating the possibility to include a fallback provision based on the future or realized €STR derivative market.
Japan		X	
Korea			
Latvia		X	Conventional bonds or Sustainable Bonds are on the agenda in medium term.
Lithuania		X	
Luxembourg		X	
Mexico	X		The Ministry of Finance already issued the BONDES D on October 5. This instrument has a reviewable rate with coupons referenced to the TIIE Fondeo. Later there are plans to issue more instruments with different characteristics and rates to build the new curve.
Netherlands		X	All Dutch government bonds are fixed rate.
New Zealand		X	
Norway		X	
Poland		X	
Portugal		X	
Slovak Republic		X	
Slovenia		X	

	Yes	No	Comment
Spain		X	
Sweden		X	
Switzerland		X	
Turkey		X	
United Kingdom		X	We have no plans at this time to issue securities linked to the new reference rate. We keep the possibility of launching new instrument types under review.
Total	**1**	**32**	

Printed by Libri Plureos GmbH in Hamburg, Germany